V. S. Naipaul

A Literary Response to the Nobel Laureate

V. S. Naipaul

A Literary Response to the Nobel Laureate

edited by

SUMAN BALA

KHOSLA

NEW DELHI

Published by
Khosla Publishing House
New Delhi 110 002

in association with
Prestige Books
New Delhi 110 058

ISBN: 81-7551-136-2

Rs. 500

Printed at Chaman Offset Press, New Delhi 110 002

Contents

A House for Mr. Biswas

Half a Life

V.S. Naipaul: A Literary Tribute

SUMAN BALA
University of Delhi

V.S. Naipaul is one of the best-known English novelists of the modern times; his popularity reached its zenith when he received the Nobel Prize for literature last year. His name for this award had been in circulation for more than ten years and all these years it was a subject of discussion and speculation, both for literary critics and his admirers. An examination of the history of his recognition as a writer reveals that almost since the time he started writing, he started receiving one prize after another. While he has received several awards, it will be worth-mentioning some of these—particularly the Rhys Memorial Prize (1958), the Somerset Maugham Award (1961), the Hawthornden Prize (1964), the W.H. Smith Literary Award (1968), the Booker Prize (1971) and the David Cohen British Literary Award (1993).

V.S. Naipaul is regarded a prophet, a soothsayer, a doom-watcher and a teller of unpalatable truths. When he was awarded the Bennett Award as early as 1980, he expressed his heartfelt satisfaction at the recognition accorded to his writings as a whole. He felt that it was an acceptance of the relevance of his vision and his art. Today, after he has received the Nobel Prize, he has been hailed as "the greatest living writer in the English language." He has been bracketed with as prestigious a writer as Joseph Conrad. Both these writers share a close literary kinship. Philosophically, they share a similar vision of life. It is in fact this Conradian vision which became central to Naipaul as he looked at various postcolonial societies.

In several ways, Naipaul is as enigmatic as Conrad. He eludes any specific labelling. While on the one hand, he is as serious as Conrad, on the other he is described as an excellent writer of the Comedy of Manners. He cannot be described absolutely as a social historian, a travel writer, a journalist, a biographer or a novelist. Many of the things that he gives expression to in his writings are result of his early contact with English literature when he was a student at the University of Oxford. He admits that he went to the books for 'fantasy' because, as he said, 'the English language was mine, the tradition was not.' The tradition of English and European literature was not essentially his own, for he was a third generation Indian English writer. He realized that he could write only about his society, for every writer needs a 'starting point' in order to project his fictional world. In terms of geography, he was located in a world that was far off both from West Indies as also India—the country of his heritage. Says he: 'To us, without a mythology, all literatures were foreign. Trinidad was small, remote and unimportant; and we knew we could not hope to read in books of the life we saw about us.' Since he did not have strong roots, he portrayed most authentically the anonymous man. Like Conrad's protagonists, his heroes are always in search of a more dignified life and they become acutely aware of their helplessness in achieving the goals they set for themselves. The existential question 'what is man' bothers him as much as it does Conrad.

II

It is primarily as a writer of diaspora and the one who gives expression to the theme of rootlessness and the crisis of identity that he is best known in the literary world. All his writings have a close relationship with his personal life. It is desirable, therefore, to have an acquaintance with V.S. Naipaul, the man. He was born in the Caribbean island of Trinidad in 1932. His grandfather had migrated from India to teach the Indian cane-workers of Trinidad. His father, Seepersad, was a journalist and a literary writer. He was a reporter in the *Trinidad Guardian* and also published a collection of short stories under the title *Gurudeva and Other Indian Tales* in 1943. His brother Shiva Naipaul was highly talented and was on his way to acquiring great popularity when he passed away in his early thirties in an accident. He published a novel entitled *Fireflies* and a collection of short stories.

Naipaul left Trinidad for England in 1950 to do English Honours at Oxford University. He graduated in 1953 and settled in England thereafter. He married Patricia Ann Hale in 1955 and decided to launch his professional career only as a writer. It was indeed a difficult resolve, for to eke out one's living by merely writing is not easy, any way. He worked as literary editor of the B.B.C. programme "Caribbean Voices" between 1954 and 1956 and reviewed constantly for the *New Statesman* between 1956 and 1960. For Naipaul, then, it was a deliberate, conscious decision to be a writer in life, despite the hazards involved in the enterprise. "I began to write," says Naipaul, "I am afraid, for no other reason than because I thought it would be nice to be a writer."

III

While Naipaul has produced several works, it is *A House for Mr. Biswas* that has given him name and fame. It is desirable to discuss this novel at some length. The novel deals primarily with two themes—the one being the protagonist's struggle to establish himself in a hostile environment through the ownership of a house and the other being the decline of Hindu culture under the impact of Westernization. In both these aspects, V.S. Naipaul bears close similarities to the African writer Chinua Achebe. *Things Fall Apart*, the most popular novel of Achebe, is the story of a hero who suffers a rise and fall because of his temperament and largely because of the culture-clash between the two societies, namely African and European. Like Achebe, Naipaul feels greatly concerned about the subordination of the Eastern culture to the Western. However, unlike Achebe, he is satirical and cynical in his approach. It will be important to mention here that Achebe's *Things Fall Apart* and Naipaul's *A House for Mr. Biswas* are regarded contemporary classics and, no wonder, copies of both these novels have been sold in millions.

In the manner of the Greeks and the Elizabethans, Naipaul prefixes a prologue to the novel. The Prologue, serving its literary purpose, anticipates the theme and the action of the novel. It reveals that the hero, Mr. Mohun Biswas, is living in a house of his own at the time of his death due to a heart attack at the age of forty-six. Ten weeks before he died, Biswas, a journalist at Sikkim Street, St. James, Port of Spain, was sacked by the *Trinidad Sentinel.*

The house in the novel stands for what life has denied to its lowborn hero in a poverty-stricken colony. Throughout the narrative, Mr. Biswas is haunted by the feeling of instability and oppression since his childhood as he is rendered homeless and frustrating-self by the accidental death of his father, Raghu, in a remote village of Trinidad. His mother, Bipti, sells the hut and the land to a troublesome neighbour and takes shelter at the back terrace of her sister's house at Pagotes. The early reading of the novel gives an immediate impression of the setting of the novel and the reader at once knows that we are transported to the land of Naipaul's birth, that is Trinidad. At first, it was a Spanish colony but later on it became a part of the British Empire. Also, we form the first impression that the people in Trinidad are economically poor and their society is not based on a strong culture. The novel is essentially the story of one man's endeavour to overcome the wasteland, the derelict land of Trinidad's East Indian people. Biswas is an unimportant man, not a traditional hero, but the overall impression that he leaves on the readers is not hazy or shadowy. He represents the twentieth century common man and the reader unconsciously identifies himself with this unfortunate person. While he faces the various vicissitudes of life, we are immediately transported to the world of absurd. In this respect, he bears a close affinity with the protagonists in the fiction of Joseph Conrad, John Steinbeck and Ernest Hemingway. Jim, in Conrad's *Lord Jim*, is a sincere and dutiful hero but the worldly forces act against him. Despite his best efforts, he fails to establish his credentials. The *Patna* episode brings disaster in his life. While other crew members escape punishment, he speaks truth and becomes a victim of circumstances. Because of his guilt-consciousness, he goes to Patusan to seek new life and opportunities. But there also, he feels disillusionment as the trust that he reposes in Brown is reciprocated by villainy. He is shot and meets his end. In the entire story of *Lord Jim*, as also *Heart of Darkness*, another significant novel of Conrad, the protagonist has to make a 'choice' and in doing so he suffers from existential angst. Man has to strive hard in order to live, but he realizes the absurdity of life and questions the very meaning of life. In the first half of the twentieth century, many writers were influenced by the philosophy popularized by Camus, Sartre and Kafka.

If we evaluate the protagonist in *A House for Mr. Biswas*, we find he partakes many of the traits of an existential hero. Biswas is at odds with the world around. Is there any God? Why do we exist? What is the meaning of life? Biswas cannot find answer to any of these questions. He is like a modern man, absolutely alienated from society, who comes to believe that there is no room for human values in a world where each individual has to struggle and suffer. Biswas, like Conrad's Jim, lives in a perpetual fear of insignificance and alienation. He chooses, at every step, the best step available to him but soon finds that he has been living in a world of illusion and though he endeavours to find reality, it always eludes him.

IV

Naipaul has great connection with India that is amply revealed in his writings. He has written extensively on India and many of his views on this country have evoked controversies. This is because he has given expression to several negative remarks on India, in books like *An Area of Darkness* and *India: A Wounded Civilization*. *An Area of Darkness* was occasioned by a journey. He had travelled to India but realized that it was a difficult book to write about. He found the experience of India too personal, too private to be turned into fiction. In any case, the description of the journey is highly absorbing, though provocative. What redeems the book is the autobiographical element that permeates the entire work. Subsequently, Naipaul has given several compliments to India in his writings, and otherwise. No wonder, when Naipaul won the Nobel Prize, it was greatly celebrated in India. Naipaul was invited to India and a grand programme was organized at Vigyan Bhavan, New Delhi, in his honour where Prime Minister Atal Bihari Vajpayee paid him a glowing tribute as one who had done India proud by winning the coveted prize.

While Naipaul has been writing for forty-five years, it was with the publication of *Half a Life* last year that he received the Nobel Prize. This novel is the story of a father and his son who fail to fully engage with life. The narrative begins in India in the 1930s when a young brahmin Willie Chandran, heeding the call of Mahatma Gandhi turned his back on his Brahmin heritage and married a woman of low caste—a disastrous union he would live to regret. Years later, Willie attends college in London, where he discovers how easy it is to conceal the truth about his mixed heritage and his parents' marriage. The narrative takes us across three continents and Naipaul reveals the way of all our experience. As Willie comes to see, "Everything goes on a bias. The world should stop, but it goes on." Interestingly, Naipaul endows his work with the heightened power of a fable.

Naipaul has been appreciated immensely both by critics and readers. He has been hailed as one of the greatest living writers in the English language, one who is an adept craftsman and master storyteller. The present volume, a collection of recent essays on his writing, aims at paying the fittest literary tribute to Naipaul, the Nobel Laureate.

Unhoused Mr. Naipaul: Some Perspectives on the Fiction of Naipaul

JAYDEEP SARANGI
Seva-Bharati Mahavidyalaya, Midnapore

As the news of V.S. Naipaul being awarded Nobel Prize came, many of us took it as an unexpected and a delayed decision of the Swedish Academy. Naipaul was surprised, "I am utterly delighted. This is an unexpected accolade!" As the news broke, every Indian felt proud of this Trinidad-born English author, who is of Indian parentage.

> Compared to the explosion of multiple realities and universes that postmodern writing places on the literary buff's plate the work of Sir Vidiadhar Surajprasad Naipaul, recipient of this year's Nobel Prize for Literature looks decidedly old-fashioned. He pursues the truth as he does it, through writing that is disciplined, precise, pared down and evocative. This makes him a loner among today's literary superstars, a sense of loneliness further ramified by his unique background and roots.[1]

Trinidad is one of the islands which together are called the West Indies. Trinidad and Tobago are the southernmost islands of the Caribbean archipelago, geologically an extension of the South American continent. Trinidad is separated from Venezuela by the seven-mile (11kms.) straits of the Gulf of Praia. Like their South American neighbours, indigenous people, mainly the Caribs and the Arawaks inhabited the islands prior to their discovery by Christopher Columbus in 1498. Trinidad was in the hands of the Spanish from the 15th century until the British captured it in 1797. It became an independent country in 1962. Naipaul's grandfather had emigrated to Trinidad from Benares (now called Varanasi) in Uttar Pradesh. Naipaul left Trinidad to study at Oxford at the age of eighteen. After the completion of his B.A. degree, he took up broadcasting as a career. Why did he leave Trinidad? In *The Middle Passage*, Naipaul wrote, "when I was in the fourth form, I wrote a vow on the endpapers of my Kennedy 'Revised Latin Primer' to leave within five years. I left after six, and for many years afterwards in England, falling asleep in bed-sitters with the electric fan on, I had been awakened by the nightmare that I was back in tropical Trinidad." His West Indies was a derelict land. The famous realist Australian poet A.D. Hope wrote of his country as a woman beyond her change of breast still tender but within the womb is dry.

Probably, Naipaul was disillusioned by the 'Tropical Trinidad.' It was a nightmare to him: "In Trinidad, from seven or eight in the morning to five in the afternoon, the heat was great, to be out of doors was to be stung, to feel the heat and discomfort."[2] In diasporic writings, the images of home, family and association connote the attempts to rebuild home (away from original home) and, therefore, exert a powerful pull on the imagination of the writers of Indian diaspora. The characters of such diasporic writings share the similar biography with the writer. Naipaul cannot be included in the same group. On the other hand, his stress is on the individual struggle to overcome change and insecurities within relationships. His fiction projects the poignant sense of cultural transition and loss. The backdrop often manifests the struggle to cope with the loss of tradition and the effort to cling to the reassurance of home.

The *Mystic Masseur* tells the story of a man called Ganesh Ramsumair belonging to Trinidad. The author describes an imaginary confrontation between the members of Creole and Indian society on one side and the sophisticated and civilized wife of the governor on the other. Naipaul ridicules the Creole society: the unsophisticated grammar, lack of aptitude or social grace. In *The Middle Passage*, Naipaul describes these people as being, "like monkeys pleading for evolution." A pidgin becomes creolized when a generation of speakers learns it as their first language. This particular sociolinguistic entity becomes relevant when the parents of different linguistic backgrounds have only pidgin as a common language and their children hear it spoken in conversations. "Pidgins and their creolization have great bearing on social and historical backgrounds of speech communities."[3] "Creoles becomes fully developed languages, having more lexical items and broader array of grammatical distinctions than pidgins. In time, they become languages as complete in every way as other languages."[4]

The Suffrage of Elvira is about a successful campaign by Mr. Harbans, a Trinidadian Hindu, to win elections from Elvira (a place in Trinidad). Suffrage has a specific cultural connotation. To the people of Elvira, it means a selfish opportunity for personal gain. The novel portrays the basic selfishness and hypocrisy of the common residents. It is this basic selfish motif that ensures Harbans' return. Baksh is bribed first in to the election; and, finally, to withdraw his candidature for the 'popular candidate.' The novel depicts Elvira with a 'destitute society without history, without achievement.' The readers find the novel interesting for the comic presentation of self-interest, basic creed and of petty ambitions which together constitute the plot of the novel.

Naipaul successfully depicts the English setting in *Mr. Stone and the Knight's Companion.* Mr. Stone is frightened by thoughts of his retirement. His world reflects the nothingness that he carries with him. The opening pages of the story are set in winter. Mr. Stone's house is sketched as an empty place. Decay and a feeling of nonentity trouble him so much that he can't even look forward to his retirement. Mr. Stone's world seems to be darker than Mr. Biswas's. The aging librarian watches his idea "licked into shape" by Whymper. His life turns everything upside down.

A House for Mr. Biswas is set in Trinidad, where the novelist was born. Trinidad, an island in the Caribbean Sea, became an independent country in 1962. Naipaul saw the dismal condition of the Indian labourers who were imported into Trinidad. The novel spans forty-six years of Mr. Biswas's life. Apparently, the novel is a family saga of Mr. Mohun Biswas, who marries into the Tulsi family. Pundit Tulsi emigrates from India to Trinidad as a sophisticated Indian. The society of Trinidad is mainly agrarian. Shipping and petroleum are the major industries of Trinidad. There is a reference to Hanuman House. The story of this novel is Mr. Biswas's struggle to get a house of his own. The story has another dimension: Mr. Biswas finds himself a misfit in Mrs. Tulsi's household. The conjugal life of Mr. Biswas and Shama never becomes a happy one. They remain like two islands in the Caribbean sea. They become emotionally uprooted. Having lost his identity to a great extent, Mr. Biswas finds his life in Hanuman House to be one of great strain because all are hostile to him. Mr. Biswas, after a history of two heart attacks, dies. *The Trinidad Sentinel* announces his death as "Journalist Dies Suddenly." Shama and her children go back to their 'empty' house.

> The Hanuman House [at Arwacas] in Trinidad is the abode of the Tulsi family which represents the old Hindu identity. The Hanuman House was established by a Pundit who happened to be an immigrant. The Tulsi household represents the old Hindu tradition in miniature. Hari, a priest for generations, performs the family ceremonies and rituals. The Creole culture and the orthodox Hindu beliefs leave room for social transmission. The novel highlights the problem of geo-political uprooting of people and the consequences of socio-cultural hybridity. The sense of 'uprooting' weakens the traditional forces. Mr. Biswas's desire to own a house symbolizes an individual's strong impulse to protect his identity.

The Mimic Men, a political novel, deals with the society in Isabella. Ralph Kripal Singh, the protagonist, passes his childhood in Isabella (in the Caribbean), goes abroad for education in England. He marries an English lady. He experiences the feeling of 'exile' in a foreign soil. Ralph Kripal Singh undergoes the same feeling even when he comes back to his newly independent motherland. *The Mimic Men* is about a hollow society and its true victims. Singh fails to settle in Isabella. He decides to settle down in London. For him, 'exile' involves the consolidation of 'forced absence.'

All cultures are hybrid and heterogeneous by nature. No one can deny the existing continuities of long traditions, linguistic heritage and sustained habitations. "Survival in fact is about connections between things."[5] 'Exile' is a status to the marginal. Men in exile search for authentic identity. Naipaul is to a great degree a cosmopolitan novelist. He is basically unhappy about the cultural and spiritual poverty of Trinidad. He feels uprooted from India, and in England he fails to identity himself with the British traditional values of what was once a citadel of colonial power.

"Naipaul grew up with an exalted idea of the Western literary canon. Unlike, for example, Salman Rushdie, whose literary references were Gunter Grass, Gabriel Garcia Marquez, Naipaul cut his teeth on the great masters of nineteenth and early twentieth century. European fiction: Tolstoy, Balzac, Stendhal, Flaubert and Proust."[6] Naipaul's colonial world is mixed and second-hand. In *The Enigma of Arrival*, Naipaul visits the reality of England like an anthropologist studying some hitherto unexplored areas. Naipaul creates an unrelenting image of the collapse of the age-old colonial ruling and the European dominance. Caribbean and Indian traditions are blended with the socio-cultural traditions encountered by the author when he settled down in England. The narrator in *The Enigma of Arrival* is concerned of his historical roots with the Caribbean. He attempts to minimize his West Indian cultural traditions, maybe for the sake of the sacrality of the canon of Western literature. The Trinidad landscape is too enclosed for him. But having come to India searching for an alternative to cultural traditions sanctified by Orientalist lore, he finds some material that he could use. *India: A Million Mutinies Now* is an enduring monument of postcolonial India. For Naipaul, Orient is not merely a map. The colonial power had exploited in the oriental countries both politically and culturally. People in the postcolonial era live in a world of inter-dependent mongrelized social entity. Naipaul's mixed cultural experience has the components of both, the East and the West. *India: A Million Mutinies Now*, a travel book, takes us from Bombay to Calcutta, from Kashmir to Madras. It is a near-true picture of a nation—"million mutinies"—on the move.

A Bend in the River gives an account of the personal relationships of an Indian Muslim. The setting of the story is a

Franco-phone African State. Naipaul traces out the personal relationships among the characters. The novel is predominantly pessimistic. It is also marked by Conradian nihilism and corruptibility of human endeavour. For Naipaul, pessimism is endemic to African environment. The president tries to combine new technology and new mythology in his concept of the new Africa. *A Bend in the River* typifies a colonial rage. This is more Arundhati Roy-like rage at the colonizer turned inside out.

Naipaul prefaces *Half a Life* with the saying: "This book is an invention. It is not exact about the countries, periods or situations it appears to describe." It is obviously a semi-autobiographical work. *Half a Life* was published just before the Nobel Prize came his way. It "portrays and evaluates the lives of the people of mixed descent in three countries—India, England and Portuguese Africa (modelled on Mozambique) and their struggle to discover their identities." The novel "delineates the traumas of a tainted and troubled past, of attempting to find some meaning and purpose of life."[7] It is a treatise on the pangs of the exiles. Exile is a mental condition—a sense of insecurity and anxiety for living 'half a life.' As Edward Said says: "The man who finds his homeland is still a tender beginner, he to whom every soil is as his native one is already strong, but he is perfect to whom the entire world is as a foreign land."[8]

Naipaul chooses to exclude himself from the countries, cultural identities and communities within which he moves. For him, the entire world is but a foreign soil. He always suffers from a basic homelessness. The story of *Half a Life* is told by three narrators. The first part of the story is told to the hero, Willie Chandran, by his father:

> Willie Chandran asked his father one day, 'why is my middle name Somerset? The boys at school have just found out and they are mocking me.'
>
> His father said without joy, 'You are named after a great English writer. I am sure you have seen his books about the house.'
>
> 'But I haven't read them. Did you admire him so much?'
>
> 'I am not sure. Listen and make up your own mind.'

> And this was the story Willie Chandran's father began to tell. It took a long time. The story changed as Willie grew up. Things were added and by the time Willie left India to go to England this was the story he had heard.[9]

The son is Willie Somerset Chandran who has the middle name after the famous English writer Somerset Maugham. Willie's father decides to join Mahatma Gandhi's crusade against casteism and to prove the point, he marries a girl of backward class. He even takes the vow of 'brahmacharya.' Willie's father becomes the father of a son and a daughter in quick succession. The daughter is Sarojini, who is named after the famous pre-Independence poet of India: "This was the story that Willie Chandran's father told. It took about ten years. Different things had to be said at different times. Willie Chandran grew up during the telling of the story." (35) Willie's father named her daughter after 'the woman poet of the independence movement' in the hope that the same blessing might fall on his daughter. The girl, Sarojini was the image of her mother. And for Willie, "It was like divine punishment." (35)

Willie and his father differ from the beginning itself. To prove the point we may refer to the discourse between them in 'A Visit from Somerset Maugham':

> His father said, 'You asked me many years ago, before I began the story, whether I really admired the writer after whom you are named. I said I wasn't sure, that you would have to make up your own mind. Now that you've heard what I had to say, what do you think? Willie Chandran said, 'I despise you.' 'That is your mother talking.' Willie Chandran said, 'What is there for me in what you have said? You offer me nothing.' (35)

Willie's father depends heavily on his friendship. He even considers his friendship as a 'treasure.' Willie's father is too optimistic to hope for Sarojini's international marriage.'

The omniscient author intervenes to narrate the next part (The First Chapter) of the story:

> Willie Chandran and his sister Sarojini went to the mission school. One day one of the Canadian teachers asked Willie, in a smiling friendly way, 'what does your father do?'

> It was a question he put at various times to other boys as well, and they had all readily spoken the various degraded callings of their fathers. (37)

Willie emerges, oddly like his father, exceptionally sensitive to the immigrant community of post-war London. He is like a protagonist in a picaresque novel. He is portrayed as a bohemian 'with nothing to his name but his promise as a writer, drifting aimlessly, groping for a voice.' Willie's London chapter is full of frightening incidents. He becomes desperate to satisfy his carnal desires. Ana guides him to satisfaction. With her, he visits a province of Portuguese Africa. (139-40)

'A Second Translation' is about Willie's life with Ana. And just as once Willie's father told him about his life, "so now, over many days of the Berlin winter, in cafes and restaurants and the half-empty flat, Willie began slowly to tell Sarojini of his life in Africa." The first day at Ana's estate house meant different to him. He felt as a stranger. He hardly knew about a colonial country in Africa. Willie met a little African maid, who greeted him in an oddly stylish manner. "So you are Ana's London man." She asked him some formal questions: 'Did you have a pleasant journey?' 'Have you had a chance to see something of the country?' and 'What do you think of the country?' At this point of life, Willie suffered from the oppression of kinship. He was not free from the nausea of disconnectedness, alienation and lack of social standards in a group of persons. He often thought back to the first day. Things were different sixty or seventy years before, "when Ana's grandfather had arrived to take over the immense tract of land he had been granted by a government that felt its own weakness and was anxious—in the face of the restless power and greater populations of Britain and Germany—to occupy the African colony it claimed." (149)

Willie's search for roots in the African state is laudable but abortive. Willie's case is not that of "weak gravity [that] keeps your dreams inside your head so that they don't go flying out."[10] Cross-cultural transmission is a complex negotiation and exchange. It is a dialogic as well as an interactive process. Willie's gravity of cultural monopoly seems to be 'weak' and queer.

Willie has similarities with Naipaul himself. Both of them suffer from nausea of cultural plantation. They live their foreign soil where they feel uprooted.

The coral reef ecosystem around the Caribbean has been drying these days. Similarly Naipaul's path to success is not all that glorious. He has been attacked for not only his anti-Islam stand/references but also his works on postcolonial change in India. Khushwant Singh claims Naipaul as the writer with elements, nobody writes like him. The way he writes English is just beautiful. He has command over the language.[11] His literary domain is not confined to the West Indian Island of Trinidad. He encompasses India, Africa, America from South to North, and the Islamic countries of Asia and of course, England. For the experts from the Swedish Academy awarding the 2001 Nobel Prize for Literature to V.S. Naipaul, "for having united perceptive narrative and incorruptible scrutiny in works that compel us to see the presence of suppressed histories," Naipaul is a literary circumnavigator. The mood of the Indian writers is upbeat. Playwright and theatre personality Mahesh Dattani praises Naipaul. He also claims Naipaul's achievement as the seventh Indian to get the coveted prize, "He is the seventh Indian to get it and the second to receive it for literature after Rabindranath Tagore. It's good news."[12] Rabindranath, the Bengali poet, got the Nobel Prize in1913 for his *Gitanjali*. Naipaul's *Beyond Belief: Islamic Excursions among the Converted Peoples* expresses his ruthless empathy for the Islamic prejudices. Sunil Gangopadhyaya, the famous Bengali novelist, feels happy over the news. "He should have won it 10 years ago. He is one of the best writers in English right now." "There is also coincidence with his latest novel and my serialized memoirs which have appeared in a Bengali magazine. It was called *Ardhek Jiban* which means half life, the title of his latest novel."[13] The author of *The Binding Vine*, Shashi Deshpande says, "I'm glad he's won and I'm happy for anyone who get what they deserve. In fact I've been reading *Enigma of Arrival* by Naipaul. His writing is unusual. As a writer, he is so good at expressing himself."[14] Naipaul's novels are materially alluring and imaginatively enchanting for the exotic cultural references he depicts in his novels. "Postcolonialism is, in a way, an assertion of cultural nationalism, or the voice of people who unheard so long, the voice of people who were formerly underdogs."[15] There are not many voices from Trinidad. Through Naipaul, a marginalised West Indian society, its people and exotic natural surroundings get represented. Social representation from all quarters of the world contribute to 'new literature.' And cultural nationalism is the hallmark of the 'new literature.'

Naipaul makes synthesis out of 'home' and 'abroad.' The meaning of values varies. There is a cultural mismatch. There is "the necessary combination of distance and intimacy with a place."[16] Migrant writers project their identity as plural and partial. Naipaul observes things both as an insider and an outsider. This is possibly, a common scene in Indian green-card holding diaspora too. Naipaul does not work for the dropping of boundaries. Like Jhumpa Lahiri, his writings are nomadic: he visits different locales and gets into these localisms. Life in exile is a trademark of Naipaul canon.

On the occasion of the First International Festival of Indian literature (18 Feb. 2002), "At Home in the World," organised by the Indian Council for Cultural Relations, Indian Prime Minister accolades Naipaul, "Though one may or may not agree with your description of India as a land of a million mutinies, I do know this nation of one billion people celebrated your winning the Nobel Prize as a proud event."[17] Naipaul, the guest of honour, says, "Literature is a part of a society that is always on the move and not that of a stagnant society."[18] He praises the ancient Indian literature and approves the dynamism in Indian English Writing.

Derek Walcott while interviewing Naipaul had asked him about his relationship with the country of his origin. Naipaul's cryptic response "I am not a cricketer" conveyed his aversion to cricket as much as his refusal to be labelled. West Indies has produced many a cricketing genius. He remains unhoused in his literary works. Meenakshi Mukherjee rightly says, "Naipaul's lack of roots is a burden that he carries with him in his restless travels around the world, as well as a weapon with which he can ironically slice up the countries he visits. It's the source of his strength as well as his acerbity."[19] Naipaul's novels are of new planetary consciousness and a new breed of cosmopolitan citizenry. He is well aware of the pitfalls of national consciousness. The diasporic and the exilic composites of the transnational writers like Naipaul should not be euphemistically termed as the writers of national consciousness only. Such consciousness may be non-existent. There is the homogenizing impulse in slotting diverse kinds of life and attitude under the insignia of nationalism. Naipaul is the odd man in the new generation of postcolonial writers who celebrate the plurality of their heritage.

NOTES

1. *The Statesman*, 21October 2001, Kolkata.
2. *Desh*, Feb. 2001, Kolkata.
3. Suresh Chandra, *Aspect of Linguistics and English Language Teaching Now* (Delhi: Doaba, 1992).
4. Fromkin and Rodman, *An Introduction to Language* (Chicago: Holt, Rinehart and Winston, 1988).
5. Edward Said, *Culture and Imperialism* (London: Chatto and Windus, 1993), p. 408.
6. *The Statesman*, 21October 2001, Kolkata.
7. Parmanand Jha, *Indian Journal of English Studies*, Vol. 39, p. 47.
8. Edward Said, *The World, The Text and the Critic*, p. 7.
9. V.S. Naipaul, *Half a Life* (London: Picador, 2001), p. 1.
10. Bharati Mukherjee, *Jasmine* (New Delhi: Penguin, 1989), p. 178.
11. *The Asian Age*, Oct. 2001, Kolkata.
12. *Ibid.*, p. 3.
13. *Ibid.*, p. 3.
14. *Ibid.*, p. 3.
15. Rama Kundu, "A Transcultural Voyage: The Agony and the Ecstasy," ed. Amar Nath Prasad (New Delhi: Sarup, 2000).
16. J. Pais Arthur, June 2, 1999, "Uncle Sam's Sisters—Jhumpa Lahiri," Calcutta.
17. Pilgrim, *India Today*.
18. *The Statesman*, Feb. 19, 2002, Kolkata, p. 1
19. *Ibid.* p. 1.
20. *Iaclals Newsletter*, Jan. 2002, p. 1.

V.S. Naipaul: The Man and the Novelist

LAKSHMI KUMARI SHARMA
Vaishali Mahila Mahavidyalaya, Hajipur

V.S. Naipaul was born in the Lion House of Chaguanas in Central Trinidad on 17 August 1932. This house belonged to an influential Capildeo family whose seventh daughter, Bropattie was married to his father, Seepersad Naipaul in 1929. As his grandfather was a resident of Uttar Pradesh (India), his title "Naipaul" is the Hindi transliteration of "Naipaul" or "Nypal" of Panday clan in Brahmins. Vidiadhar Surajprasad Naipaul started his primary education at Chaguana's Government school and stayed there for more than one and half year. In 1938, his father was transferred to Port of Spain. Consequently he moved to Tranquillity Boy's school where he distinguished himself in the Exhibition Examination and in 1942 boys of this school won seven out of twenty-one exhibitions. Thus he got a free access to "Queen's Royal College at Port of Spain where he continued his studies from January 1943 to April 1949 specializing in French and Spanish.

He has published many books which include travelogues, short stories, novels and some collected articles. Under his travelogues come his three books entitled *The Middle Passage* (1962), *An Area of Darkness* (1964), and *India: A Wounded Civilization* (1977). *The Middle Passage* is a final testimony to the integrity of the Trinidad and Tobago Government on one hand and to the integrity of Naipaul on the other. *An Area of Darkness* shows that Naipaul is deeply concerned with the drives of the Indian civilization and culture. He suffers badly from the tension between identification and alienation, between belonging or not belonging. The final impression that he carries is that old India is a mixture of pride and pretensions, sensibility and brutality, incompetence and inefficiency. The India he saw was like an onion with one skin after another of pretence—at the heart—negation, nothing. *India: A Wounded Civilization* is nothing but a complement to an *Area of Darkness*. There is more of anguish than anger in Naipaul's observations on India, and they are prompted by his concern for the survival of the values nurtured by the ancient civilization of India.

Under short story come his two books. *A Flag on the Island* (1967) is a collection of eleven short stories. The stories are well made and are cast in the conventional mould. The themes are varied; some of them are related to the plight of the Hindus in the West Indies troubled with Christianity; some others explore the feeling of alienation among London suburbanites and his pre-occupation with pets. Throughout the multiplicity of subjects, Naipaul achieves coherence, precision, wit, humour and satire which establish him as one of the creative writers in English. There is a combination of several strands of different cultures in Naipaul's personality. He is a Trinidadian by birth, Indian Brahmin by descent and Western by education and attitudes. Therefore, he is well-equipped to feel into their consonances and dissonances and it is mostly their incompatibilities that provide him with themes which his creative imagination dramatizes in the novels.

The novels of Naipaul form a pattern around a central theme. They are attempts to articulate an ever-growing vision of rootless and displaced humanity in quest of home and a congenial central milieu to drive their roots in. Naipaul's systematic exploration into the moral urges and drives characteristic of Trinidadian Hindus and others receives an added poignancy from the fact that Naipaul, himself a Trinidadian, is engaged in urgent search for a home from which he feels to have been displaced. But as is evident from *An Area of Darkness*, he meets with frustration and disappointment in his attempts to recover and restore to himself the lost original home. The fact that he repeatedly comes back to the task of understanding and discovering for himself the reality of India shows that the pull of the values of his forefathers is quite strong.

It is instructive to contrast Naipaul's angry or anguished outburst against the anachronism of Indian habits of thinking and patterns of beliefs in his travelogues like *An Area of Darkness*, *India: A Wounded Civilization* and newspaper articles collected in *The Overcrowded Barracoon* with his genial amused good natured irony in his novels. His liberal imagination and compassionate humanity combined with his sharply critical perceptions of the social and moral concerns of the present day Trinidadian Hindus give us detached, dry but humane pictures of abiding human comedy. Naipaul seems to suggest that there is no escape for human beings from one or the other kind of subservience to social and moral authority. All societies have their characteristic means and ways of holding their members in bondage whether colonial or metropolitan, advanced or tribal. Naipaul's choice of themes, his attitude to life around him, his belief in language and its communicative powers, his preoccupation with social reality mark him as 'contemporary' rather than a 'modern' novelist. The distinction between the 'contemporary' and the 'modern' was first drawn by Stephen Spender in his book *The Struggle of Modern*. According to him, a novelist engaged in the critical explorations of the social and political circumstances of his age is a 'contemporary' novelist. His exploration is, of course, performed with intense moral concerns for the finer possibilities of human beings. These 'contemporaries' protest against those elements in the social life which altogether thwart human aspirations for humane and moral order. There is a strong line of such contemporary novelists in the history of English novel. Dickens, George Eliot, H.G. Wells and Galsworthy are some of the major novelists of this category. In respect of themes, forms, techniques and language, V.S. Naipaul stands out as a novelist who has broken new grounds with admirable virtuosity and grace.

Naipaul, like every conscious artist, was in search of a creative congenial tradition. While discussing the relationship between his writing and the tradition of England and European literature, he admits to have read Dickens, Charlotte Bronte, Conrad, Swift, Dryden and Shakespeare and he finally comes to the conclusion that they, instead of giving inspiration to write, make it difficult for him to be fair to the society around him. "I went to books for fantasy," he says and what he found in Dickens and Jane Austen only succeeded in making him "despairingly conscious of his poverty and haphazardness of my own society. I might adopt Dickens to Trinidad; but it seemed impossible that the life I knew in Trinidad could ever be turned into a book." There has been no influence of any European novelist on V.S. Naipaul and even if there is some, it appears to be very slight, unconscious and general. The distinctly different overall tone with which Naipaul introduces himself in the tradition of contemporary novels sets him apart from other novelists. But he himself acknowledges a teacher who exercised a crucial influential on him and made him aware that it was possible for him to write seriously about his own society. This teacher was none else than his father, S. Naipaul himself, whose short stories in *Gurudeva and the Other Indian Tales* exerted considerable influence on his works. The predominant themes of entrapment and escape in his novels have connections with the themes of these stories. Naipaul admits his indebtedness to his father and dedicates his first published novel, *The Mystic Masseur*, to his father's memory. He writes:

> Something of more pertinent virtue was needed and this was provided by some local short stories. These stories perhaps a dozen in all, never published in Trinidad, converted what I saw into "writing." It was through them that I began to appreciate the distorting, distilling power of writer's art. Where I had seen a drab haphazardness they found order where I would have attempted to romanticize, to render my subject equal with what I had read, they accepted. They provided a starting point for further observation, they did not trigger off fantasy.

The passage shows that the influence of the father on his son is very strong, conscious and particular. Naipaul's own way is the way in which every creative artist adopts and uses tradition available to him. In his case, there are two traditions—the native tradition of story-telling and European tradition of novel. Naipaul has sought to assimilate the European tradition into the rapid bloodstream of his sensibility nurtured by the tradition to which he was born. His understanding of Dickens and his adaptation of Dickensian technique were necessarily conditioned by his awareness with his own culture and the knowledge of his people. Thus, in Naipaul's way of relating himself to two traditions, we find an interesting example of relation between the individual talent and a cross-cultural tradition. It requires a sound critical sensibility to assess the native strengths and weaknesses of the native and alien tradition for the purpose of making their use in the interest of art.

Colonial Consciousness in V.S. Naipaul

M.R. ASHOK
S.V. University, Tirupati

Commonwealth literature today signifies much more than a mere monolithic oversimplification that anything written in English with superficial similarities which is shared by a number of national literatures, especially those in multi-lingual literatures of India and partly subdivisions of Africa. The modern trends and evolutionary appetite of the contributors represents a consciousness which bestows a reality that cannot be overlooked. This stems from the obvious fact that there is a tremendous diversity and divergence which has cumulatively yielded the typical product of 'colonial consciousness' in literature and history.

Literary writings in English which caused an intellectual awareness in the Commonwealth countries has enabled various writers to establish and assert their individual creative urges and aspirations. This has led to many common forms continually breaking into brilliant shapes according to Patrick White in *Voss*. There is a move to inspire interest and a desire to explore these further.

The writings of V.S. Naipaul can be aptly considered in the present context for he gives very powerful expression in terms of the 'colonial consciousness.' In his fiction, he lays stress on the Indian immigrant's dilemma, his troubles and travails, problems and plights in the rapidly changing Caribbean world. Coulthard discusses the common characteristics which shaped the creative sensibility of writers like Naipaul for grappling with the issue of colonial consciousness. He comments: "The historical background in all the islands has followed the same pattern: discovery and conquest by the Spaniards; extermination of the native

Indian population and their replacement by slave-labour from Africa; the introduction of sugar and the world of the sugar estate, both during and after slavery: and independence are at varying dates (Haiti first in 1804 with Jamaica and Trinidad gaining their independence as late as 1962). All the islands have known the common experience of colonialism, exploitation, poverty and economic frustration. In all the islands, racial discrimination has been a problem and racial resentments and complexes continue to be an important factor. The last twenty five years have seen the growth of a middle class in all the islands, living largely on borrowed values (either American, British or French) and an intelligentsia seeking urgently a spiritual and cultural orientation of its own."[1] It is evident that the West Indian novel is a creative derivative of a society influenced predominantly by European landlords, traders, functionaries and African slaves apart from a promiscuous section of indentured Indians.

Thereby a hybrid society came into existence like the one of the Caribbeans exposed to innumerable challenges of self-discovery, self-recognition and self-assertion after prolonged subjection and cultural deprivation. The literature of the region attempts to give articulation to their inmost aspiration and yearnings, distress and diffidence of an emerging nation. Hence, this is very powerful and pulsating literature encompassing a vast amount of felt life experiences concerning the menace and the comfort of discovering origins.

George Lamming, a much acclaimed West Indian novelist, has enumerated on three important events in the history of the Caribbean islands: "The first event is the discovery . . . the next event is the abolition of slavery and the arrival of the East-India and China in the Caribbean Sea. . . . The third important event . . . is the discovery of the novel by West Indians as a way of investigating and projecting the inner experience of the West Indian community." The West Indian novel symbolizes articulation in a powerful way, the complexities and sensibilities of a race dogged by disillusionment and riddling uncertainties.

V.S. Naipaul strives at presenting the indentured Indian immigrant's hapless, hopeless predicament in the West Indian context. The root cause for colonization occurred on account of an unfortunate coincidence in the political history of the world, when slavery was abolished in 1833. There was a crisis which precipitated a need for recruitment of cheap labour by the Planters. As a consequence, a steady string of shiploads of Indian labourers was transported to many parts of the world, not excluding the Caribbean. Hugh Tinker observes, "They arrived as coolies, and in many people's eyes they are itinerant coolies still. For slavery is both a system and an attitude of mind. Both the system and the attitude are still with us."

Tinker also mentions Lord Russell's stipulations of 15 February 1840 fearing these mass transfer of labourers from British India as highly improper, as it might perpetrate two harms, one of the loss of lives, the other of starting anew a fresh system of slavery! Naipaul viewed this act of uprooting Indian peasants, most of whom had not even dared to venture beyond the confines of their tiny village hamlets, as tremors prior to a devastating shock leading to indentured repercussions in their consciousness. Moreover, he describes the intimate close-knit harmony in life shared by Indians, however poverty-stricken and evil ridden their society may be. They show an extraordinary sense of traditional values and undisrupted community life, both of which are prone to becoming the first causalities in the event of a cultural shock accompanying change into a new environment. Through their economic exploitation and cultural disorientation, their psyche is crippled, rendering them orphan and destitute.

The Indian segment anywhere in the world constitutes a sizeable portion of the total population. Naipaul throws light on the indentured slave's descendents, whose world and world-view have been ruthlessly fragmented time and again, grossly affecting the sense of wholeness of existence. Thereby they are doomed to grapple with a perennial cultural vacuum as also face various natural and human hostilities in consequence. Commenting on this society, Naipaul declares: "A peasant-minded, money-minded community, spiritually cut off from its roots, its religion reduced to rites without philosophy set in a materialistic colonial society: a combination of historical accidents and national temperaments has turned the Trinidad Indian into a complete colonial, even more philistine than the White."

The thematic exposition of Naipaul's novels, especially of the first two phases, aims at exploring failures, futility, isolation, dispossession, rootlessness and value baselessness of an unanchored community. Treatment of this subject of cultural crisis has met with enthusiastic writers contemplating on the West Indian immigrant's lot. Several prominent spokespersons like Samuel Selvon, Wilson Harris and Shiva Naipaul, besides poets like Derek Walcott, Hendricks and Meryn Morris, have dwelt on this aspect. V.S. Naipaul is outstanding in his contribution through his detailed and illuminating analytical studies of this crucial issue. Most of his works concentrate on defining and ascertaining "the setting, the historical time, [and] the racial and social complexities of the people concerned."

To Naipaul, the novel offered a convenient channel as a form of social inquiry, much less than a mere pretext for writers surrogating and sacrificing it as an opportunity for indulgent autobiography or a platform for bragging about themselves. His fiction can be perceived as a homogenous and artistic blend of a creative interpretation of the past while offering a rich criticism about the contemporary life. Hence, it emerges as an authentic account of the agony and the pride, the trials and tribulations of his people. Both the Negro and the Indian suffer dislocation but the fate of the Indian is worse. His experiences are more acute, pathetically tragic, far more bewildering and his problems of adjustment exceed all the above. Drawing the distinction of attitudes between the two immigrant communities, Naipaul states:

> Much of the West Indian Negro's drive arises out of his desire to define his position in the world. The Indian, with no such problem, is content with his narrow loyalties. . . . Indian politicians have created Indian radicalism out of a harmless egoism. Negro racialism is more complex. It is an overdue assertion of dignity; it has elements of bitterness; it has something of the urban mob requiring to be satisfied with bread and circuses. It has profound intellectual prompting as well, in the realization that the Negro problem lies not simply in the attitude of others to the Negro, but in the Negro's

> attitude to himself. It is as yet confused, for the Negro, while rejecting the guilt imposed on him by the White man is not able to shake off the prejudices he has inherited from the White man.

One may contradict Naipaul's neat distinction, but the problems of Indian immigrants are a glaring, stark reality. The task of giving a faithful picture of them was not an easy one. This was further heightened by the complicated fact that the Caribbean society underwent uprooting more than once. In his *Autobiography*, Naipaul confesses:

> So there was a migration from India to be considered, a migration from within the British Empire. There was my Hindu family, with its fading memories of India; there was India herself. And there was Trinidad, with its past slavery, its mixed population, its racial antagonisms and its changing political life; once part of Venezuela and the Spanish empire, now English-speaking, with the American base and an open-air cinema at the end of Bogart's street.

Naipaul has spared no pains to etch the dilemma of the Indian immigrant's fractured consciousness consequent to factors like transplantation, exploitation and rootlessness. George Steiner opines: "the modernist movement can be seen as a strategy of permanent exile." He further says that Nabokov, Burgess and Beckett occupy a pivotal position in this movement. Meenakshi Mukherjee contends that Naipaul be considered as belonging to the same fraternity patronizing "their apprehension of reality [which] has been affected by the experience of more than one country and conditioned by exposure to more than one culture."

Naipaul's early novels which include *The Mystic Masseur* (1957), *The Suffrage of Elvira* (1958) and *Miguel Street* (1959) serve to bring about the tradition-ridden, decadent society built precariously upon the degrading and demoralizing facts of colonialism. It is a world devoid of scientists, engineers, soldiers or poets. The people, by and large, lack any cultural ties with their heritage. The deprived yet captivating world is projected here. The confusion of chaotic lives and values without any norms to guide the community are depicted in symbolic terms. In his novel, *Miguel Street,* the past in this society is generally non-existent, a thing without a name and the state of affairs likened to the stray mongrel dog, as a befitting symbol suggestive of the life led by the people.

The Mystic Masseur presents a unique picture of the West Indian society, its crises and challenges in a more systematic way. As M.K. Naik puts it aptly, "Naipaul's main aim in *The Mystic Masseur* seems to be to exploit the comic absurdity in the lives of the transplanted Indians in the West Indies." *The Suffrage of Elvira* is another novel wherein he examines the functioning of democracy in a world where it has no sanction as per tradition. Commenting on the Indian democratic stance, he remarks: "Formal politics answered less and less, became more and more formal; towards the end it had the demeanour of a parlour game, and became an affair of head counting and floor-crossing." Naipaul seems to be thoroughly cognizant of the pitfalls of a nascent democracy. Although politics and electioneering constitute the central theme of the novel, there are other more important considerations for Naipaul in this novel. He presents scenes dealing with family misunderstandings, neighbourly quarrels, breaches of etiquette, lovers meetings, peeping-toms, and several other incidents and events that do not appear to be an integral part of the main political theme. They however shed light on the ways and manners of the people.

The Mimic Men (1967) is far more substantial than his earlier works. The narrative is in the form of dramatized reminiscences. Incidentally, it also presents a detached understanding of a violated, colonial society. This novel attempts to explore "the ways in which the conscious individual in a given society establishes modes of mediation between himself and his experience." In a heterogeneous community like the West Indies, an individual faces multiple problems of adjustment.

Similarly, the subject of the novel is more than mere politics, marriage or race. It is nothing short of a vision of 'disorder,' 'placelessness' and breakdown of human relationship in the world of the 'mimic men.' Commenting on Malgonkar's novel, *The Princes,* Naipaul draws our attention to "the Indian withdrawal and denial," which according to him "is part of the confusion of Indian Anglo-India." This withdrawal, denial and confusion of values is the lot of the other colonial people too.

Naipaul takes absolute care in presenting a lurid picture of the West Indian society. It is one which is hopelessly disorganized and torn asunder by its conflicting loyalties. Though it is a small world, its issues are 'more complex' than in any normally civilized society. Here, everyone's motives remain unclear and these motives and alliances shift rapidly.

To conclude, the West Indian's dilemma is not sorted out by redeeming graces of what Naipaul calls 'racial sense,' the absence of which he holds responsible for the present day India's problems. In Naipaul's novels, the physical and cultural setting acquires a significant role. Speaking up for the uprooted persons he attempts to create a colonial consciousness in this ambiguous New World.

WORKS CITED

The Journal of Commonwealth Literature, 13/3 (April, 1979).

S.K. Desai, "History against History: Commonwealth and Colonial Consciousness," *The Literary Criterion,* 116/4 (1981), pp. 34-43.

William Walsh, *Commonwealth Literature* (OUP, 1973), p. 51.

G.R. Coulthard, *Caribbean Literature: An Anthology* (London, 1966), pp. 10-11.

Kenneth Ramchand, *The West Indian Novel and its Background* (London, 1970), p. 162.

The Pleasure of Exile (London, 1960), pp. 36-37.

A New Slavery (OUP, 1974), p. 383.

The Middle Passage (London, 1962), p. 89.

India: A Wounded Civilization (London, 1977), pp. 18-19.

Autobiography, given in *Gentleman* (Feb, 1984), p. 45.

Extraterritorial (Penguin, 1969), p. 26.

C.D. Narasimhaiah, "Inside Outsider," *Awakened Conscience: Studies in Commonwealth Literature* (New Delhi, 1978), p. 86.

An Area of Darkness (London, 1964), pp. 66-90.

William Walsh, *Commonwealth Literature,* p. 60.

Commonwealth Fiction, ed. R.K. Dhawan (New Delhi, 1988), pp. 128-56.

Naipaul and His Dialectic on India

RAMA DEVI
S.K. University, Anantapur

Naipaul, who writes from the position of "perpetual exile," enjoys the unique status and posture of a professional outsider that enables him to be a prophet, soothsayer, doom-watcher at the same time and utter unpalatable truths which sound too macabre and uncomfortable for the general taste. In order to strip the new postcolonial societies of their pretences and defensive mechanisms, he assumes the role of a "Social Deconstructionist." As Gail Minault points out, Naipaul sees "through a glass darkly and yet face to face."[1] The reader is at once put off by his dark vision of human frailty and attracted by his eye for the telling detail. It is this attribute of his writing which has enabled V.S. Naipaul to shape the travelogue into a finely honed instrument of personal expression. Even in his travelogues, his choice of subjects tends to be highly personal. Just as has been said by D.H. Lawrence that one sheds one's sickness in one's novels, writers like Naipaul—who is a complex of multiple identities—seem to resolve their existential dilemmas in their travel writings. Naipaul travels to discover his own identity to come to terms with his own sense of homelessness and rootlessness, adopting detachment as the only possible response to his situation.

Rootlessness is not merely at the base of' Naipaul's identity but also happens to be his subject matter thus "detached and yet attached, colonial and yet metropolitan, seeing darkly and yet face to face, Naipaul has evolved a style which juxtaposes opposites."[2] Quite in line with his ambiguous identity are the ambivalence and mixed feelings that he rouses in his reader as certainty is something of a luxury for the modern man to afford.

Naipaul's constant quest for identity and ethnic roots during his visits to India, his ancestral land, has resulted in a kind of philosophic acceptance of his separateness from India and at the same time some inexplicable, yet strongly felt, link with India but for which he would not have made so many visits that have culminated in the writing of four books—one fictional and three non-fictional. He observes in *An Area of Darkness* (1962), "I had learned my separateness from India and was content to be a colonial, without a past, without ancestors."[3] The search and the journey he undertakes to the land of his forbears three generations away is by its very nature a romantic theme. The roots, when found, turn out to be "gnarled, sterile, and the journey, frustratingly antiheroic."[4]

Behind the personal account, one can sense the moral concern and the anguish that Naipaul's concern for India brings to the fore. The anguish he feels is due to the 'culture shock,' due to the people's attitude and their lack of a sense of history, growth, their 'ability to retreat, the ability genuinely' not to see what was obvious. (188) But Naipaul cannot be accused of being 'uninvolved' and 'unconcerned,' given his own question, movingly raised, "which Indian would be able to read the history of his country for the last thousand years without anger and pain." (202)

Naipaul's hazy childhood impressions about Hinduism—"a vaguer sense of caste, a horror of the unclean"—play a decisive role when he confronts the living India in the twentieth century:

> Men had been diminished and deformed; they begged and whined. Hysteria had been my reaction; and a brutality dictated by a new awareness of myself as a whole human being and a determination, touched with fear, to remain what I was; it mattered little through whose eyes I was seeing the East, there had as yet been no time for this type of self-assessment. (13)

The sights and sounds of India often made an assault on the wholeness and integrity of one's personality. At the very beginning of *An Area of Darkness*, Naipaul makes clear the emotional dilemma of his involvement with India as an involvement that qualifies the resultant nihilism. At the very beginning he says, "to give to anger and contempt was to know a later self-disgust." (10) Then he reminds himself, "contempt was what I had to fight against, to give way to that was to abandon the self I had known." (45) Thus self-analysis and self-monitoring of responses ensue from him incessantly as he moves through his 'area of darkness.' By way of recording the failure of his attempts to come to terms with India, in *An Area of Darkness*, Naipaul realizes that racial similarities had no meaning and that his Trinidadian upbringing and Western education had rendered him a colonial without a country, an international man, a product of an empire that had withdrawn. Thus Naipaul launches an act of purgation of his system of all dreams of possibility, his soul of India, in his first book on India, *An Area of Darkness*. His sense of disquiet reaches the climax in the last chapter.

The journey to his ancestral home which he had put off for a whole year, and his final encounter with Ramachandra, what was left of his grandfather's pedigree, are in a way his encounter with himself that part which recoils from itself and fills him with self-disgust, the part which had learnt "through the stresses of a long residency in England" (188) to be self-sufficient, self-sustaining and alone. The book which begins with a sense of quest leads him through self-disgust to position of self-discovery.

In *India: A Wounded Civilization* (1977), written next, Naipaul moves away, from a preoccupation with self to a more objective discovery of India. The powerful adjective, 'wounded,' in the title is reminiscent of Jessie Weston's *From Ritual to Romance*. It has references to something maimed, cursed and rendered impotent from an earlier state of potentiality and vitality evidently due to spiritual stupor, lack of personal dignity and responsibility, and the tendency to mimic the west. The title reveals an uneasy sense of personal loss and society in the mind of the writer. Naipaul adopts a pragmatic approach in this book to prove his point on the postcolonial society. What he sees and hears in India are related to men who reflect or transmit culture, to concepts, and assumptions such as "Dharma" and "Karma" at the back of the Hindu attitudes. He finds Gandhi and R.K.

Narayan as more or less representing the old morality, and Vijay Tendulkar and U.R. Anantha Murthy as reflecting the incipient "new morality," whereby individuals realizing the inadequacy of past myths strike out on their own. By saying, "It [India] isn't my home and cannot be my home, and yet I cannot reject it or be indifferent to it,"[5] he is hinting at the spiritual flux in which he finds himself while he is face to face with India, which, at the same time, is not of divided loyalties but of divided energies.

> Naipaul says of Gandhi in *An Area of Darkness*: [Gandhi] emerged a colonial blend of East and West, Hindu and Christian. Gandhi never loses the critical, comparing South African eye, he never rhapsodizes. . . . Sanitation was linked to caste, caste to callousness, inefficiency and hopelessly divided country, division to weakness, weakness to foreign rule. This is what Gandhi saw, and no one purely of India could have seen it. It needed the straight simple vision of the West. (73-74)

This acquires new significance in the light of how Naipaul comes to liken himself to Gandhi, in his *India: A Million Mutinies Now:*

> Growing up in far off Trinidad, I had no idea of class or religion, none of the supports and cushions of people in India. Like Gandhi among the immigrant Indians of South Africa, and for much the same reasons, I have developed instead the idea of the kinship of Indians, the idea of the family of India. And in my attempt to come to terms with history, my criticism, my bewilderment and sorrow, was turned inward, focussing on the civilization and the social organization that had given so little protection.[6]

Thus Naipaul manages to arrive at a kind of self-therapy by forging a new relationship with a violently rejected past. Naipaul continues to take India personally in his book too. This time he comes with a sense of tragedy and urgency, with the new habit of contemplating man as both metropolitan and non-metropolitan. He relegates himself to the status of listener, his critical eye giving way to an ear willing to listen and understand. He finds himself supported by the people he talks to. He uses people's voices, their personal stories and their own witness in order to give a chain of voices that illustrate every phase of Indian life. What he had not understood in 1962 regarding the country's progress and remaking and restoration comes to him through these accounts. He is able to see what must have been necessary to create a Bengali reformer like Ram Mohun Roy and Mahātma Gandhi. He comes to see the British peace after the 1857 Mutiny as a kind of luck, as a time of intellectual recruitment that set India on the way of a new kind of intellectual life during which India was given new ideas about its history and civilization. Naipaul opines that the freedom movement reflected all of this and turned out to be the truest kind of liberation:

> the freedom it [freedom movement] brought has worked its way down. People everywhere have ideas now of who they are and what they owe themselves . . . what was hidden in 1962, or not easy to see, what perhaps was only in a state of becoming, has become clearer. The liberation of spirit that has come to India could not come as release alone. In India, with its layer below layer of distress and cruelty, it had come as disturbance. It had to come as rage and revolt. India was now a country of a million little mutinies. (517)

These million mutinies to Naipaul are the beginnings of self-awareness, beginnings of an intellectual life, already negated by old anarchy and disorder. These mutinies are supported by twenty kinds of group excess, sectarian excess, religious excess and regional excess. Naipaul, after his close encounters with the insiders of all these little movements or excesses ranging from the Dalit movement in Bombay to the Dravidian movement in Tamil Nadu to the Naxalite movement in Calcutta to the Sikh movement in Punjab to the Shiv Sena movement in Maharashtra to the Hindutva movement, tends to take a tolerant and even a rhapsodic view of all these little wars. These mutinies seem to be suggestive of the presence of a central will, a central intellect, a national idea which did not exist 200 years before. In professing thus, Naipaul seems to come very close to the votaries of Hindutva movement who express a similar faith in India.

Naipaul who had earlier used the qualifier 'wounded' deriving its significance from Jessie Weston to title his second book on India in order to hint at the maimed and doomed situation in which India found itself in the 1970s, now comes to view the wounds of the past as likely to be healed by the present and future. And none of India's wounds, now, seem to him as deep as that caused by the great 'Hindu defeat,' the subjection of India to foreign rule, and its consequent emasculation. From a vision of the past as a wound, Naipaul carries three conflicting and at times interacting components in his personality of being a Trinidad colonial, an English metropolitan, a person of Indian ancestry and moves in his self-exploration towards new restoration and vision of wholeness. In his confrontation with India, in this work, he visualizes a more whole world than a mere country. There is visible a growing compassion and a wish to understand that are stronger in Naipaul's writing of this book. 'Women's Era' (Section VIII) of the book clearly illustrates the new compassionate vision attained by Naipaul in this book.

Naipaul grew up with his own ideas of the distance that separated him from India. He was far away from it to cease to be of it. He knew the rituals but couldn't participate in them. "But I was near enough to understand the passions: and near enough to feel that my own fate was bound up with the fate of the people of the country. The India of my fantasy and heart was something lost and irrecoverable." Just when he was beginning to feel that there was no one in India who felt like him, about India, Naipaul happened to come across Vishwa Nath, who says to Naipaul, "When I read the history of India, I weep sometimes." (399) He further says, "we [Indians] have been subdued, subjected to torture, conquest--but no body has been able to kill us off. That has been the strong point of our civilization." (399) Vishwa Nath's women's magazines, especially, *Woman's Era*, carried the same tone of reassurance about it. These magazines also carried a special passion—an outcome of a mixture of his homespun, his sense of history, his reverence for Gandhi and seemingly contradictory rejection of religion. Naipaul attributes the success of *Woman's Era* to the fact that it did not intimidate its readers. Naipaul further says about *Woman's Era*:

> A recurring theme of its stories was the discovery by a woman that the great shame she feels about her poor relations. And *Woman's Era* never shamed its readers. In its stories, its recipes, its photographs . . . it acknowledged the conditions in which its readers lived; . . . Perhaps that recognition in itself was a kind of glamour; . . . With that recognition, there was always reassurance. It could be said that reassurance was the dominant tone of *Woman's Era*. . . . *Woman's Era* invites its readers to a special, shared world. The editorial tone is one of concern, almost love. . . . And when I got to know the editor, Vishwa Nath, I found that this tone fairly reflected his idea of a mission. (411-12)

Of all the people whom he meets and talks in the course of his visit to India, it is with Vishwa Nath that Naipaul tends to identify himself to some extent:

> I used to go to the press, and set type by hand—for play. My father loved printing, and I also loved printing. When I was in the eighth class, when I was eleven, I had decided that I would publish magazines. I felt he was speaking for me. In colonial Trinidad, at about the same age, I had developed--largely through my father, a journalist—a love for print the shapes of letters, the variety of typefaces, a wonder at the way words were transformed when handwriting turned to type. Out of a love for that process I had decided to be a writer, with perhaps less idea of what I was going to write about than Vishwa Nath—in the ferment of India in the 1930s—had of the magazines he was going to publish. (414)

Vishwa Nath is iconoclastic and at the same time concerned about the family, the old social order and the hinge of civilization, which he wanted to preserve and strengthen. The reason why he had started *Woman's Era*—the very name a counter-blast to Woman's lib—was to fight for the sanctity of the family. The tears for the past, the iconoclasm, the fear of chaos coming again, the strong nationalist feeling, the homespun, with the over-riding love of print that had come down from the ancestor who applied a new kind of scholarship to the everyday India he knew have all gone to make *Woman's Era* a success. To Naipaul, *Woman's Era* is nothing but an expression of "a purely Indian social order much lower down, offering instruction and reassurance and a subtle transformation of the hard real world, to women just emerging, women whose lives were a tissue of ritual and given relationships, and didn't want to rebel or dream." (419)

The compassionate narrative vision in this book enables him to capture the theme of India collapsing, mutinying, and reaching after a final integration. It is his ability to look for the sense of life in a mutinous spirit order that is a significant aspect of Naipaul's writing. Even in the midst of apparent chaos, he sees a semblance of continuity, coherence and harmony. Thus the million mutinies come to symbolize the dawn of a postcolonial society for Naipaul. Naipaul feels that "the mutinies were not to be wished away. They were part of the beginning of a new way for many millions, part of India's growth, part of its restoration." (518) He happens to trace behind these mutinies defeat, humiliation, shame, anger, pain given which it is hardly surprising that he sees Babri Masjid as expressing Babar's contempt for India and asks us to understand the passion behind its demolition. Behind this destructive passion, he sees ideas of country and pride and historical self-analysis that have at last dawned upon some Indians. The new attitude expressed in this book brings to light a new Naipaul with 'a central will, a central intellect, a unifying idea' suggesting that the conflicting components of his identity are not to be wished away as they have been responsible for his growth and restoration and achievement of the particular truth he had in his mind all through.

NOTES

1. Gail Minault, "Through a Glass Darkly: Naipaul's Postcolonial Travel Accounts," *Osmania Journal of English Studies* (V.S. Naipaul Special Number, 1982), p. 15.
2. *Ibid.*, p. 24.
3. V.S. Naipaul, *An Area of Darkness* (London: Penguin, 1964).
4. T.R.S. Sharma. "Naipaul's Version of Postcolonial Societies," *Osmania Journal of English Studies*, p. 29.
5. V.S. Naipaul. *India: A Wounded Civilization* (New Delhi: Vikas, 1977), pp. 8-9.
6. V.S. Naipaul *India: A Million Mutinies Now* (London: Minerva, 1990), p. 399.

Naipaul's Vision of Indian Diaspora and Trinity of Indian Travels

H.S. LAL
Feroze Gandhi College, Rae Bareli

The word 'diaspora' means 'distribution.' It also means the dispersion of the Jews among the Gentiles after the period of their exile. In the present times, Diaspora refers to the study of ethnic and racial communities living far away from their native places or homelands. Now we hear and read about the Asian, the African, the Indian, the British and the American Diaspora. The Indian Diaspora is used by many writers in the context of ethnicity of Indians who migrated to foreign lands. Such Indians belong to the first generation expatriates who still treat India as their homeland because of religious faith that they have, and the cultural heritage they possess. Rootless though they are, they still feel deep sympathy and attachment.[1]

Who is an expatriate? An expatriate lives outside his country and the expatriate literature is written by authors as aliens in a foreign country. Yashoda Bhat analyses the main features of expatriate literature characterized by "descriptions of incessant travel, displacement and homelessness. At the heart of an expatriate is a growing restlessness which makes him launch on 'temporary journeys.' 'Flights' and 'escapes' are common features in expatriate life."[2]

The sense of flight from the homeland gives a psychological relief from uncivilized surroundings, religious fundamentalism, obsolete rituals and outdated modes of living. The expatriate writers present authentic pictures of depression and alienation. Most of the expatriate writers, hence, share "the cross cultural existence, the cultural shock, and the cultural encounter—it may be cross religious, cross lingual, cross racial or cross-ethnic, often results in identity crisis. There may be stages of cultural alienation and confrontation only to be followed later by acculturation and cultural actualization and sometimes in genuine cultural assimilation. Several novels on the theme of expatriate experience deal with a depiction of the 'run-on the mill issues.'"[3]

The literature of Indian Diaspora is produced by many writers who are permanent overseas residents popularly known as Non-Indian Residents. These writers are Salman Rushdie, Bharati Mukherji, Amitav Ghosh, V.S. Naipaul, Hanif Kureishi, Jhumpa Lahiri, Geeta Mehta, Rohinton Mistry, Himani Bannerji, Chitra Bannerji Divakaruni etc. in whose writings Diaspora achieves the unintended purpose of celebrating marginality and embracing virtually multiculturalism and diversity. Most of these writers belong to Indian cultural heritage but are settled in the United Kingdom, Singapore, Canada and African countries. They treat India as their homeland but have adopted overseas life-styles; they feel disgusted and alienated. G.S. Sharatchandra, an Indian scholar settled in America, remarks in his short story:

> Though India is always on my mind, there is no link that connects the sudden stop my life came to there and my new self. I leaped from one to another, and in between I left nothing but a vacuum. Only imagination and memory, when I need, act as my bridge. (232)

V.S. Naipaul is an expatriate writer. His journeys to Trinidad, England, Iran and India may be physical but they have mental and intellectual reflections of his moods and sensibility. He escaped to London from the dirt and dust of Trinidad. He travelled to the West Indies, Africa and America but finally settled in England. His visits to these countries refer to his quest for order, creativity and homeland.

Naipaul was born on 17 August 1932 in a family of an Indian immigrant in the central locality of Trinidad. He took a degree from the University of Oxford in 1953, and in 1955, he got a part-time job in the B.B.C. The trinity of his travel writings is: *An Area of Darkness* (1964), *India: A Wounded Civilization* (1977) and *India: A Million Mutinies Now* (1991). These travel writings have established Naipaul as a critic of India and an anti-Indian expatriate. He criticizes Indian customs, insignificant religious practices, hypocritical notions and meaningless spiritual ideas. Naipaul possessed a romantic view of India in his consciousness. The India of his childhood, of Hindu culture, of beautiful temples and colourful festivals helped him build up a dream homeland. He was aware of his ancestral roots. He once remarked: "The particular Diaspora where my work begins, if I can use this word for the migration of my ancestors which took place just over a hundred years ago." (*The Times of India*, June 21, 1994)

In *An Area of Darkness*, Naipaul describes his visit to the village of his grandfather in Uttar Pradesh. His grandfather was a poor Brahmin. With the help of an 'arakatia,' a recruiter, he went to Trinidad and worked in a sugar factory; in addition to his profession he also worked as a Benaras-trained pundit. Gradually he prospered and accumulated a huge property.[5]

V.S. Naipaul had a romantic dream of his homeland. He allows India to appear on the canvas of his memory and imagination. But he was separated from India by two generations. Nonetheless, India had been the background of his childhood.

These books which constitute his travel writings refer to an independent genre. The trinity of Indian travels received aggressive notes from Indian scholars and critics for his anti-Indian projection. In this context, Naipaul remarks: "I am profoundly Indian in my feeling, profoundly in my sensibility—but not in my observations." The problem of V.S. Naipaul is that he remains an Indian in feeling and sensibility but tries to judge his homeland on western modes of life. His travelogues have a theme of quest for roots. His response is like an Indian and at the same time he views India as an outsider. This dilemma is a complex problem; and it refers to his identity-crisis.

The travel writing has its own tradition. Without travel, expatriacy is not possible. In Trinidad, V.S. Naipaul suffered from creative barrenness and in search of creative fertility he travelled to England where he found himself an outsider. He travelled to distant lands and gathered varied experiences of nationalities, cultures and civilizations. His travels gave him new dimension of thoughts and ideas. Travel also gives a new kind of perception of antiquity and modernism. V.S. Naipaul's travel writings blend history, anthropology, philosophy, sociology and ethnography. *The Middle Passage* (1960) is the first book that launched his career as a travel writer. It accounts for his return journey to England where he settled permanently and from where he went to many countries in search of order, stability and cultural roots. As an outsider in London, he suffered from rootlessness but found literary stability. Today London is the centre of international activities and a place of many expatriate writers.

An Area of Darkness (1964) follows the model of his first travel writing *The Middle Passage*. In 1960s, his first visit to India was based on romantic stories told by his relatives in the West Indies. On his visit to India, Naipaul suffered from cultural shock when he encountered degrading and depressing human conditions. The beginning of the novel posits a very disheartening picture of the customhouses and Bombay docks. He felt aghast with uncivilized red-tapism of Indian bureaucracy in early Sixties. His two bottles of whisky that he bought from Alexandria was immediately seized because he had no transport permit. To custom authorities he put a query: "But what is transport permit? . . . Help me. Where can I get this transport permit?"[4] The reply was disparaging and humiliating. V.S. Naipaul felt frustrated. Bombay docks had been his Gateway to India. The most noticeable feature of *An Area of Darkness* is its narrative that exposes the filth, degraded people, decaying social condition and apparent stupidity of Indians living in different cities. His portrayal of Goa and Goanese present a very unpleasant picture. He states:

> For the people of Goa, as for house of Imperial Rome, defecating is a social activity, they squat close to one another, they chatter. (25)

V.S. Naipaul's book is a displaced autobiography. He presents his total disgust: "It was a journey that ought not to have been made, it had broken my life in two." (37) The conflict is between the myth and the acute obscenities perceived by him. He wishes to discover his roots in India that is a country of his childhood's romance, memory and imagination. *A Wounded Civilization* refers to V.S. Naipaul's agony and his vision of his homeland that is based on paradoxes, lassitude and feelings of shame. The extreme poverty and illiteracy compelled thousands of Indian peasants and farmers to emigrate to Africa, Trinidad, West Indies and Guatemala where they worked as labourers. The title of the book is ironical and satirical. V.S. Naipaul criticizes the imposition of Emergency. Emergency after Independence showed India's incapacity and intellectual depletion. The entire book narrates India's political and social events during his visit in 1975. On his visit he was more interested in finding out the sources of India's culture and tenets of civilization. The history of India and its story of invasions by foreigners present the marks of wounds and ruins. *India: A Million Mutinies* was published after thirteen years of his second travel-writing *India: A Wounded Civilization* that refers to his framework of revision of his past visits. He visited India between 1988-99. The last travelogue runs into 520 pages. This is a work of great enquiry. He wishes to correct his errors of the past observation of his homeland. He finds India a country of limitless energy and power and a land of strong determinations. The book is also a realization of the writer's inadequacy to understand India in right perspective. The large part of the book contains interviews. In his interviews, he interacted with people of different sections of society. He could see the other side of the Indian milieu completely different from the area of darkness.

The narrative of the trinity of the Indian writings presents anxiety and tension realized, felt and perceived by the novelist. The trinity of Indian travel writings posits his vision of a country of the third world. His narratology presents panoramic view of historical, cultural and ethnic institutions and the influencing forces of Western world and the scientific advancement. His Diaspora depicts frustration, agony, sense of alienation, rootlessness and writer's own fraudulence. V.S. Naipaul is frank in his revelation. His vision in the first book is anti-India, in the second writing, it deals with decline, ruins and wounds and in the last travelogue it propounds Naipaul's vision of reconciliation. *An Area of Darkness* defines his personal chemistry of imagined Hindu India and disparity that existed between actual and ideal. His imaginary places proved as shadows in his onward journey. *India: A Wounded Civilization* expresses the pliant attitude and Naipaul's existential loss. *India: A Million Mutinies Now*, is a different version of his homeland. Naipaul's vision of Indian Diaspora has a sense of immediacy.

NOTES

1. A.L. McLeod, ed., *The Literature of the Indian Diaspora* (Sterling: 1999), p. 137.
2. Yashoda Bhat, *V.S. Naipaul: An Introduction* (Delhi: B.R., 2000), p. 57.
3. *Ibid.*, p. 63.
4. V.S. Naipaul, *An Area of Darkness* (Penguin, 1970), p. 253.

Narrating the Self: Vikram Seth's *From Heaven Lake* and V.S. Naipaul's *Area of Darkness*

D. MAYA
Government College for Women
Thiruvananthapuram

Travel literature as a genre occupies hardly any space in literary criticism. The absence is unwarranted considering the rich corpus of interesting works in the area, contributed by writers of eminence. In the trail of Robert Louis Stevenson's *The Amateur Emigrant* and Melville's *Typee*, we have the classics of twentieth century travel-writing—Eric Newby's *A Short Walk in the Hindu Rush,* Norman Lewis's *Golden Earth* and Graham Greene's *Journey without Maps.* The commonwealth contribution to the genre has been no less remarkable. George Woodcock's *Asia, Gods and Cities,* Michael Ondatje's *Running in the Family,* J.M. Coetzee's *Waiting for the Barbarians,* V.S. Naipaul's *Area of Darkness,* Vikram Seth's *From Heaven Lake* are works that can stand on par with the best travel-writing.

This paper focuses on two much acclaimed and brilliant pieces of travel writing—Vikram Seth's *From Heaven Lake* and V.S. Naipaul's *Area of Darkness.* As travelogues, these do not merely map the geoscape but become an index to the personality of the writer. Vikram Seth, the young Indian poet and novelist, was a student in China when he made the journey to Tibet and Nepal with very little money in his pocket and the stringent regulations of the Chinese and Tibetan governments barring his freedom. V.S. Naipaul, hailing from Trinidad, was already an established writer when he visited India, a land linked to his past by ancestral roots. A sense of place, a strong consciousness of history and graphic and vivid descriptions of the land and the people distinguish both narratives. As a record of subjective impressions, the tone of the discourse in travel-writing is determined by the persona of the traveller-writer, the land is transformed according to the perceiving, narrating self. The contrast between these two travelogues is too glaring to be overlooked. The eco-friendly spirit of Seth approaches the land he surveys with a sense of total abandon and brings out gems hitherto undiscovered; Naipaul, burdened by colonial prejudices, poises a harshly critical lens on the land and the people and unearths dirt and filth alone. Levi Strauss remarked: "The first thing we see as we travel round the world is our own garbage, flung into the face of mankind."[1] Seth succeeds in escaping the self and tunes in with space; Naipaul is trapped in the self, in its prejudices and bitterness that colour and blind vision. The reader journeys into the inscape of the traveller's experiencing self which sets the dominant tone or 'rasa' of the work.

'Adbhuta,' the sense of wonder, generated by the poet's delight in the heavenly marvels of nature, dominates Seth's work and is transmitted through highly lyrical language. Seth is in harmony with the rhythm of the land and as he hitch-hikes from Sinkiang to Tibet and Nepal, his uninhibited delight in the land he traverses seeks expression though occasional lyrical spurts. The oppressive heat of Turfan and the taxing regulations of Chinese officialdom hardly curb Seth's enthusiasm or disturb the dominant 'rasa' of the work. To him, as to his father, "greenery and flowing water" formed the "idea of paradise."[2] The cartography of the land mapped by Seth has its spots of picturesque beauty. They come to life under his sensitive and poetic touch. Turfan's overwhelming heat and donkey carts form a relief to highlight the beauty of the landscape.

By his vivid descriptions, Seth invests place with a distinct personality of their own. Xingiang with its crystal channels of running water (called karez) that play hide and seek by disappearing underground and surfacing at some point; Tian Chi or Heaven Lake "an area of such natural beauty" that poets choked for space elsewhere in China, could enjoy solitude and ease there

(20); and Xian that brings a sense of deja vu by reminding him irresistibly of Delhi with its broad streets, shop-fronts with small canopies leaning out over the pavements and the bicycle-riding, white-shirted population. Seth's description of Heaven Lake is graphic:

> Heaven Lake is long, sardine-shaped and fed by a snow-melt from a stream at its head. The lake is an intense blue, surrounded on all sides by green mountain walls, dotted with distant sheep. At the head of the lake, beyond the delta of the in-flowing stream, is a massive snow-capped peak which dominated the vista; it is part of a series of peaks that culminate, a little out of view, in Mount Rogda itself. (22)

The poet's spirit as he languishes in the luxury of nature's plenty is one with that of Confucius, the sensitive sage who approves of the disciple whose only desire in life is to bathe in the river Yi in Spring and to enjoy the breeze and go home singing poetry. A strong sense of history is evoked by the museum, the collection of calligraphic inscriptions, sites of prehistoric monuments, the pool where the Emperor Ming Huang first set eyes on the courtesan Yang Gui Fu (who disrupted the Tang empire and cost him his throne), the tomb of Empress Wu and the vast underground labyrinth with its thousands of life-size soldiers and horses in clay in the burial place of Qui Shi Huang, testifying to the megalomania of the first great unifier of China and to the amazing skill of artists over 2000 years ago. The dull monotony of the architecture sanctioned by the socialist government in the cities of Lanzton, Beijing and Guangzhon with "street of standard shop-cuboid following street of standard shop-cuboid" (37) and the unvarying repetition of design in workers' flats, government offices, parks, bookstores or even street lamps, is projected in sharp contrast. Nature in its elemental fury confronts Seth when they cross Dunhuang where the Dang River reservoir was flooded by heavy rains. Nanhu or South Lake presents another arresting picture of beauty. Nanhu is a deep blue lake in a tree-packed oasis, cast like a pearl in the midst of an arid land. Seth discovers there are two lakes, a larger, broader, very clear lake below and above it a narrower, serpentine lake of yet more amazing cleanliness, almost as pure as Heaven Lake. To Seth, it is paradise on a hot day.

The traveller's sense of exhilaration and wonder at the pristine beauty of nature is transmitted to us through the brilliant description of landscape as they reach the point of maximum elevation climbing front Chidam Basin—a point at which world itself seemed to slope, a declivity that stretched for a hundred miles. The breathtaking beauty of the landscape gives way to the sheer wonder of geological transformations:

> nude dunes, unconnected by sand, completely isolated one from another; then black bills, oily and stony, slowly becoming wrinkled and clay-like; later lakes of distant blue; with a band of sparse vegetation in front and a red strip of soil nearest us, like the uninvited tricolour of an artists' republic. (72)

At an altitude of 4000-5000 metres on the Qinghai-Tibet plateau, the thin air, the sharp sunshine by day and the intense cold at night make the traveller feel awfully sick, but the zone of flowers in the Tangula Range, the lush greenery of Tibet and the gorge and cliff and turbulent river in the trans-Himalayan range are enchanting enough to drown all thoughts of illness and physical exhaustion. The descent from the Thongha Pass to Nilamu and Zhangmu marks a shift from alpine meadow to semi-deciduous forest. The valley surrounded by peaks on all sides with streams gushing like waterfalls and a frothing river below makes Seth burst into Tennyson's lines:

> A land of streams! Some, like a downward
> Slow-dropping veils of thinnest lawn, did go. (165)

For him, there is enchantment in flowing water. Water is "the most unifying of the elements that ties land, sea and air in one living ring." (165)

The sensitivity to the splendour of nature, the total emotional surrender to it, and the disregard for personal discomforts make the narrative a whole-hearted tribute to nature. It is a paean of unstinted praise from a pilgrim at the temple of Nature. It is noteworthy that Heaven Lake or Mansarovar, a pilgrim centre for followers of four religions—Hinduism, Buddhism, Jainism and the Tibetan Bonpal—has for Seth only the significance of a place of spectacular natural beauty.

One endearing aspect of the itinerant is his nostalgia for home and family, even amidst the delights of travel. This comes home with all intensity when he reaches Kathmandu where the similarity with the Indian landscape—terraced fields of rice, banana trees and flame-of-the-forest—and even the indigo-coloured wrapping of a match-box evoke the longing for home. As the journey nears its end, there is the sense of fulfillment and the expectation and longing for home—sentiments appropriate to any travelogue.

Tension and resolution, character and insight—the characteristics of the novel—are absorbed into Seth's narrative. The tension caused by straitjacketing regulations, and a visa that threatened to expire in a few days and the terrifying fury of nature posing obstacles at the most unexpected moments, keep us in suspense till Seth touches the soil of Nepal. The effect of the narrative is cathartic for the writer as well as the reader. Overriding every other sentiment is the poet's uninhibited enthusiasm, the "utsaha bhava" generated by his joy in the unalloyed beauty of nature. The descriptions of nature in heightened language, sustain this 'bhava' which has its source in the 'adbhuta rasa.'

Naipaul's approach to India—the land where his ancestral roots lie—has none of the openness or receptivity of Seth. Here, the traveller, clogged by colonial prejudices, positions himself as a representative of the west, vindictively judging and condemning the land and the people—the 'other'—the uncultured natives, crawling in filth and mimicking the west. The first reaction of the traveller-writer sets the tone of the entire narrative. The falling away of Europe and the impingement of the East mark for him "the chaos of uneconomical movement, the self-stimulated din, the sudden feeling of insecurity, the conviction that all men were not brothers and luggage was in danger."[3] As the East reveals itself feature by feature, he pours out his disgust through sketches of squalor, filth, noise and confusion. Part I of the book is an unrelieved expression of disgust—of 'jugupsa,' the 'sthayibhava of Bibhatsa rasa'—generated by sights displeasing and unwholesome to the traveller and the narrative is the discussion of it in language that hardly conceals the feelings behind. It is 'anista-sravana-darsana-parikirtana.' After he meets the Indian, the very concept of man has to be revised. Naipaul writes: "From Athens to Bombay another idea of man had defined itself by degrees, a new type of authority and subservience." (13) The English names on the boards in Bombay provoke unease "at the thought of the mute animal crouching on the floor at the master's back." (16) The place for unclaimed baggage in the Customs House which is worse than a junkshop; the caste system that brutally degrades the latrine-cleaner; the bureaucratic paraphernalia that taxes and exasperates the tourist; "the smugness, the imperviousness to criticism, the refusal to 'see,' the double talk and double think" (16) in the Indian character are only a few of the factors that rouse the indignation and revulsion of the writer.

The narrative abounds in graphic pictures of filth and squalor as though they are the sum total of Indian reality. The villages with "the narrow, broken lanes with green slime on the gutters, the choked back-to-back mudhouses, the jumble of filth and food and animals and people, the baby in the dust, swollen-bellied, black with flies, but wearing its good-luck amulet" (45) forms just one among the dismal portraits presented. There are indignant outbursts against the Indian "mimicry"—the imitation of the English—which is "incongruous and absurd," because it is a mimicry not of England, a real country, but of the fairy-tale land of Anglo-India, of "clubs and sahibs and syces and bearers." (57) The author feeds his disgust on the picture of Indians defecating on the streets, near the railway tracks, on the beaches, hills and rivers banks. Gandhi is to him the "failed reformer" (73) because though he saw India clearly with a colonial's eye and looked down into the roots of the static, decayed society, the picture of India that comes out of his writings and exhortations over more than thirty years still holds and this, according to Naipaul, is the measure of his failure.

In *From Heaven Lake*, speaking about the relations between India and China, Vikram Seth remarks: "on a personal level, to learn about another great culture is to enrich one's life, to understand one's own country better, to feel more at home in the world, and indirectly to add to that reservoir of goodwill that may, generations from now, temper the cynical use of national power." (178) It is this sensitivity to appreciate and understand another culture, and essential humanity that makes enduring personal relationships possible and makes travelling an enriching experience. Unfortunately, Naipaul seems to be in want of these two qualities. His jaundiced eye perceives the external details, but the spirit of the place is lost on him. His culture-clogged self foregrounds vision and impression. His distorted understanding of the message of the *Gita* is a typical example. The supreme lesson of "nishkama karma" advocated by the *Gita* is interpreted as "each man to his function, his private contract with God," (78) reducing people to islands in themselves. Indian passion for making speeches, for gestures and symbols also become targets for his incrimination. To quote Naipaul, "Symbolic dress, symbolic food, symbolic worship: India deals in symbols, inaction. Inaction arising out of proclaimed function, function out of caste." (80)

The prejudices of the self determine and limit understanding so that travelogue becomes revelation of the writer's self—his prejudices, his inability to enter into the spirit of the land or to gain an insight into it. As C.D. Narasimhaiah asks in his famous essay "V.S. Naipaul: A Split Sensibility": "The theme being India, does Mr. Naipaul make a genuine effort to 'explore' it by, what T.S. Eliot calls, surrendering himself to the object in front of him? Or, is he not, to invoke Eliot again, overpowered by an excess of his own emotions?"[4]

It is amazing to note that even the section on Kashmir (Part II) does not evoke any warmth of response from the traveller. Historical information, detailed descriptions of day-to-day discomforts in the hotel where he stays, comments of elemental Hindu rituals and religion, descriptions of flagellants in religious frenzy and the pilgrimage to Amarnath are rendered in a detached and critical tone, without any emotional involvement. The only place where he lets himself yield to the splendour of nature is when Naipaul declares:

> Yet a special joy had been with me throughout the pilgrimage and during all my time in Kashmir. It was the joy of being among the mountains; it was special joy of being among the Himalayas. I felt linked to them; I liked speaking the name. India, the Himalayas; they went together. (167)

This is however a temporary shift in mood, as the later accounts of his visit to the ancestral home in the village of the Dubes and his concluding remarks on India reveal. Naipaul comments:

> India had not worked its magic on me. It remained the land of my childhood, an area of darkness; like the Himalayan passes, it was closing up again, as fast as I withdrew from it, into a land of myth; it seemed to exist in just the timelessness which I had imagined as a child, into which for all that I walked on Indian earth, I knew I could not penetrate. (252)

Looking back on his journey just twenty-four hours after the Indian episode, he says: "It was a journey that ought not to have been made; it had broken my life in two." (265)

"When I think of China, I think first of my friends and only then of Qin Shi Huang's tomb," (36) says Seth. His journey became a pleasurable experience because of the beautiful friendships he formed on the way. His essential humanity enabled him to journey into the heartlands of China and it is with pain that he records the effects of the cultural revolution that almost destroyed the cultural heritage of China, and created a self-centred and insensitive generation brought up on Mao's sayings. Naipaul's self, caged and distanced by its own prejudice, fails to achieve any relationship of significance during his one-year tour in India. Relationships turn sour or exist precariously on the verge of collapse. The relationship with Aziz in the hotel on Dal Lake never runs smooth; with the Sikh what promises to be an amiable relationship snaps irreparably; even civility is discarded in his dealings with Ramachandra Dube, the present head of his ancestral family.

The darkness that reduces India to an "area of darkness" issues from within the traveller's persona. The detached style that exudes disgust is characteristic of the dominant mood or rasa of the work. Heaven or hell resides within the perceiving self and it needs the empathy of a sensitive mind to gain an insight into the spirit and culture of an alien land, The cartography of the land is mapped by one's own self and in the process travelogue becomes a narration of the self, as these two works signify.

NOTES

1. Qtd. Keith Fraser, "Introduction," *Worst Journeys: The Picador Book of Travel 1991*, ed. Keith Fraser (New Delhi: Rupa, 1993), p. xvii.
2. Vikram Seth, *From Heaven Lake: Travels through Sinkiang and Tibet* (London: Chatto and Windus, 1983), p. 8.
3. V.S. Naipaul, *An Area* of *Darkness* (1964; New Delhi: Penguin, 1968), p. 10.
4. C.D. Narasimhaiah, *The Indian Critical Scene: Controversial Essays* (Delhi: B.R, 1990), p. 99.

An Area of Darkness: The Document of Diasporic Experiences of V.S. Naipaul

SUREKHA DANGWAL
H.N.B. Garhwal University

Nearly every Indian writer—or writer of Indian origin writing in English--seems to have decided that the object of his and her imagination has to be the mother country. In recent times, terms which are gaining popularity are 'diaspora' and 'expatriate.' At the core of diaspora literature is the idea of the nation-state. It has the "ambiguous status of being both an ambassador and a refugee."[1] Both the roles demand opposites: while one requires the projection of one's culture and the ability to enhance its understanding, the other seeks refuge and protection and relates more positively to the host culture.

The cultural borders perceived by most diasporic writers are quite understandably drawn along national lines. In a world without nation-states, these writers would have merged with others who deal with cultural confrontations of all kinds. But diaspora literature focuses on cultural states that are defined by immigration counters and stamps on one's passport. The diasporic community in world literature is quite complex. It has shown a great mobility and adaptability as it has often been involved in a double act of migration—from India to West Indies and from there to Africa and then to Europe or America on account of social and political resources.

To deal with this kind of double-triple diaspora, the meetings of disparate cultures occur on various geographic levels: village-city, city-city and country-country. For the writers of 'diaspora literature,' however, cultural rendezvouses are restricted to those between countries. This is obviously because the authors are themselves dislocated along national lines. Writers like Salman Rushdie, Bharati Mukherjee, Jhumpa Lahiri, Rohinton Mistry and V.S. Naipaul write from their own experience of hanging in limbo between two identities: non-Indian and Indian. The diasporic Indian is "like the banyan tree, the traditional symbol of the Indian way of life, he spreads out his roots in several soils, drawing nourishment from one when the rest dry up. Far from being homeless, he has several homes, and that is the only way he has increasingly come to feel at home in the world."[2]

Naipaul is a victim of double diaspora as his grandfather migrated from India to Trinidad in 1880; since then, his family has lived there. And after that Naipaul himself settled in England. He went there as a student at Oxford University College and, after that, settled there. He had a strong desire to settle in England since his childhood. The sense of expatriateness was in his blood because he was born and educated in a country which was not his own and now he is residing in England. Being a victim of double diaspora, he cannot call any place his home. He can only be a visitor wherever he goes. For him, India can only be a country of his ancestors, not of his own generation. And Trinidad, where he lived, became a country because of colonialism and for England he is just an alien. So the blood, which is moving in his veins, belongs to one country, while he lived in another country and settled in the third country.

The crisis of unbelongingness is always a feature which one cannot ignore while reading Naipaul. He is like other West Indian writers who is disinherited by all traditions and exposed to all problems of becoming a writer. There is a strong desire of independence and identity in his writing. His works have connection to the Caribbean literary tradition from which it arose. His works give a sense of his biography of departure from the constructive closed background of the Trinidadian society of the open literate and cosmopolitan culture of the world of England. He finds that Trinidadian society is very hostile to him and England is the place where he could make his career and become a writer. So his works are concerned with contemporary reality. After receiving Nobel Prize for literature this year, he may be called a writer of the twenty-first century. As a writer, he agrees with the values and preoccupations of the dominant western culture. He is not a writer of the typical West Indian protest novel. He does not take fiction as a tool of revenge against all vices but he is interested in giving reality to his works through his own experiences.

Naipaul could not reconcile with Trinidadian or Caribbean society. He condemned those societies as backward. He did not write anything in favour of these societies. To him "as popular myth, that world was permeated by fear, deceit and treachery."[3] He thinks that colonial society was the product of colonizers and the culture and knowledge of those societies has come from outside:

> He hated the narrow, circumscribed, brutal life which surrounded him in colonial Trinidad with its limited possibilities, small range of profession, notorious political corruption and racial and religious conflict. . . . Indians among whom he was raised lived in a social world of their own uninvolved with the races. The Trinidadian of African descent appeared to have no traditional culture of their own and modelled themselves on the English. . . . The local whites had produced nothing of lasting values, were drunkards, uneducated and privileged. They had the best jobs.[4]

Though he hated those societies but as a colonised being he felt humiliation because colonizers always exploited colonised people.

Naipaul's view about Trinidad is that it is the culture of mimicry. His *Middle Passage* describes his passage to his home country amongst a motley crowd and his efforts of establishment with West-Trinidad seemed to him complex. People of these islands used to take education only to secure themselves, they never wanted to be familiar with books for knowledge. Therefore, he could not live long in Trinidad and went to London to settle.

In London, he remained an outsider and never felt at home in his first twenty years. London is a cold country and everything happens there within the doors--people do not want to know each other. Naipaul feels that he knows very little about England and has few friends there. He feels that in Trinidad he knew more people but in London it is not possible. He writes:

> The privacy of big cities depresses me. There are no communal pleasures in London. Between the activity and the response there is always the barrier of self-consciousness. You go to a restaurant or a night-club, you eat, you watch, you pay, you come out and look for a bus, feeling you have wasted your money. The theatre is a disappointment. . . . You watch, you come out in the interval to smoke or have a drink, you watch again, and it is all over. You might have been at home, before the television set. However gay the musical or farce, however good the acting, you come out alone into the cold street, private sitting in a bus full of grim people who have left their pleasure behind them in the threat . . . the communal element is not there; all you have is a remote spectacle. . . . I get more pleasure from going to a cinema in Trinidad.[5]

This statement of Naipaul makes it clear that he was not happy in London also. He was always disappointed with theatre in London, which shows the barrenness of his life there.

He went to London at the age of eighteen as a colonial who wanted security. But he grew up there. There he had his second childhood because in London he began to think and understand the world from another point of view. Though the people of England also wanted security because they were attached with America, they were very aware about American happenings, while for him even the American Black Power movement is a sort of television revolution. He felt that Blacks in England have worse situation than the American Blacks, because in England these are West Indian Blacks, who are people of no representation. They are lost people. Though he has criticized London many times but he always gives credit to London because he feels that England is the country of which he could be a writer. He always appreciates English which is the language used by peoples of most countries of the world.

He had to leave Trinidad for other reasons also. In Trinidadian society, Britishers had the most highly regarded culture; Blacks were politically dominant during his lifetime there. And Indians who were in a foreign land, of a different colour, spoke a different language, had a different religion and for many years had no opportunity for education in English. "Indians were until recently at the bottom of the Trinidadian, social, economic and political ladder, mostly rural farmers and labourers; even Hindu marriages were not recognized by law."[6] The Indians remained separate in Trinidadian society.

Naipaul lived in London as a diasporic. He went there because he had no other place to go. England was everything in the life of colonized people, so he preferred London. Though he used to think that he was writing about a world that was fairly whole, he had no society to write about. He had to write differently and to look at the world with a fresh and different attitude because as he wrote, he did not know whether he would have readers or not.

His sense of alienation is depicted in most of his writings. He has remained a stranger among the people and this sense can be found in his writing, whether novels or travelogues. He has always written about the problems of Indian diaspora, whether his subject is Trinidad, London, East Africa or India. In *A Bend in the River*, Salim, an alien settled in Africa, faces many problems. In *In a Free State* also, Indians feel alienation and loneliness among a foreign race. His "fiction is designed to convey to the readers the experiences of a particular situation in which alienation and absurdity occur in contemporary life."[7] Mostly he has given the description of third world and for him that is the world of colonies, which has been composed by the immigrant people. These people as a labour went there with their particular culture. They have still no root there and large part of world population, living in those colonised islands, have sense of inferiority and they were forced to accept the Western values.

An Area of Darkness (1964) is a record of his impressions of his one-year stay in India during his first visit. In this book, he explored the land of his origin, thinking that he might live in India. This is the story of his disillusionment and recognition that he was now a homeless product of colonialism and the new world. He has given a record of all his visits to different cities in India. His minute observation of people and their behaviour, customs, societies are also presented in this book.

An Area of Darkness is divided into eleven chapters. The first five chapters are related to Naipaul's personal experience, his establishments and conversation, while other chapters are his examination of India's history. In the prologue, "Traveller's Prelude: A Little Paperwork," he gives expression to his views about East, which are totally negative. He says that East is full of dirt, disease, undernourishment and hawkers. The streets are also narrow, filled with tiny shops and crowds and horns of motor cars have made the street worse. He seems very sure that other people also encounter such embarrassment and problems as he did. He feels exhausted and totally depressed at the very beginning of his first visit to India as he has to go here and there to get liquor permit, transport permit in order to take back his two liquor bottles which were seized by custom. He makes clear in the prologue that he could not be happy in this country.

The book can be divided into three parts. The first part consists of four chapters which give autobiographical details about how his grandfathers went to Trinidad as indentured labourers. He heard about India from his grandfather in his childhood. The second chapter is about India's poverty: "India is the poorest country in the world." According to Naipaul, India is full of beggars, all family members are involved in begging. Indian life is just a mimicry of the west. Naipaul also discusses the rigid caste system in India and the superiority feeling in the Europeans in this chapter. The third chapter 'The Colonial' describes Naipaul's darkest views about India.

There is no sanitation arrangement in the country. He also compares Europeans and Indians in their sanitation arrangement.

The fourth chapter is about his experiences in the house of Mrs. Mahindra, for whom he had been a paying guest. Mrs. Mahindra is so much crazy for foreign things and foreigners that she insisted on his accompanying her to the market to buy curtains.

The three chapters in part II present his Kashmir experiences, observations of people and their behaviour. In the third part of the book, he feels quite happy to be separated from India and "to be a colonial citizen without a past and ancestors" because he is very disturbed seeing the conditions in India.

So there are mainly two subjects, linked with each other in this book: one is Naipaul and the other is India. They progress with each other. But Naipaul fails to find the India of his childhood's imagination and he discovers India's "overwhelming reality." He came to India in search of some stability but having seen the conditions here, his imagination about India was wounded and distracted. Thus *An Area of Darkness* "mixes autobiography and ethnography, interweaving impressions of the author's personal journey in his ancestral land and observations of Indian culture and society."[8]

In *An Area of Darkness*, Naipaul has presented the experiences of an exi!e. The exile, who feels the pain of leaving home, goes into a world of new possibilities. It results in self-fragmentation. He came to India to find a home but here also he finds himself a diasporic.

In the first chapter "A Resting Place for the Imagination," he remembers his childhood days in Trinidad. All sorts of people lived there and everybody ate their own kind of food, they had their own ceremonies. Other people used to criticise Indian multi-racial societies. He gives sense of isolation felt by Indians on that island. He criticises London which is a country of mist, rain and forest. Nobody would want to stay there because it seems unfamiliar. He had to work hard to come to London and felt lost there. According to him, London is a good place for getting lost. He became only an inhabitant of a big city—he just passed his time there. In his writing, he successfully described characters like himself, who face problems of permanent exile, a refugee, a homeless citizen of the world, and an extranational writer.

His diasporic view is that England is not proper England as it expressed itself in Trinidad and India. These colonies can not be related to England, because real England is the source of inspiration while in these countries he has become very disturbed as he finds mimicry of England that there are English names of the things as well as of human beings. Indian colonial mimicry seems false to Naipaul. It is not only mimicking of West but a mimicking of colonialism also.

In *An Area of Darkness*, Naipaul compares Trinidad to India and Trinidad appears comparatively simple and happy:

> Colonial India I could not link with colonial Trinidad. Trinidad was a British colony; but every child knows that we were only a dot on the map of the world, and it was therefore important to be British: that at least anchored us within a wider system. It was a system which we did not find oppressive; and though British in institution and education as well as in political fact, we were in the New World, our population was greatly mixed, English people were few and kept themselves to themselves, and England was as a result only one of the countries of which we were aware.[9]

Here he compares India with Trinidad but his isolated sense and diasporic sense reflects strongly. That even children on the island know that they were nothing in the map of the world. They were forced to take an established recognition, which they used to take only in England. The people did not have their own identity and those mixed people, who came to that island from different parts of the world, were always attracted by England. They did not have their own particular education and for everything they depended on British.

Naipaul compares Britishers with Americans also. He says that the language of BBC news cannot be understood by a man while American radio was marvellous, modern and easy for everybody. On that island, British soldiers seemed foreigners because communication was not easy with them. They seemed very ugly in Trinidad and they had little money and little sense of propriety. On the whole he did not like Britishers on that island but England was the only country for him to settle. His long residence in England made it possible for him to withdraw completely from nationality. He writes: "it had convinced me that everyman was an island, and taught me to shield all that I know to be good and pure within myself from the corruption of course."[10] But after his first trip to India, he had to re-examine himself and his career as a writer. Because not having been raised in England, not being a white Englishman, he could not write novels about the British class system. He began to think over the conflict between freedom and security in his own life and in the decolonized world.

A colonial being has always a sense of difference. In *An Area of Darkness*, Naipaul suggests that in India nobody feels such differences. He describes his experiences in India that in the dress and appearance he cannot distinguish himself from the Indians. While "he wants to be different as the complex of Indian-Caribbean-Briton that he is,"[11] in India, he finds nothing to distinguish himself. He writes:

> Now in Bombay I entered a shop or a restaurant and awaited a special kind of response. And there was nothing. It was like being denied part of my reality. . . . I was faceless, I might sink without a trace into that Indian crowd, I had been made by Trinidad and England; recognition of my difference was necessary to me. (43)

He is not different in his colour or in his dress but in his attitude and temperament and outlook. And because of his different attitude towards India, he feels himself separate from those Indians.

He made a night journey in the company of a Sikh, who draws out Naipaul's darkest feelings. He feels some companionship with that Sikh because Sikhs look different in India in their dress, appearance and minority just like Indians looked in Trinidad. Through the Sikh, he expresses his confusion, embarrassment and dislike. That night journey opens his wounds of exile as he sees Sikh's eyes wild with humiliation and anger, whenever the Sikh notices that people are staring at him. The Sikh told him that Sikhs began to decline since Ranjit Singh and since partition. Through all this, Naipaul feels his own foreignness. The Sikh feels that there is no particular country for them; similarly Naipaul feels that the exiled Indian does not have any land. He associates himself with that Sikh in India.

Naipaul is a socialist who analyzes the manners and morals of people in decaying as well as developed societies. His views are that there is disturbance, instability and anxiety prevailing in these societies. His own "expatriate status makes his work 'interstitial' in that they capture the texture of the lives of the people of both the cultures at the very crack between culture."[12] The worlds depicted in his other novels have endless variation of the "cargo cult."[13] The people who inhabited his novels are "mimic men" and they try to achieve European power and success by imitation of the European culture. The result is that there is frustration, disappointment and disillusion in their life. Though he has not favoured imperialism of white European because slavery and imperialism were terrible crimes. He thinks that Africa, India and Islam are practised form of slavery. Indians have often been the victims of Africans and Islam. Many of his novels reveal his dislike for white liberals.

He finds in India that Indian people respect their past only because foreigners have appreciated it. So Indian people feel that their past was really great. In *An Area of Darkness*, his concern is primarily with that unique kind of colonial mimicry which he found in India. He observes that external impact of England on India is evident mainly in architecture, but internal impact is deeply rooted in the Indian psyche.

His perspective has been shaped by the humiliations of his youth in Trinidad and it is also influenced by his consciousness of being Indian and that humiliation which Indians suffered. It was the weakness of India that its people went as indentured labour to Black-dominated Trinidad and other colonies. So alienation and displacement become recurrent in his writings. He never stopped to remind himself of his Hindu origin. There was always a longing for Hinduism in his heart which is reflected in his writings.

The Loss of El Dorado is about a search for a cultural and national identity and to free itself from the "catastrophic idolatry and blindness to one's own historical and philosophical conceptions and misconceptions which may bind one within a statuesque present or a false future."[14] And in his *An Area of Darkness* he sees his travel "as analogous to those of the diaspora as displaced Indian's journey through the modern world attempting to create a home elsewhere."[15] He has made it clear in his work *The Middle Passage* that he was not a West Indian; and in *An Area of Darkness*, he says that he wants to be neither an English nor an Indian, both's victories have no meaning for him.

Nissim Ezekiel criticises Naipaul. But for Naipaul, India is a country of those people who have packed themselves within the life of death, negation, disturbance and he himself is happy to escape. He feels sorry to have travelled here. He is satisfied to be a colonial rather than an Indian. He is disturbed because when he came to India, he was not prepared for the poverty, aimlessness and disease which he saw here. *An Area of Darkness* ends with these lines:

> The world is illusion, the Hindu says we talk of despair. . . my experience of India defined itself more properly against my own homelessness, that I saw how close is the past years I had been to the total negation, how much it had become the basis of thought and feelings . . . illusion could only be a concept and not something felt in the bones . . . I could never adequately express and never seize again. (266-67)

NOTES

1. Jasbir Jain, ed., *Writers of the Indian Diaspora* (Jaipur and New Delhi: Rawal, 1998), p. 11.
2. Bhiku Parekh, "Some Reflections on the Indian Diaspora," *Journal of Contemporary Thought*, Baroda, 1993, p. 106.
3. Selwyn R. Cudjoe, *V.S. Naipaul: A Materialist Reading*, (Amherst: The University of Massachusetts Press, 1998), p. 124.
4. Bruce King, ed., *V.S. Naipaul* (England: Macmillan), pp. 5-6.
5. Robert D. Hamner, ed., *Critical Perspectives on V.S. Naipaul* (London: Heinemann Educational Books, 1979), p. 11.
6. P.K. Rajan, K.M. George and Others, ed., *Commonwealth Literature: Themes and Techniques* (Delhi: Ajanta, 1993), p. 7.
7. Shashi Kamra, *The Novels of V.S. Naipaul: A Study in Theme and Form* (New Delhi: Prestige, 1990), p. 39.
8. Timothy F. Weiss, *On The Margins: The Art of Exile in V.S. Naipaul* (Amherst: The University of Massachusetts Press, 1992), p.116.
9. V.S. Naipaul, *An Area of Darkness* (London: Penguin, 1968), p. 188.
10. *Ibid.*
11. Niaz Zaman, Shawkat Hussain et al, ed. *Essays on Commonwealth Writing* (Bangladesh: University Press, 1991), p. 130.
12. N. Rama Devi, *The Novels of V.S. Naipaul: Quest for Order and Identity* (New Delhi: Prestige, 1996), p. 132.
13. Larry David Nachman, "The Worlds of V.S. Naipaul," *Salmagundi*, 54 (Fall 1981), pp. 66-67.
14. Wilson Harris, "Tradition and the West Indian Novel," *Tradition, The Writer and Society: Critical Essays* (London: New Beacon), p. 36.
15. *V.S. Naipaul*, p.11.

Perceptions of Indian Women in *India: A Million Mutinies Now*

NAMRATA RATHORE

India was made when the British took over. It was then that we, the people residing within its cultural boundaries, were first addressed as 'Indians'; and our cultural individualities were first termed 'Indian.' It was a term that loosely encompassed all that was un-English and un-European before it acquired its current socio-political connotations. To say today that there exists a distinct identity that is 'Indian,' we need to answer for ourselves some of Edward Said's questions:

> When did we become "a people"? When did we stop being one? Or are we in the process of becoming one? What do these questions have to do with our intimate relationships with each other and with others? (qtd. in Bhabha, 7)

The term 'Indian' comprises ideologies in transition, ideologies trying to reinvent themselves, ideologies that are at times strangely intertwined and invariably contingent. The term 'Indian' in itself being of such a transient nature, it is dangerously misleading for any discourse to be based on a set notion of the 'Indian Woman.' Naipaul has wisely overlooked the mythical Indian woman and her baggage of motherhood, service, and sacrifice that she carries with herself all through her life. He has recognized that there exist within womanhood such varied categories that women can best be understood as people belonging to different strata of society who have been "othered" within the dominant patriarchal society at different levels and to different degrees. They are people trying to reclaim their 'personhood' differently on account of the difference in their individual economic, political, social and sexual conditions.

Naipaul's first statement is made on the cover jacket itself which shows that the woman is moving and she is moving with her children. There is none come to see her off, she looks ahead as the baby suckles at her breast, waiting for her sons to move with her belongings. She is tired but the determination writ all over her face cannot be missed. The picture leaves numerous questions in its wake: Where is she? What is she looking at? Where is she going? Will the boys be able to carry her belongings? What are the things she wants to carry with her? Why is she alone? The answers to all these questions form the content of this non-fiction work. The story of the woman is the fabric on which Naipaul has etched his picture gallery. He has also shown that it is this fabric that is shred when a 'million mutinies' break out.

The first section titled 'Bombay Theatre' presents a cross-section of the urban middle class women in metropolitan Bombay. These women are sometimes seen, sometimes heard and sometimes felt by their very absence. Mr. Patil's and Mr. Namdeo Dhasal's mothers are elderly women whose entire existence was contained in their roles of wife and mother. Mr. Patil's mother was proud of her son's achievements and didn't want to intrude into any of the serious business her son might have to deal with. (18) Her greatest ambition was 'to bring the Ganpati image home from the image-maker's with a musical band.' (21) Having been able to do that she considered herself and her sons blessed. Namdeo's mother had suffered much and 'had had a breakdown.' (109) She moved around the house shadow-like, silent. Their journeys were nearing their close and these women hadn't yet had a taste of their personhood. The second generation of women Mrs. Raote, Mrs. Ghate and their sisters-in-law are different from them. Unlike their mothers, they are educated and have chosen their own spouses. Their 'love marriage' and education has given them a greater say in family matters. Mrs. Raote is a working woman. Her sister-in-law is a doctor. Mrs. Ghate stayed home but did not succumb to her husband's ideologies. In spite of her husband's disinterest in religion, she kept a puja-box in the kitchen. Her sister-in-law is educated, has a career, and has married for love braving much opposition.

These women have begun to realize the need for financial independence. They are still docile wives and sacrificing mothers but they have begun to explore themselves. Mrs. Ghate's Puja-box bears testimony to that. Mallika represents the third generation women. She knows her self, her potential. She seeks and expects more from marriage than what Mr. Patil's mother or Mrs. Raote ever did. She is a poet and she marries the poet in Namdev. She marries him because he called her 'comrade' and he gave her the 'red salaam.' (105) She never could fit into the role of the shock absorber that Namdev assigned to her after their marriage. She thinks and she writes what she thinks. Her autobiography *I want to Destroy Myself* screams: 'Male ego is the most hideous thing in our present society. Women find quite a pleasure in boosting it. . . . I do not believe that for anybody called Namdeo I should surrender my entire life.' (109) Her conflict arises out of the clash between her clear perception of the failure of her marriage and her love for Namdeo. Her 'obsession with the man and his poetry and his cause' had made her lose her freedom. (109) The choice between love and freedom will not probably be made by Mallika and by so many of our women caught in similar situations but the process of self-assertion has certainly begun. Mallika has her views on the law too and believes that 'a mother should have a right to her child.' She is afraid that even if she leaves Namdeo, he would get the custody of their son once he was past seven. The fear of losing her son along with her love keeps her from seeking divorce. The landmark to be noted here is the realization of conflict which was altogether absent earlier. The hope lies in Mallika's dream of bringing up the child to be a better, sensitive human being: 'I don't want the child to grow up like his father—the negative aspects.' (108) With Mallika's story, the visit to the 'Bombay Theatre' comes to an end. The reader has viewed the contemporary Indian women in the numerous roles that she appears in on the stage of life.

'The Secretary's Tale' with its 'Glimpses of the Indian Century' takes a long look backward. In Rajan's story, we meet his mother. Rajan's father, a Brahmin was a widower twice. 'He lost his first wife, and then he married a second time, so that his second wife could look after his first two children. When his second wife died, leaving in turn two or three children, he was forced by his relations to marry a third time. In those days such marriages were not difficult.' (123) On his third wedding, Rajan's father was forty-three and his mother eighteen. She died eleven years later at the age of twenty-nine, her stepdaughter had nowhere to go when she was deserted by her husband. 'This was in January 1948.' (126) In spite of their helplessness, these women managed to pass on to Rajan a perspective very different from that of his father. On being told at an interview that he ought not to have left Calcutta and 'should have stayed at least for the rasgolla-like women there,' Rajan 'told off one of the interviewers' even at the risk of being rejected for the job. He felt it 'too degrading to women.' (131) When he married in 1985, his was a 'civil marriage—no dowry, no give, no take.' (134) His wife was a simple, independent woman. In the professional sphere, Rajan says he hadn't risen beyond what his father and grandfather could rise to, at the beginning of the century, but as a sensitized human being he has certainly made a huge leap across the century.

"Breaking Out" is the breaking out of the Indian woman from the shackles of ignorance and subversion. It is the map of the journey of her evolution. Scientist Subramaniam's grandmother 'divided the world into three parts: *Raja seemay*—the Mysore State; *Kumpani seemay*—the Company's Land; and beyond these two areas was the rest of the world.' (152-53) In such a world was born Kala's grandmother. Married at eleven, she wasn't very different from Subramaniam's grandmother but her daughter studied till class 10 and dreamt of being a doctor. Her dreams and her taste for a more fulfilling life cost her marital happiness. She turned into a 'chattel.' 'She had no time to herself . . . she could make no decisions . . . somebody always decided for her.' (178) She bore physical and mental abuse. She was never able to break free but she taught her daughter Kala 'how important education and financial independence are.' (180) As a result 'Kala was in a position to make her own life . . . she had her job; she was free to come and go.' (175) Naipaul sees in it a very positive 'historical progression' which Kala missed out on account of her emotional involvement with her mother's life. (180) It is true of the Indian woman too. She has been 'breaking out' slowly, through generations. The possibilities available to the Indian women today could never have been dreamt of by their grandmothers. With more and more women 'breaking out,' 'little wars' were bound to follow. (207) These wars that occurred at different levels were mainly between the many selves of the Indian women. The social structure that they had broken came back to haunt them. Manyammai left her home in opposition to marriage and continued with her teacher-training course. She later married Periyar who had founded the Self-Respect campaign and campaigned amongst other things, against the disabilities of women. She managed the campaign till her death. Mrs. Veermani, in spite of her 'traditional and demure and self-effacing' manner was a dutiful server of the self-respect cause. (272) 'Little Wars' were also fought by menstruating women and girls who were segregated during their periods in a special room in a corner of Kakusthan's Brahmin colony. In spite of their so-called 'polluting' effects, they went out to work through the 'wicket gate at the back of the colony' and dared 'pollute' the men's world by their presence. (247) In Sugar's story, we hear of middle-class Brahmin ladies who opt for jobs and stay unmarried rather than push their fathers to bankruptcy in arranging for their marriages. They don't see marriage as a goal.

Emerging 'After the Battle' is Chidananda's wife, a discerning woman who dissuades her husband from taking up an upmarket job as it would turn them into 'a different kind of people.' (290) Torn between his 'Jekyll and Hyde' existence, Childananda experiences deep anguish in bringing together the westernized life-style demanded by his job and the cultural yearnings of his soul. Finally, deeply disgusted, he says to himself what his wife had warned him of in the beginning. 'What have I done to myself?' (292)

Arati, a schoolteacher went through her battle in her family's opposition to her marriage with Dipanjan. Although she had been sympathetic to the Naxalite cause in the beginning, she thought it foolish to take the revolution to the people. 'The poor in India believed in their fate . . . that . . . had set the revolution back by 40 years.' The position of women in England had further shaken her up 'given the choice, she would have continued to live in England—this feeling of freedom, and recognition of her as an individual.' (317-18) Another product of 'Little War' is Ashok who found the matrimonial preliminaries of 'bride-seeing' humiliating and very disturbing. He was troubled as 'the girl apparently had no say in the matter . . . everybody was waiting. . . . On these occasions it's all weighted in favour of the boy, and the girl's family occupies the inferior position.' (330) He said no to the process. Later, he found solace in a self-choice marriage. At 'the End of Line' we have in Parveen the Indian woman breaking through the power structures. Optimistic, up-right and confident with her ambition of entering 'secular' politics, she knows exactly where she is going. (363)

'Woman's Era' begins with Naipaul's first encounter with Russell's *Diary* and the different griefs it inspired in Rashid and himself. It questions the authenticity of documented history that assumes without question a sequence of events 'built around the ascendancy of men.' (Fogel, 99) This is Naipaul's prelude to a chapter which deals with the life of Indian women and its projection in various women's magazines. In his meetings with the editors of women's magazines, he discovers the tough life of the urban lower-middle class earning women members of a family.

> She's up at the crack of dawn . . . to fill the water for the day . . . does the morning chores, filling the tiffin-carriers for husband and children after giving them tea, breakfast . . . then she is off to work herself. A very long train journey. . . . She hardly gets a seat. . . . She gets off from her office at 5.30 or six. . . . Before getting to the bus or station she would buy her vegetables or whatever she needs.

> . . . Then the dinner, then a bit of the children's homework. . . . Then she has to think of the water again. (405)

Naipaul's encounters with *Femina, Eve's Weekly, Savvy* and *Woman's Era* lead him to the same question with which he began. Who writes for whom? And with what authority? Are these magazines actually addressing the women? Who is their target audience? Here once again, Naipaul comes across the extreme heterogeneity within womanhood. '*Femina* is for the older woman. *Savvy* is for the city bred woman, from eighteen to thirty.' (408) *Eve's Weekly* is unconventional in its outlook as compared to *Woman's Era.* If readership is any indicator of effective communication, *Women 's Era* with its highest readership tops the list. Its editor is Vishwa Nath—a man who holds iconoclastic views on religion but is strangely conventional, even stereotyped in his concern for the role of the woman in the family. Probably the ambiguity of the editor's personality struck a concordant note with the doubts and confusions of women just emerging from their shells. What to hold on to? What to let go? What to strive for? What to fight against? Plagued by these questions and caught in the whirlwind of change, taking cautious little steps, these women found comfort in *Woman's Era* because it 'did not intimidate its readers . . . it acknowledged the conditions in which its readers lived; and it never went beyond those conditions . . . with that recognition, there was always reassurance.' (411) It told its readers how to conduct themselves at formal dinners, how to write a letter, how to entertain guests and all this with a tone that was 'one of concern, almost love.' (412) The paradox regarding women and her world which can be easily understood as coming from a male editor trapped in his own ambiguous vision was well accepted by women caught within similar visions of themselves and their worlds. 'Offering instruction and reassurance, and a subtle transformation of the hard real world, to women just emerging, women whose lives were a tissue of ritual and given relationships, and didn't want to rebel or dream.' (419) It gave them an honest woman's view of herself, hence recognition.

It is from here that women had started acknowledging their existence and had begun to expand their 'space.' It is from here that they later dared to rebel and dared to dream. It is in its wings that a thousand Nandinis and Kalas still wait to make their entries. What Naipaul says of India is also true of the Indian women. If the 'twentieth century restoration of India to itself had taken time,' it would take time for women to be restored to themselves. The transition cannot be a very smooth one. Kala's mothers will have to go through oppression, Mallikas will have to be stifled before there can emerge a Kala. The harrowing experiences of womanhood and the struggle is not to be 'wished away. . . . They were a part of the beginning of a new way for many millions, part of India's growth, part of its restoration.' (518)

This brings Naipaul to the end of his book and as the reader closes it shut one knows the answers to all those questions which had struck one in the beginning. The woman on the cover is the Indian woman just emerging from her grandmother's role, looking at nothing, looking through everything, looking within herself for reassurance. She is travelling to get her 'personhood.' The boys, her children, will carry her belongings: like Ashok and Kala. Mallika's son at her breast will not grow up to be like his father. The woman is alone because she has to make this journey herself. No one else can make it for her. It reminds us of Emma Goldman's words, from *The Tragedy of Woman's Emancipation:*

> History tells us that every oppressed class gained true liberation from its masters through its own efforts. It is necessary that woman learns that lesson. . . . It is far more important for her to begin with her inner regeneration, to cut loose from the weight of prejudices, traditions, customs. The demand for equal rights in every vocation of life is just and fair; but, after all, the most vital right is the right to love and be loved. (qtd. in Jordan, 19)

We may 'accept the call to liberation through our own activity, but loving, or getting oneself loved may be the very thing that stands in the way of acting against tradition and custom and the prejudices of those we love.' (Jordan, 19) This also brings us face to face with the 'subject-object dichotomy' of women. In determining the position of women as the subject of discourse, one needs to keep in mind that we are all different persons in relation to the various people in our lives. The subjectivity of women is constantly in flux. As Kristeva says, we are no doubt permanent subjects of a language that holds us in its power. But we are subjects *in process,* ceaselessly losing our identity, destabilized by fluctuations in our relations with the other to whom we nevertheless remain bound in a kind of homeostatis.' (qtd. in Kumar, 6) The very identity of women is determined by a society's 'shifting discourse of sexuality' which is in turn socially and politically constructed. (Kumar, 20) The Indian woman is constructed by discourse but she is not a 'passive recipient' of the discourse. (Kumar, 21) She is an amalgamation of a collaborator, generator, receptor and dissident within the socio-economic-political structures of dominance.

Naipaul has perceived Indian women negotiating change in her situation. He has presented them in relation to their individual 'spaces within which women act.' (Kumar, 19) A woman who may appear totally powerless as a part of the entire social set up is not so at all places and at all times. Naipaul has presented her in those spaces, in those personal capacities from where she has begun to subjectify herself. She is shown as working towards her own empowerment. In some cases, the woman acts but does not speak: as in the case of Rajan's mothers and sister. In other cases she speaks but does not act: as it is with Mallika. Naipaul has effectively uncovered the tremendous potential of women which may not show up explicitly to the undiscerning eye accustomed to 'cross-sectional' analyses. The Indian woman is moving towards change. This movement has begun within the family—the space most intimately known to women. It is from here that she has begun to challenge all structures of dominance. It is from here that she has begun to enlarge her 'space.' We have to only give her time.

WORKS CITED

Bhabha, Homi K., ed. *Nation and Narration.* London: Routledge. 1990.

Fogel, Robert William and G.R. Elton. *Which Road to the Past? Two Views of History.* New Haven: Yale University Press, 1983.

Jordan, Elain. "Enthralment: Angela Carter's Speculative Fictions." *Plotting Change: Contemporary Women's Fiction*, ed. Linda Anderson. London: Edward Arnold, 1990.

Kumar, Nita, ed. *Women as Subjects.* New Delhi: Stree, 1994.

V.S. Naipaul, *India: A Million Mutinies Now.* London: Vintage, 1990.

A House of One's Own: A Study of V.S. Naipaul's *A House for Mr. Biswas* and Toni Morrison's *Beloved*

PASHUPATI JHA
I.I.T., Roorkee

Since the days of Adam's expulsion from the Garden of Eden, man has been looking for a house; this primal search for shelter has become so much deeply entrenched that it has turned out to be an archetypal aim of all individuals. The present paper makes a modest attempt to analyse this eternal quest for a safe haven, specifically in one novel each of the two Nobel laureates, namely, *A House for Mr. Biswas* by V.S. Naipaul and *Beloved* by Toni Morrison. Despite the temporal and spatial gaps between these two novels, there is a common concern to own a house of one's own in both of them. In the first novel, the yearning for an independent house is equated with asserting one's own identity independent of others material and moral support. Thus, there is a constant refrain on the part of Mr. Biswas: "I am going to get a job of my own. And I am going to get my own house too."[1] The novel depicts the bitter struggle of Mr. Biswas to own a house of his own where he is free to act and think in his own way. So house becomes a symbol for selfhood unfettered by outside checks and balances. In Toni Morrison's *Beloved*, the meaning of a house for the black slaves is even more primal, passionate and profound—it stands for an urge for security, for freedom from bondage, from mental and physical molestation and torment. Unlike the first novel, here the quest for house is more comprehensive because it is working on both personal and communal levels. This paper presents an analytical study of these two novels focusing on the common core of possessing a house of one's own as a means of individual as well as familial salvation.

Mr. Biswas is a "classic loser"[2] since his birth itself in the house of penniless parents, Raghu and Bipti. He is born with the evil sixth finger and therefore the attending maid declares him to be an ominous baby, who would eat its own parents. The prediction proves half-true when Raghu is drowned in the river while looking for his missing son. Reduced to skeleton and dotted with eczema scars due to malnutrition and neglect, Mr. Biswas looks a grotesque figure. Not only that, he grows into a clumsy, careless boy who cannot look even after a calf. When he goes to school, he is ridiculed by his own teacher, Mr. Lal, who compels him to write on the blackboard that he is an ass before his entire giggling classmates. When sent to Pandit Jairam for learning the Hindu rituals so that he can earn something later in life, he makes a mess of everything by easing himself on his kerchief one night and throwing the excreta on the sacred tree of the Pandit. Thrown out from there too, his mother requests Ajodha, a distant relative, to employ him as an assistant in a rum shop. There too, the chief salesman Bhandat taunts and teases him so much that he takes a peculiar way to avenge himself by mixing his own spit in each bottle of the rum. Accused wrongly of theft there, and beaten by Bhandat, he runs away from the place and becomes a sign-painter.

Although sign-painting is satisfying his creative craving, it also brings him to Hanuman House of the Tulsis at Arwacas where he falls for Shama, one of the fourteen daughters of the matriarch, Mrs. Tulsi. This occasional lapse entraps him for life into a mismatch and misadventure. He gets a shelter over his head but at the cost of his self-identity; the Tulsi daughters live in the same big house along with their husbands and children. For bare sustenance, they have to mortgage their soul to Mrs. Tulsi and her manager-cum-relative Mr. Seth. A born rebel, this arrangement is unsuitable for Mr. Biswas, but where is the alternative? Should he also die "in a crumbling mud-hut in the swamplands" like his maternal grandfather? (15) Or strive for a better future for himself which can satisfy both his body and spirit? When one of the brothers-in-law of Shama suggests him to become a driver, the proud Mr. Biswas shouts back, "Give up sign-painting? And my independence? No, boy. My motto is: paddle your own canoe." (107) It is this independence of mind that leads to many of his troubles; but its strength also sustains him all through his struggle.

But till he is in Hanuman House or elsewhere supported by Mrs. Tulsi, he has no say in even such personal matters as naming his first-born daughter. Unusual as he is, he selects a very long name Sarojini Lakshmi Kamala Devi, combining a lot many traits in his darling daughter. But the name given to her finally by Hanuman House is Savi. What galls Mr. Biswas further is that on the birth certificate, the occupation of the father is given as labourer by the dominating Mr. Seth. But even in this depressed and dejected mood, his absurdly eternal optimism does not leave him that some nobler purpose is awaiting him. So he forgets his sorrow by reading Samuel Smiles and Marcus Aurelius. When his shopping business arranged by the Tulsi household ends in fiasco, he is dispatched to another Tulsi estate as a driver-cum-sub-overseer to live in one dingy, dark room which is part of a row of similar rooms occupied by labourers. It is here that his suppressed desire to own a house again surfaces with full force: "As soon as he saw the barracks Mr. Biswas decided that the time had come for him to build his own house, by whatever means." (206) From this point onward, the dream-picture of a house becomes his constant companion:

> He wanted, in the first place, a real house, made with real materials. He didn't want mud for walls, earth for floor, tree branches for rafters and grass for roof. . . . He wanted a galvanized iron roof and a wooden ceiling. He would walk up concrete steps into a small verandah; . . . And his house would be painted. The roof would be red, the outside walls ochre with chocolate facings, and the windows white. (210-11)

But for the time being, he has no means to fulfill his dreams; if he cannot provide a full house to his children, he at least can gift them a doll's house. So Mr. Biswas buys a pretty little box-house for his darling daughter, Savi, as a Christmas gift. For him, this thrilling mini-house is a momentary consolation for its final shape in future. But jealous Padma, the wife of Seth, fabricates a macabre story that such a gift had earlier killed a charming girl. Other women and children of Hanuman House are also full of ire against this doll's house, compelling Shama to finally break it to pieces in order to maintain harmony in that big house. But this shocking event jolts Mr. Biswas from within. This breaking of the mini-house breaks something very substantial inside him:

> The doll's house did not exist. He saw only a bundle of firewood. None of its parts was whole. Its delicate joints were exposed and useless. Below the torn skin of paint, still bright and still in parts imitating brickwork, the hacked and splintered wood was white and raw. (219)

He rages at Shama in full fury, but his anguished cry in the wilderness of Hanuman House remains largely ineffective. Gradually, he decides that he has to think seriously now of constructing his own house, otherwise he would remain rotting in the barracks at the Green Vale and his family would remain mortgaged to Hanuman House. If he fails to build the house now, he can do it never. Without a house and identity of his own, he begins to suffer from a sense of existential annihilation: "The future he feared was upon him. He was falling into the void, and that terror, known only in dreams, was with him as he lay awake at nights." (227) As he cannot wait any longer, so he hires George Maclean, carpenter-cum-builder, to construct a house for him. He begins to think not only of the house, but also of a garden in front of it adorned with blooming flowers. As soon as the bare structure of that house is ready, he is very much pleased with himself, "it was a pleasure to Mr. Biswas to stand below the roof and be in shade where only the day before, only that morning, there had been openness." (261) As the fate would have it, that house is almost washed off in a torrential rain coupled with a howling storm. The remnant portion of the house is burnt down by the wicked labourers over whom he has been an overseer. So much attached to this ramshackle house, its ruin makes Mr. Biswas almost insane. He along with his family is to be brought back to Hanuman

House where he takes a very long time to recover from his material and mental loss.

Life in Hanuman House is quite unsuitable for him. He finally marvels how he could survive that horror of watching his own house tottering before his eyes. In order to boost his morale, Ramchand, his brother-in-law, comes from Port of Spain telling him that his genius is not suitable for this backward place. In his enthusiasm, Ramchand addresses Sushila, one of the daughters of the House, very lightly, making Chinta to comment rudely: "However much you wash a pig . . . you can't turn it into a cow." (301) This taunt enhances the hurt of Mr. Biswas who has already been listening to such teasings by the inmates there. So, he finally decides to leave Hanuman House and its periphery forever and try his luck in the capital city: "He was going out into the world, to test it for its power to frighten. The past was counterfeit, a series of cheating accidents. Real life, and its especial sweetness, awaited; he was still beginning." (305) This great escape is equated with the historical escape from Nazi tyranny because, in the Port of Spain, the younger son of Dehuti narrates the story from his book related to "an escape from a German prison camp in 1917." (310)

In the capital city what strikes him first is the utter independence of each individual; almost habituated of living under the authority of either Mrs. Tulsi or Mr. Seth or even both, the sight of men and women moving freely in the city refreshes him for something novel: "And now he saw the city as made up of individual, each of whom had his place in it." (316) His early attempts to get his own place there is only a partial success in as far as he gets the job of a sign-painter only with the *Sentinel*, where he wants to become a journalist with some name and status. But later Mr. Burnett gives him a lot of things to write as a specimen report; so much of caricatures and cranks about the Tulsi family are stored in his mind that Mr. Biswas writes many funny and interesting pieces. Thus finally he wins a place in that paper as a reporter; now he has to "recover" his family living behind with the Tulsis from their dominance (327). The authoritative Mrs. Tulsi dictates her own terms for that recovery, that Mr.

Biswas will have to rent the town house of Mrs. Tulsi for eight dollars a month and Shama has to collect rents from other tenants too. As a reporter, Mr. Biswas has now become quite famous and so, for the first time, Shama takes "a wifely interest" in his dress and appearance (330).

But everything is still not alright with Mr. Biswas; he has no house of his own and this is made to him more clear when Mr. Seth once destroys his garden for making a place for his own lorries. When Anand, the only son of Mr. Biswas, goes to his school, his friends tell him that his father is still a low-ranking employee and not the famous writer he boasts of. Here is a conversation between Shama and Mr. Biswas:

> 'Lawrence say that his father is your boss.'
>
> There was silence.
>
> Mr. Biswas sat on the bed and said, 'Lawrence is the night editor. Nothing to do with me.'
>
> 'He say they have you like an office boy in the office.'
>
> 'You know I write features.'
>
> 'And he say that when you go to his father house you have to go to the back door.' (379)

In this way, Mr. Biswas is again forced by his circumstances as well as by his own obsession, to build a house near the Shorthills, which again is accidentally burnt down, compelling him to return again to the town house of Mrs. Tulsi. There the situation has worsened now because it has become over-crowded; after the return of Owad as a doctor from England, the entire Tulsi clan gathers in the same house. Moreover, the proud Owad once insults Anand; a very sensitive child as he is, Anand for the first time tells his father to give up that house: "Pa. We must move. . . We must move. I can't bear to live here another day." (551)

So, Mr. Biswas finally buys a townhouse, in Sikkim Street, from a solicitor's clerk in five thousand and five hundred dollars. Although he is cheated because the house is badly built, "a hodgepodge, a poorly assimilated assortment of ill-coordinated elements,"[3] the entire family has a sense of satisfaction. In the case of Mr. Biswas, this house gives him a deep sense of victory that he has finally succeeded, despite his humble origin, not only in having a house but also in owning a car of his own. Thus, it is truly said that Naipaul provides convincing pictures "of ordinary people who exemplify extraordinary reality."[4] But, evey big success has a bigger price tag. Mr. Biswas has exhausted all his mental and physical strength to reach there and, as a consequence, he suffers a heart-attack. Even then, he and his family are fully enjoying this new status of owning a town-house. Mr. Biswas introspects:

> How terrible it would have been, at this time, to be without it [house]: to have died among the Tulsis, amid the squalor of that large, disintegrating and indifferent family; to have left Shama and the children among them, in one room; worse, to have lived without even attempting to lay claim to one's portion of the earth; to have lived and died as one had been born, unnecessary and unaccommodated (13-14).

He suffers another stroke and dies at the early age of forty-six, almost in the same condition as the father of the novelist, Seepersad, who is Naipaul's model for Mr. Biswas. Like Mr. Biswas, Naipaul's father was also a journalist and had to live for many years in the house of his mother-in-law. Because of such autobiographical elements, it is rightly remarked that Naipaul "finds personal resonance with the world views of the dispossessed, the former colonial subjects now cast on their own resources."[5] Despite this sudden death, the life of Mr. Biswas is not a complete waste. At his funeral, people from all races come to mourn his loss because his writing has made him so popular. The achievement of Mr. Biswas is made clear to the reader by the writer also on the last page of the novel:

> Downstairs the doors of the house were open. The door that couldn't open had been made to, and its hinges dislocated. The furniture was pushed to the walls. All that day and evening well-dressed mourners, men, women and children, passed through the house. The polished floor became scratched and dusty; the staircase shivered continually; the top floor resounded with the steady shuffle. *And the house did not fall.* (589-60, emphasis added)

Thus the entire novel aims at depicting "the unaccommodated man's repeated attempts to find a stable location in a ramshackle and random world."[6]

While in *A House for Mr. Biswas*, despite the importance given to it, house is still an object, a non-living need for the living, in Toni Morrison's *Beloved*, house is a living entity, a vital part of human existence. Among all the important characters of the novel, Denver is the least formed one; even then she understands the importance of house in the life of the black people: "Shivering, Denver approached the house, regarding it, as she always did, as a person rather than a structure. A person that wept, sighed, trembled and fell into fits."[7] In the context of the eldest member of her family, Baby Suggs, her grandmother, house has been a consistent aim of her life. For her, living in Negro farms under this or that white master has been a series of torture. One example of such a sexual exploitation is pointed out by the simple fact that her eight children had six fathers. Because she has no house of her own, she cannot keep her children with her—they are either sold or dead or have simply disappeared. She has no track of them, she simply remembers their names—Patty, Rosa Lee, Ardelia, Tyree, John, Nancy and Famous. Only Halle remains with her at Sweet Home, a slave settlement owned by Mr. Garner. A slightly enlightened white master, he has given the option to Halle to work outside his allotted hours and days, even through holidays, to earn the freedom for his old mother. Only freedom from bondage may lead to another desire—a house where one can live according to one's wishes.

Baby Suggs, first, does not understand what freedom means for an old woman over sixty with a limp in the leg. But when she becomes free, she knows then "that there was nothing like it in this world." (141) Raped repeatedly in her youth and overworked even in her old age, she has forgotten the taste of life, her senses have become numb but just after the first flush of freedom, each part of her body comes to life again after a long gap:

> But suddenly she saw her hands and thought with a clarity as simple as it was dazzling, "These hands belong to me. These *my* hands." Next she felt a knocking in her chest and discovered something else new: her own heartbeat. Had it been there all along? This pounding thing? She felt like a fool and began to laugh out loud. (141)

She shifts to 124 Bluestone Road on a nominal rent; though the house does not belong to her officially, for all practical purposes it is hers only. There she waits for the arrival of Halle, his wife Sethe, and their children. Sethe comes with her children, but Halle unfortunately does not make it. It is found out that when under the authority of the Schoolteacher, the new master of Sweet Home, a few white urchins pin Sethe down and drink her milk from her exposed breasts, this sight becomes so shocking for Halle that he loses much of his sense, and after that no one knows his whereabouts.

With a very large heart where all the blacks can be accommodated, her house at 124 Bluestone becomes "the nerve center and the heart of the black community."[8] As Baby Suggs wants a wider house, where yet larger number can be collected, she has to go to the Clearing, an open space in the nearby forest, and use it as her area of work. It is this place that becomes her focal point of action. From there, she delivers her famous speech to all the blacks gathered there, to inspire them to love their black body, every part of it like "life-holding womb and your life-giving private parts." (89) She is fully aware of the utter subjugation of the black body by the whites resulting into its loathing by the slaves. So her first task is to revive blacks' interest in their body, the house of all their action and emotion. Therefore, she repeatedly tells them to love their flesh, lungs, legs, neck, and even the dark liver. More than everything else, she tells them to love their beating heart because that is the prized possession of the entire race, still uncorrupted by the white influence. She finally exhorts them to love one another. It should be noted here that while in Naipaul possessing a house is at best a personal or familial question, in Morrison it is as much a personal quest as it is the communal need. The Clearing is a house for the entire black community. It is from here that Baby Suggs becomes a symbol of black courage and when she dies, she is remembered by the whole of the black people.

For Sethe, a house of her own, where she can safely keep her milk and children intact, is of vital importance. When Paul D sees the horrible condition of her back turned to pulp by constant whipping and asks her whether they were beating her by the lash of cowhide, her repeated answer is that they stole her milk as if beating is nothing when compared to her biological function of feeding her own child. Living in a slave-house means physical and sexual exploitation of terrible magnitude, so she kills her daughter Beloved to save her from future disgrace. This part of the novel is the most moving one. The novelist explains everything behind this shocking murder of a two-year daughter:

> That anybody white could take your whole self for anything that came to mind. Not just work, kill, or maim you, but dirty you. Dirty you so bad you couldn't like yourself anymore. Dirty so bad you forgot who you were and couldn't think it up. Though she and others lived through and got over it, she could never let it happen to her own. The best thing she was, was her children. Whites might dirty *her* all right, but not her best thing, her beautiful, magical best thing—the part of her that was clean. (251)

This murder is based on a real-life event of 1856 when an escaping slave-woman tried to kill her children to save them from slavery. One can easily understand that this type of mercy killing would have been out of question if Sethe had a house of her own.

On the metaphysical level, the return of Beloved in the form of a spirit after many years, is also the result of her craving for an affectionate house where she can get the unconditional and unfettered love of her mother. On that level, it may be explained that even heaven could not provide her a homely touch, thus she has to return to her mother so that she can experience her growing up in a domestic atmosphere: "I don't want that place [heaven]. This is the place I am." (123) Even Sethe is so much attached to 124 Bluestone that when Paul D, one of the co-slaves of Sweet Home, tells her to leave this haunted house, she fails to understand any logic behind such a foolish suggestion: "This house he told her to leave as though a house was a little thing—a shirtwaist or a sewing basket you could walk off from or give away any time." (22) Sethe has so much attachment to any house that even at Sweet Home, she used to bring a fistful of flowers to her kitchen where she has to do all the menial jobs for Mrs. Garner. That used to make her "feel at home." (22)

For Sethe, home is where one can act on one's own sweet will without needing permission from any one else. Even at Sweet Home, she was not permitted to do everything of her choice in the kitchen, there it was the reign of Mrs. Garner, even if disarmingly tender. So, she is having the feel of freedom only at 124 Bluestone. This is obvious to Paul D, who understands Sethe better: "He knew exactly what she meant: to get to a place where you could love anything you chose—not to need permission for desire—well now, *that* was freedom." (162)

Paul D, who has been a slave for almost all his life, understands, like Sethe, the importance of house—not only as a geographical space where one is secure from outside authority and weather, but also as a place where one can get human warmth and affection associated with a family life. So when Denver objects to his sharing her mother's room and love, he tells Sethe to convince her daughter that love, when shared, expands: "Tell her it's not about choosing somebody over her—it's making space for somebody along with her." (45) He himself cannot recollect his mother and has never seen his father. Youngest of the three half-brothers—from the same mother but from different fathers—he is sold to Mr. Garner when hardly a boy. After twenty years of grinding slavery at Sweet Home, he tries to run away from the tyranny of the Schoolteacher, the new master at the slave farm. Unfortunately, he is caught and severely punished by tying his tongue and hands down with iron chains. He is finally sold to another master where he is imprisoned in a cage-like box and made to work without stop like mules. He has to put up "with anything and everything just to stay alive." (221) After years of intolerable misery, he comes to 124 Bluestone where, with Sethe and Denver, he can get both home and family love:

> Sethe, if I'm here with you, with Denver, you can go anywhere you want. Jump, if you want to, 'cause I'll catch you, girl. I'll catch you 'fore you fall. Go as far inside as you need to, I'll hold your ankles. Make sure you get back out. I'm not saying this because I need a place to stay. That's the last thing I need. . . . But when I got here and sat out there on the porch, waiting for you, well, I knew it wasn't the place I was heading toward; it was you. We can make a life, girl. A life. (46)

And he comes true to his words, reviving the dead-spirit of Sethe when the ghost of Beloved leaves her finally. He convinces her to do away with her past and look for a better and happier future, telling her, "You your best thing Sethe. You are." In sudden realization, Sethe cries out, "Me? Me?" (273) Thus the novel, which is otherwise so full of tragic events, ends on a note of refreshing life with a lot of new possibilities of a cosy and affectionate homely living.

Although the backdrop and time-frame of *A House for Mr. Biswas* and *Beloved* are apparently poles apart, yet there are striking similarities too. Both the novels deal with displaced and dispossessed characters, marginal men and women with stunted opportunities, but striving hard to find out a local habitation where they can lead their own life. In Naipaul, they are emigrant Indians forced by circumstance to earn their bread and find a place worth the name in alien Trinidad. In Morrison, time recedes further back; her characters are Africans forcibly brought by and sold to whites to work on slave-farms of America. In the first novel, the escape is from Hanuman House; in the second, it is from Sweet Home. In both the cases, the movements of characters lead them to several stop-gap places. The state of "nowhereness"[9] and "semipermanency"[10] that one finds in Naipaul's novel, is common to Morrison's work too. It is because of this state of flux demanding a loyalty to some outside authority, is not acceptable to the characters of these novels, so they make their best attempts to achieve a place of their own even if with tenuous foothold. Among the many reasons for these two novels being masterpieces, one definitely is their depiction of this primal passion of man to own a house of his own.

To conclude this paper, I quote a few lines from the simple yet archetypal song sung by Amy in *Beloved*:

> Through the muck and mist and gloam
> To our quiet cozy home,
> Where to singing sweet and low
> Rocks a cradle to and fro (81).

NOTES

1. V.S. Naipaul, *A House for Mr Biswas* (1961; rpt. New Delhi: Penguin, 1992), p. 67.
2. Siddharth Singh in a review of the novel, *Connect!* September 18, 2000, http://www.sawf.org/newedit/edit09182000/Bookrev.asp, p. 2.
3. William L Sachs, "V.S. Naipaul and the Plight of the Dispossessed," http:www.religion-online.org/cgi-bin/relsearchd.dll/show article?item_id=1354, p. 6.
4. *Ibid.,* p. 3.
5. *Ibid.,* p. 2.
6. Meenakshi Mukherjee, "A House for Mr. Naipaul," *Frontline*, Vol.18, Iss. 22, Oct. 27-Nov. 09, 2001, http://www.flonnet.com/fl 18 22/18220520.htm, p.3.
7. Toni Morrison, *Beloved* (London: Vintage, 1997), p. 29.
8. Nancy Jesser, "Violence, home, and community in Toni Morrison's *Beloved*," *African American Review* (Summer 1999), http://www.findarticles.com/cf_0/m2838/2_33/55577123/print.jht ml, pp. 12.
9. Veena Singh, "V.S. Naipaul's *A House for Mr. Biswas*," *The Quest*, 15:2 (December 2001), p. 32.
10. *Ibid.*, p. 31.

A House for Mr. Biswas and *Half a Life*: A Comparative Study

VANDANA DATTA
University of Bihar

In many ways *Half a Life* seems to be a sequel to *A House for Mr. Biswas*. Not only does it take off where the latter ends, it also explores into some of the same themes. As *A House for Mr. Biswas* concludes, the son, Anand, has left for England for his studies. This provides the opening for *Half a Life*—Willie Chandran is happy to leave his parents and his country for the London of his dreams. What follows leaves a lot to be answered but one thing is clear: the central concerns of the two novels are much the same. What strikes one immediately is the father-son ambivalence deftly portrayed with sympathetic understanding. Writing about his works, Naipaul once happened to remark: "I begin with myself, this man, this time I begin from all that and I try to investigate it, I try to understand it. I try to arrive at some degree of self-knowledge, and it is the kind of knowledge that cannot deny any aspect of the truth."[1]

Autobiography then provides the raw material for all of Naipaul's novels. To him the novel is "a form of social inquiry,"[2] an exploration not only of individual history but also of social and political history. It is probably his commitment to deliver the truth that makes him disparage made-up stories. Obviously the question arises, why fiction at all then? Why fictionalize autobiography and history? Why not render them just as they are? Naipaul's answer is: "An autobiography can distort, facts can be realigned. But fiction never lies: it reveals the writer totally." The 'wonder' of fiction lies in "the unsuspected truths turned up by the imagination."[3] So it happens that his novels *The Mystic Masseur*, *The Mimic Men*, *The Enigma of Arrival*, *A Way in the*

World, *A House for Mr. Biswas*, to name a few, are overtly autobiographical. But his latest novel *Half a Life* is, as he claims at the very outset, 'an invention.' Nevertheless themes and patterns recur. Language and sometimes even phrases repeat themselves. The protagonists present different facets of Naipaul's personality so that every novel is an attempt at self discovery. *A House for Mr. Biswas* is undoubtedly the most personal of all his novels. The character of Mr. Biswas is done on his father, Seeprasad Naipaul, and much of the novel is about his struggle to establish himself on his own—the house is an assertion of his identity and his refusal to succumb to the demands of his wife's family. It is at the same time, the story of his son, Anand, who is born and brought up in his mother's extended family. Anand is a shy and sensitive boy who has felt all the humiliations and antagonisms that his father suffers in the Tulsi family. The little boy's heart warms out to the father though he does not say anything. Mr. Biswas, on the other hand, for quite some time remains oblivious of his son's existence. Staying away from the Tulsis, he has missed his son's childhood and it is much later that he learns to appreciate Anand's sympathetic gestures. What develops is an ambivalent father-son relationship which forms the basis of the emotional structure of the novel.

There is a recurrence of events in the lives of father and son. Like Anand, Mr. Biswas too has grown up in the absence of the father, depending upon the benevolence of the extended family of his mother. He has suffered all the humiliations that Anand suffers now. He is therefore able to reach out to the boy gradually. And Anand responds with feeling. Once during one of his visits to Hanuman House when Mr. Biswas defends Anand against what he thinks to be an unjust punishment, Anand is "unwilling to let him leave. He said nothing, he simply hung around the bicycle, occasionally rubbing up against it."[4] Both father and son understand each other perfectly well. Mr. Biswas is "touched by the boy's fragility" and Anand is aware of his father's loneliness. In a later incident, the little boy is able to sense the 'clouds' that have gathered on his father's mind while Shama is unable to realize the gravity of the situation. Once again Anand has just one line to say, "I staying with Pa" (278) and he keeps his word. His mother and sisters go back to Hanuman House but he stays on with Mr. Biswas. In their brief stay together, they come close to each other. Mr. Biswas indulges in providing parental care—he makes toys for Anand and gives him lessons and urges him to "Remember Galileo. Always stick up for yourself." (280) He teaches Anand the lesson of self-assertion, a lesson that he always repeats to himself even when face to face with the toughest of opposition from Hanuman House. But his breakdown is too much for Anand to cope up with. The little boy cannot take the delirious condition of his father and is suddenly left all alone. This loneliness, coupled with his father's weakness, arouses in him anger and fear and he cries to be taken back to Hanuman House. It is Hanuman House that provides refuge to Mr. Biswas in this condition. But once he recovers, he leaves for Port of Spain. Things change for him all of a sudden. Lady Luck smiles on him and he gets the job of a reporter on *The Sentinel*. His stories earn him a name and even in Hanuman House he is now looked up to as a figure of some standing so much so that Mrs. Tulsi offers him her house at Port of Spain to live in with his family.

It is with their arrival at Port of Spain that Mr. Biswas starts supervising the education of his son. His love for Anand makes him determined to secure him a life much better than his own. He says this in so many words: "I don't want you to be like me." (374) In other words, he is helping his son in escaping from his world, his kind of life, from himself. There is this understanding between father and son that the father is training the son to leave him. Mr. Biswas takes keen interest in Anand's education, his college activities, his writings—all this is a preparation for the boy's escape, to attain the fulfilment Mr. Biswas—or in real life Seeprasad Naipaul—was deprived of. Thus father and son have a very close bond. They share each other's weaknesses. There is a flip side too to this bond. Both of them are extremely sensitive, get angry easily and can hurt each other in the most callous way. So it happens that once pricked by Mr. Biswas' overzealous efforts at disciplining him, Anand throws back his father's words at him: "When I get to your age I don't want to be like you." (465)

It is interesting that in *Half A Life*, Willie's father tells him the same thing: "We have to think of your higher education, Willie, you mustn't be like me."[5] In fact, *Half a life* takes off where *A House for Mr. Biswas* ends. But in both cases the love-hate relationship of father and son forms one of the central concerns of the novel. Willie's father detests himself for having a son with a 'backward' taint. Willie feels that his father's life, which he calls a 'life of sacrifices,' is one of fraud and deceit. He also feels that his father is a coward who could never own up his weaknesses and failings. His hatred of his father is revealed in very obvious terms in his stories of 'King Cophetua and the Beggar-Maid' and of the selfish brahmin, ironically named 'A Life of Sacrifices.' But later on, as he grows up and faces life on his own terms, he develops some understanding for his father. When he gets the same formal, cold type-written letter from the 'great writer' that his father had got, he is able to sympathize with his father: "I misjudged my father. I used to think that the world was easy for him as a brahmin and that he became a fraud out of idleness. Now I begin to understand how hard the world must have been for him." (58) Again, he thinks of his father with compassion even in the midst of his sexual encounters: "I rested my right hand on her thigh as long as I could, and I thought with sorrow and now without personal shame of my poor father and mother who had known nothing like this moment." (205)

It is here that *Half a Life* comes a long way from *A House for Mr. Biswas*. Years ago, Naipaul had made a disarmingly frank confession: "I cannot write sex. . . . I would be embarrassed even at the moment of writing. My friends would laugh. My mother would be shocked, and with reason."[6] But *Half a Life* is unabashedly about relationships, about fulfilment—sexual fulfilment—in relationships. The whole novel is about Willie's adventurousness from one sexual encounter to another in search of fulfilment. His relationship with his wife Ana provides him some stability in life but sexual fulfilment comes from his affairs with Graca. But in the end, there is only disillusionment. In fact, there is a contradiction of some sort in his relationship with Ana right from the beginning. From the very moment he sets foot in Africa along with her, he has this nagging feeling that he won't be staying there for long, a feeling that stays with him all through the eighteen years he spends there. And though it is for the first time that he feels emotionally secure with someone, there is the feeling of being trapped. The fuss that he makes over his passport is evidence enough that he may just escape one fine morning.

Marriage is a trap for Mr. Biswas too. In the beginning, he is fascinated by Shama, a charming girl of sixteen and enjoys boasting to his friends that he has a girl. To prove his adventurous manliness, he puts down a note for her. Her reaction to the note and also her behaviour with a customer at the shop put him off. He is immediately disenchanted of Shama and ashamed of his note. But the piece of paper is already in the hands of Mrs. Tulsi and he cannot retrieve it. Marriage, therefore, becomes for him a trap laid by destiny. There are no illusions, no expectations right from the beginning. Rather, there is a sense of being caught in a future from which there is no escape. The irony is that Mr. Biswas agrees to the marriage against all reason, something that he regrets all his life. "How often, in the years to come, at Hanuman house or in the house at Shorthills or in the house in Port of Spain living in one room, with some of his children sleeping on the next bed, and Shama, the prankster, the server of black cotton stockings, sleeping downstairs with the other children, how often did Mr. Biswas regret his weakness, his inarticulateness, that evening! How often did he try to make events appear grander, more planned and less absurd than they were!" (91) There is no doubt the regret that "there could be no romance at Hanuman House." (93) There is also the humiliation, the degrading manner in which sons-in-law are treated at Hanuman House. It is only later when Seth tells him in plain words that he realizes that marriage of daughters is a deal for the Tulsis. "You come here, penniless, a stranger. We take you in, we give you one of our daughters, we feed you, we give you a place to sleep in. You refuse to help in the store, you refuse to help on the estate." (109)

It is this fact that Mr. Biswas refuses to bend that redeems his character that redeems the absurdity of the evening when he agreed to marry Shama. He is a fighter all through. Born with handicaps—he had six fingers and was born in the wrong way—his childhood is marred by the pundit's predictions about his unlucky sneeze and that he would be the cause of his father's death, which unfortunately turns out to be true. The death of the father is a disaster for the family and they have to depend on the benevolence of the well-to-do relatives. It is amidst the humiliation of these circumstances that Mr. Biswas grows up. He tries out various jobs. His training as a pundit ends abruptly due to his 'misdemeanour.' He works in a rumshop for some time and then takes up sign-painting which brings him to Hanuman House. He very soon understands what is expected of him there, but his pride, his self-respect stand in the way. He refuses to be ordered about by the Tulsis. In fact, he makes it clear very soon that he does not want to live in their house. But the experiment at 'Chase' fails. The next job on the estate ends even more miserably. But nothing deters Mr. Biswas from going on trying, howsoever comic his efforts may seem to be. Naipaul intends this comic effect and perhaps therefore, even as a child, Mr. Biswas is referred to as Mr. Biswas, not once by his first name—Mohun.

It is his job on *The Sentinel* that gives him the independence he had always wanted. Even the Tulsis start respecting him now. But in Port of Spain too, it is the house of the Tulsis that he is living in. Having a house of his own is not just a dream for him. It becomes a symbol of his identity, of the strength of his personality with which he asserts and refuses to give in—getting a house is his greatest achievement in life. He would have been extremely miserable if he were to die in the house of the Tulsis. So what if the house has an absurd shape, so what if the cellotex panels on the eaves have fallen away, so what if the staircase hangs at the back, open, with only a banister, and sheltered by unpainted corrugated iron, so what if the house has no back door at all? Without the house it would have been terrible "to have died among the Tulsis, and the squalor of that large, disintegrating and indifferent family; to have left Shama and the children among them, in one room; worse, to have lived without even attempting to lay claim to one's portion of the earth; to have lived and died as one had been born, unnecessary and unaccommodated." (14)

The story of Mr. Biswas thus comes a full circle, that of Willie Chandran doesn't. *Half a Life* ends on a note of disillusionment. There is no elation of achievement as in *A House for Mr. Biswas* where the hero gains a sense of identity. Here there is a total loss of personality. It is about people living artificial lives and so there is no satisfaction in the end. Rather, there is a sense of being lost. Both brother and sister—Willie and Sarojini—come together in the end after having made a mess of their lives. Like Mr. Biswas, Willie is also born with handicaps. But his handicaps are not physical like those of Mr. Biswas; his handicaps are social. He is the son of a low-caste mother. His father is a Brahmin but one who has degraded himself miserably, one who had aspired to greatness, to what he calls a 'life of sacrifice' but ends up living out the most dull, drab and ordinary life. To prove his point, he had married a low-caste woman but himself remains a victim of this unhappy union all through his life. The birth of his children instead of bringing him joy makes him feel all the more guilty of his actions—he blames himself for the 'backward' taint on their faces. Willie has grown up despising his father and he desires to go far away from him. But unwittingly he follows his father's footsteps. Getting away from what he knew is what his father had done. Getting away from what he knows is what Willie embarks upon as he leaves for England. And it is not a scholarship like Anand that takes him to England but the kindness of a member of the House of Lords who had visited his father's ashram just after independence. And once he reaches England, he does not do anything meaningful. He allows his life to drift away as it may. Though he is at the college of education, he is not really serious about it. As he tells Roger, he is only 'marking time.' (81) For sometime, he continues giving radio talks but abandons it soon. His stories are published. But he doesn't continue with writing either. His sister, Sarojini, is right about him when she says that he is selfishly wasting his life in London 'doing this little thing and that little thing and not knowing why you are doing anything.' (115) She pointedly says that Willie is an idler like their father. And even when he gets his degree, it will not be something really worthwhile. "You will get a little teaching job and hide away here for the rest of your life?" (116)

It is here that Sarojini touches at the truth, for hiding away is what Willie has really been doing all the time. He has come to England to hide away from his parents. He tries his hand at stories in school but his father sneers at him for them. Later on Roger says, that they are not real, 'the writer has secrets. He is hiding.' (83) He rewrites the stories, this time with success and they are published. But Willie cannot continue with writing either. His writings now lead him to looking at things, especially his family, his parents and his life in a way that he is unable to face. He hides from his friends too because he has been making love to their girlfriends. Having a girlfriend of his own is something for which he does not have the courage. His stories, however, do win him a girlfriend. Ana, his first true love, is drawn to him through his stories. And once again Willie runs away from life. He follows his wife to her home in Portuguese Africa to live under her protective wings. It takes him eighteen long years to realize that "now the best part of my life has gone, and I've done nothing. . . . I have been hiding for too long." (228) It is on this note that the novel ends—so far Willie had depended on Ana, now he leans on Sarojini's strength. Sarojini's personality has blossomed in a big way. She is now a mature, self-confident and authoritative woman—one who has learnt from and grown with the experiences of life. Willie has done simply nothing. Though in the end there is the realization of his failure, there is no hint as to what he would do to make good the damage done. Precious time has been lost. Those years cannot come back. It is for him a painful realization indeed that he is forty-one and has achieved nothing. There isn't a trace of the fulfilment that one gets in *A House for Mr. Biswas*. The latter is an epic, there is a fullness of vision and an achievement of completion. In comparison, *Half a Life* seems to be sketchily conceived and gives the impression of a half-hearted effort. Naipaul does not seem to have put himself into it. Though most of the issues and themes taken up are common to both of them, *A House for Mr. Biswas* is a class apart It is a great prose epic that can compare favourably with the best novels in the world.

NOTES

1. V.S. Naipaul, "Introduction," *East Indians in the Caribbean: Colonialism and the Struggle for Identity* (New York: Krause International, 1982), p. 7.
2. V.S. Naipaul, *India: A Wounded Civilization* (New York: Vintage, 1978), p. 189.
3. Qtd. Lillian Feder, *Naipaul's Truth* (New Delhi: Indialog, 2001), p. 18.
4. V.S. Naipaul, *A House for Mr. Biswas* (London: Penguin, 1992), p. 236.
5. V.S. Naipaul, *Half a Life* (London: Picador, 2001), p. 43.
6. V.S. Naipaul, qtd. Gamini Salgado, "V.S. Naipaul and the Politics of Fiction," *The New Pelican Guide to English Literature*, ed. Boris Ford, Vol. 8: From Orwell to Naipaul (London: Penguin, 1988), p. 312.

A House for Mr. Biswas: An Autobiographical Study

BHAGABAT NAYAK

V.S. Naipaul, the master novelist and expatriate literary circumnavigator, occupies a significant position between cultures and countries, defines his position in his internalized nostalgia by his observation of the disintegration and hypocrisy of the Third World. He is preoccupied with the varieties of dislocation, migration, exile, the idea of being unanchored and displaced and the enigma of a disorientating experience in the explosive and disconcerting realities of the postcolonial world anywhere, everywhere. "He is like a living university" with an urge to visit monuments, museums, landmarks, and libraries without much joy has known like any colonial what Fielding, Dickens, Lamb and Thackeray have failed to help him find personal or autobiographical correlatives. In his search for identity in his fiction, he has the poignant recollection of his life and ancestry that evokes the slow dereliction of an unwanted one, betrayed and cheated into a contract of indenture, and further disowned by the communities. He is "eternally an outsider—an Indian in the West Indies, a West Indian in England, and as described by many . . . a nomadic intellectual in the nondescript Third World."[1] He has assured his position as the most polemical among the contemporary writers who has inherited the collective unconsciousness of the Indian ethos in the erstwhile colonies of British imperialism with a zeal "to strive, to seek, to find and not to yield." Being a Brahmin gypsy and a nomad, he acknowledges his "colonial Hindu self," and as a man and writer suffers from the pangs of alienation, hating the oppressor and fearing oppressed, but tries to establish his identity by converting autobiographical materials into poignant fiction on the tradition and cultural affinities with Trinidad, England and India. With the Swiftean vision of the life-consuming aspects of all colonial and postcolonial societies, he has characterized his posture as that "of Whitman's nigger" always "looking down."

With the decline of the British imperialism and the rise of the American power bloc in the second half of the twentieth century, the world has seen mass migration, expatriation and varieties of exile, which have given new shapes to individual and national cultural experiences. Naipaul was born in the country town of Chaguanas in Trinidad in 1932 in a large Brahmin family of Indian origin in the state of Uttar Pradesh, had his early education at the Port of Spain, and then went on scholarship to Oxford with "a feeling of privilege." From his very childhood, Naipaul had found his father to be a victim of the limited, poverty-ridden, backward Hindu world for his career in journalism and story writing in his diaspora identity. He had also realized the factors that had denied his father to be a potential writer. Yet he says in an interview with David Bates about his departure from Trinidad and his early struggles to be a writer which bear a correspondence with his father's last attempts:

> The writing that has mattered most to me is that of my father. . . . It taught me to look at things that had never been written about before, and seemed dull in life, yet when transformed to paper became very surprising. A great deal of my vision of Trinidad has come straight from my father. Other writers are aware that they are writing about rooted societies; his work showed me that one could write about another kind of society.[2]

Naipaul does see in his own literary reminiscences of Trinidad his father's imprint, his abortive quest to transcend the limits of a rural, orthodox and ritual-ridden locality. He has never thought of his future except as a writer. Unlike most of the writers, he presents his autobiographical materials in most of his novels, either consciously or unconsciously. His development, achievement and success rest mainly on his four novels—*A House for Mr. Biswas* (1961), *The Mimic Men* (1967), *In a Free State* (1971) and *Guerrillas* (1975). "In case of *A House for Mr. Biswas*, the knowledge that the central figure is derived from

Naipaul's father, a journalist and short story writer and that most of the important events in the novel actually took place is likely to lead the unwary reader into seeing the author as a 'realistic' novelist in the limiting sense."[3] Naipaul's autobiographical narration in *A House for Mr. Biswas* is a "private epic" and is to be taken as a literal version of his life. The hero of the novel, Mr. Biswas, is not an accomplice or passive participant in his own colonization but a victim of the manipulation and machinations of others who seek to keep violence or rebellion away like Ganesh in *The Mystic Masseur* and Ralph Singh in *The Mimic Men.*

A House for Mr. Biswas is Naipaul's most personal book that is shaped after his father's stories, a vital portion of his heritage to his son who considers them "a unique record of the life of the Indian or Hindu community in Trinidad in the first fifty years of the twentieth century. Through his father's stories, he was learning a great deal about the writer's craft as they gave him a way of looking, an example of labour, a knowledge of the literary process, a sense of the order and special reality. The novel is the fictional version of experiences Naipaul has recalled in later autobiographical surveys which he describes as "very much father's book . . . written out of his journalism and stories, out of his knowledge."[4] Mr. Biswas as Naipaul's autobiographical revelation appears not only as an over-reaction to a specific concern, but more fundamentally as the "fear of extinction," the annihilation of the self that his father continued to endure and transmitted to his son. In reconstructing his father's life, he has traced the inception of his own process of self-creation on different planes in both tone and intention, theme and breadth, alienation and identity. "Mr. Biswas may be colonized in the physical, economic and political sense, but his emotional urge for freedom, his sensibility to humiliation and slavery are signs of a temperament that bristles with rebellion subversion." Naipaul locates the circumstances, . . . socio-cultural and historical in character, that go into the making of Biswas's experience of a community caught somewhere in the larger process. Mr. Biswas makes humanly interesting and compelling the immediate existential and socio-cultural themes in a transparent and natural style."[5]

The novel presents a three-fold meaning in its autobiographical technique; first we see how Seepersad's encircled life in extended Hindu clan eventually dwarfed his ambitions to be a writer; secondly, how Naipaul himself through a "cathartic moment" attained through his father's life, internally feared a similar fate; and finally, Mr. Biswas's being colonized under conditions which are specific to his setting and background. The novel portrays the tentative approaches and withdrawals of the early relationship between father and son. Naipaul reflects his father's and his own life in Mr. Biswas and his son. Thus, the novel appears to be a double autobiography in which Mr. Biswas is modelled on Seepersad Naipaul's life and career and Anand, his son whose life and career run parallel to V.S. Naipaul's. Mr. Biswas is the prototype of Naipaul's father who had passed his ambition on to his eldest, brilliant son with a determination to prove himself. His sketching of Anand is not much different from his creator as his "fictious progeny." In the novel, the portrayal of Anand as a "separation of man from writer," and a most poignant recreation, evokes reactions to his father—longing, attachment, fear, rage and reconciliation on individual and historical past. Naipaul says that *A House for Mr. Biswas* was "created out of what I saw and felt as a child."[6] These perceptions and feelings emerge in Anand's gestures, in his silences and laconic responses, in his sudden exclamations of anger and oblique expressions of affection and loyalty. Episodes in the novel appear autobiographical in external detail elucidating his inner life and his internalization of his father's "fear of extinction" along with his vocation. Naipaul's aim in the novel is as much to recall a world of imaginative fullness on the lines of Dickens, George Eliot and Hardy to connect it with the void of unidentified and unqualified Caribbean experience.

Mr. Biswas's story is largely an odyssey of restless questing where the shifting locales are metaphors or analogues for his soul states. He is Naipaul's compassionate version of the being condemned to wander the world in his own psyche. He appears before us as a "visible man" in truer light like in Dostoevsky's *Idiot*. Naipaul writes him from his own experience with "a new reality" that transcends distinctions between fiction and non-fiction and stakes a claim to permanence. It is interesting to note that the novel is modelled on Naipaul's father's short story. "They named him Mohun." The novel is the most moving auto-biographical work that draws upon an experience totally based on layered levels of alienation and exile. The birth and early life of Mr. Biswas is ridiculous because he is born in the wrong way with unfavourable horoscopic signs, including a sixth finger and "an unlucky sneeze." At his birth the midwife warned: "Whatever you do this boy will eat up his mother and father" and the pundit interprets midnight, the time of Mr. Biswas's birth, as "the inauspicious hour." The pundit urges that Mr. Biswas be kept away from the tree and water—particularly water—and prescribes his father Raghu, not to see his son for twenty-one days. He adds that the child will be a lecher and a spendthrift and possibly a liar as well; he must be kept away from water. Mr. Biswas's first name Mohun ironically means "the beloved, and was the name given by the milkmaids to Lord Krishna," (17-18) and he has a variety of absurd, clownish and grotesque experiences. John Thieme rightly comments: "By giving Biswas a name accorded to one of the avatars of Vishnu, Naipaul ensures that his central character is viewed in an ironic light; he establishes him as a Hindu mock-heroic figure."[6]

Like Mr. Biswas, Naipaul shows himself induced by 'karma' and to be caught in a love-hate relationship with Hinduism, and estimates Mr. Biswas's struggles to define himself by his tripartite vocation: to build his house, to succeed as a journalist and to prepare his son to leave home for study. Naipaul's realization of fate is associated with the Hindu quest in a milieu where there is a strong belief that the individual is determined by forces beyond his control. Mr. Biswas's pattern of subjugations and slave-like roles is perhaps Naipaul's own fictional invention, while allowing himself considerable licence to alter the overall meanings. The disorder, hostilities and squalor that destroyed the inner peace of his father and resulted in Naipaul's bewilderment was "jumbled without sequence." Both Seepersad and Naipaul were deprived of father's presence in early childhood, and both were dependent on the arbitrary benevolence of their extended families. In the novel, this similarity initiates an empathy that slowly develops between Mr. Biswas and Anand. Mr. Biswas taught Anand a lesson in self-assertion, a challenge he himself will not relinquish despite all obstacles. During Mr. Biswas's visit to Arwacas, when he is living apart from his family at Green Vale, a sugarcane estate owned by Tulsis, Anand is generally shy with him, avoiding any physical contact. Mr. Biswas feels the subjection of his son in the loneliness of his exile. Likewise, Mr. Biswas's changing roles as a worker, labourer and an employee of the Tulsis are versions of his arrested growth in Green Vale, The Chase, Shorthills, and in Hanuman House itself. These perceptions and feelings he has presented in Anand's gestures, in his silences and laconic responses, in his sudden exclamations of anger and oblique expressions of affection and loyalty. On the other hand, Mr. Biswas is tormented by the feelings of depersonalization, gets hallucinatory visions, and struggles with his wife Shama and children to have a house. He tries to disguise his terrors and hostility to Shama, pretending that his strange behaviour is due to illness. When the father and son stay together, their roles remain ambiguous in his distress and rare capacity; he makes toys for Anand and teaches him bits of religion and science. Different family episodes in Mr. Biswas's life at different circumstances are, however, fictional in chronology and setting and depict the psychological condition that determines Naipaul's assimilation of his father's fear or the abyss, the "subsidiary gift" of his dual legacy. This appears similar in bringing a parity between Naipaul's and Biswas's family, as behind Naipaul's scattered memories of his father and the family disorder, there lies interestingly his parallel struggle in London, away from Trinidad past, to fix a moment that would crystallize and make intelligible the mass of unorganized autobiographical materials at his disposal.

Naipaul's fictional portrayal of Anand's unconscious identification with his father reveals psychological affinities that he does not probe into in his autobiographical writings. Seepersad's wish to write an autobiographical novel too remained unfulfilled. The great amount of pain, suffering and humiliation that Seepersad went through is understandably part of the second generation post-indentured Indians in Trinidad. Naipaul describes this in his family relations when he describes Mrs. Tulsi, Seth, Tara, Ajodha, Pundit Jairam, Owad and of course, Shama, a replica of his own mother and a rich family's daughter.

Naipaul has written *A House for Mr. Biswas* at a different creative stage in his career, a stage when he did not have the later contemptuous and negative view of human experience. Anand's need to identity with the father is revealed in brief but important incidents. Naipaul's articulation of early life in his Caribbean experience is based on close observation and details that he presents in the novel. At the same time, the cultural and historical experience of colonialism and postcolonialism in different forms dominated the island that Mr. Biswas left, a fictional transmutation of a variety of dominance under imperial arrangement in servitude. Mr. Biswas's hunger for knowledge, his singularity and playfulness, shocking to the Tulsis, are attractive qualities to the child who had been deprived of a father's example. Biswas's remoteness grows through his fantasies and reading of the novels of Hall Caine and Marie Corelli. His literary heroes like in his countries where ambitions can be pursued and have meaning, but he is trapped in an absurd place without romance.

Beginning with *A House for Mr. Biswas*, Naipaul transmits his father's legacy to many of his fictive characters. He expresses his view of the world in a structure at once naturalistic as "The substance of the novel has to do with the transformation of Mr. Biswas, a slave to place, history and biography, into free man, the sign and realization of that emancipation being his house."[8] The rising graph of Mr. Biswas's life in a big joint family is led by his father, Raghu, who died by drowning in a village pond while searching for his son. So also Anand's danger of drowning is more decisive. For Anand, the threat of drowning becomes the subject of its first original composition. "The threat of annihilation has demanded a truth to his actual experience that his education would deny."[9] Mohun's two brothers were sent away as sugarcane labourers and his sister Dehuti went to stay with her aunt, Tara. Mohun and his mother Bipti went to Pagotes and there they were accommodated by Tara. During his school days he became friendly with Alec who inspired him for the career of a sign-painter. His little education again inspired him to be a Pundit but later he was expelled by the Hindu priest Jairam from his house for greed and misconduct. Mohun went back to his mother and realized the predicaments of a man without a house of his own in disappointment. Later, he was given a job in a wine shop by Ajodha's (Tara's husband's) brother. It was a bad luck for him as he was accused by Bhandat of stealing a dollar from his pocket. He was sacked and later became a signboard painter coming in contact with his schoolmate, Alec. When he came to paint signboard during his Hanuman House days, he painted signs for Tulsi Store and came in contact with a rich, orthodox widow Mrs. Tulsi who was running the house and store with her husband's brother, Mr. Seth. This enabled him to come in contact with Shama, a young shop assistant whom he married hastily in the tradition of the Hanuman House. Walsh writes: "Everybody lived at Hanuman House in complex relationships and transient alliances, the purpose of which was to placate the authorities and to slide through life unnoticed. In this cruel, conic world, both crowded and solitary, bullying and servile, Mr. Biswas kept alive a mere glint of independence and self by refusing to be either a suave or a mild victim."[10]

Mohun was trapped among the Tulsis whom Naipaul describes a "totalitarian organization family." The matriarchal dominance by Mrs. Tulsi in every affair—politics, religion and occupation indicates a feudalistic/totalitarian set up and its iron rule recoils on Mr. Biswas's inner self-respect and desire for freedom. Thus, "Biswas is the first of his family to break with the feudal-capitalist hierarchy and forge an individual identity."[11] He finds himself a complete misfit in Mrs. Tulsi's household. Shama could not understand him till he purchased a house of his own and found his marriage with her unsuccessful. He tells Shama that the Hanuman House was "a real zoo where all kinds of animals dwelt." Later Mr. Seth saves him from a debt by paying the amount to an Insurance Company.

Mr. Biswas's discovery of his vocation seems to be redemption from his fear of extinction. Anand observes that his father's achievements impress even Mrs. Tulsi, who suggests that he and his family share a house with her and one of her sons in Port of Spain. It is here that Mr. Biswas like Seepersad Naipaul begins to supervise his son's education, to temper Anand's impatience so like his own. He was trapped by his obligations to his wife and four children. Mr. Biswas never gives up his struggle against his own internalization of the historical forces that threaten his autonomy; he is part of the Trinidadian Indian community, yet he constantly questions its customs and values. As a reporter and later as a welfare officer, he adapts to the "widening world" into which he has ventured. But in his own house where he finally lives with Shama and his children remains as his monument. Naipaul begins Mr. Biswas with himself as a centre that comprises his background, his education and his vocation. He often refers to the disadvantages of growing up in the colonial society of Trinidad overshadowed by a mysticized ancestral past from India. But in the composite portrait of the writer that emerges from the body of his work, this point of departure seems a blessing. Mr. Biswas's struggle against the Hindu fate, dramatized on more secular level as his quest for self-realization, takes the form of his attempt to emancipate from the old Hindu world of the Tulsis. Biswas's rebellion is less a revolt against Hinduism in favour of western individualism than a revolt against the orthodox Sanatanist Hinduism of the Tulsis in favour of the reformed Hinduism of the Arya Samaj, whose missionaries greatly influence him when they visit Trinidad. On the evidence of his Indian travel books, one might expect Naipaul to adopt a more committed stance and to attack the inertia he feels lying at the heart of Hinduism, but in the novel his art remains one of detached ironic observation.

The autobiographical concerns of Naipaul heavily influence the story and structure of *A House for Mr. Biswas*. The shaping of the story is conditioned by Seepersad's life and works but the immediate circumstances of Mr. Biswas's life pattern among Tulsi's household and estate are triggered by what Naipaul implies by saying that his father was "obsessed by circumstances of his birth." Mr. Biswas's struggle against Fate looks initially as if it will be a battle against the version of his Karma provided by his horoscope, when he brings about the drowning first of Dhari's calf and then of his father as a result of having disobeyed the warning not to go near water and appears to be incapable of averting his predetermined destiny. However, as he gets older and becomes more self-conscious, he begins to rebel against the constraints placed on him by his immediate environment. He tries to choose for himself, but his choices are a negation rather than an affirmation. He appears to be condemned to repeat himself from situation to situation and every house he occupies is frustratingly alien to his special vision of his own house. Escaping the actual realities of slavery, Mr. Biswas carries his colonized consciousness within him, in the way Naipaul had carried alienation and distancing within him from Trinidad landscape and through his knowledge of the present Third World realities. It appears that "Biswas's alienation is the consequence of his vivid imaginative life created and sustained by the alien influences of his education and his reading which channelise his ambitions unrealistically."[12] When he finally acquires the house on the Sikkim Street, St. James, Port of Spain, he discovers that the romance of the house is destroyed by the disappointing reality of despair. The house is an object and emblem of the loss of his El Dorado—the "golden dream" of his life. Houses become the places of his confinement as he moves "from one house of strangers to another" during and after his staying. He becomes constantly tired in his life and thinks all action is futile in his restless quest for the dream house. Time flies by "bringing disaster closer, devouring his life." (586) He runs down like an old, tired machine. We see death and darkness rising in him. During the last months of his life, his emotional states are marked as the consequences not only due to strokes but also to a life-time struggle and unbearable tension made by his indomitable spirit and a few gratifying successes. His actual dramatic journey from society to social reality is based on Naipaul's rational and existential bias and unlike his existential struggle in his mental landscape for freedom from restraint.

Mr. Biswas may be called a legendary figure from his infancy to death. No doubt Naipaul's feelings of rootedness, life of exile that results in personal insecurity and cultural instability are presented in the versions of Mr. Biswas's experience. Being alienated from all walks of life and unable to belong either to England or Caribbean, Mr. Biswas becomes a man without a side, surrounded by buffoons and impelled to be something of a tragic clown. On the whole, Mr. Biswas reflects Naipaul's struggle to assimilate his Indian past, his own complex and personal history, his continual self-evaluation and self-criticism, and sometimes his excessive reactions and the core of creative intelligence from his authorial vision. With a determination to express the truth of his experience, he exposes in his autobiographical references the identity of his pain and anger and his occasional churlishness, to consider his judgements and to correct his vision. Alienation characterizes the affinity between the protagonist and the narrator as they are marginal men in whom body and soul are in conflict. Alienation or rootlessness is related to the loss of and quest for identity. It is the loss of identity that results in alienation. The house into which Mr. Biswas and his family move near the end of the novel before his death and where he dies not long after, reflects the naivete of his owner and the petty corruption of his society. Naipaul's truth is that the self that speaks to the reader in the novel does not divulge details of his domestic or social affairs, but it is clear that his "innermost self" has, to some extent, been formed by his interaction with the worlds he has explored in Mr. Biswas's exhausting fight against the Tulsis. On the other hand, Naipaul makes a deconstruction of European colonialism in the novel for the reconstruction of the Caribbean culture, in its hybrid forms, in his imaginative revisioning of cultural history for a cultural transformation.

The very use of the title "Mr." for Mohun Biswas in the novel acknowledges the dignity and struggle for identity by owning a house is both existential and universal. Ultimately, the 'house' turns out to be the image of fulfilment, a release from years of slavery and tyranny of extended family. In the searching for a house, "He plays at little because he is unable to live it."[13] In the colonized, pre-independence Trinidad society, a white-collar job and self-respect were rare things to achieve and in this kind of social milieu, Mr. Biswas is denied the honour or satisfaction of absorbing into the Hindu world or to represent it in the outside world. Mr. Biswas's sense of belonging is a pre-requisite of assuming an identity. This is why "The 'House' in this novel is a symbol not for 'rootedness' but for freedom—freedom from slavery and oppression."[14] Identity needs one's social and cultural base to be established which seems to be in crisis with his status as an outsider, a victim of denial, betrayal and tyranny. The fear of 'extinction' that haunted Seepersad and haunts Mr. Biswas is connected with the positive, inner vocation that can sustain a man. But Seepersad's fear which got transferred to Naipaul became quite real for the young and aspiring writer. He knew that fear could only be combated by the exercise of vocation.

Naipaul often refers to the disadvantage of growing up in the colonial society of Trinidad shadowed by a mysticized ancestral past in India. But in the composite portrait of the writer that emerges from the body of his work, the point of departure at times seems a blessing. The sort of fictional biography of his journalist father and father-son life history as presented in the novel seem quite autobiographical, and hailed as a three generation novel carries the responses on mixed, chaotic and disorderly Caribbean set up. In this regard, Bruce King aptly remarks: "In the case of V.S. Naipaul there is a triple alienation since the author is dispossessed from several cultures and possible homes. Having rejected his Brahmin past, the small decaying world of Indian Trinidad, the lack of sophistication of Creole Trinidad, the provinciality of the West Indian middle classes, Naipaul was unable to find in either England or India the high, purposeful culture he desired. Subsequently he has become the voice of the modern expatriate and of our time in feeling unattached, unillusioned, without purpose, an observer of the world's follies, especially those problems which have resulted from the end of empire and the withdrawal of European rule from the Third World. Naipaul's work appeals to those who have felt the effect of rapid secularization, nobility and social change; the resulting world is large, overcrowded and yet an empty space."[15] Mr. Biswas is taken to be representing a 'universalist' and a transcultural vision of man's rootlessness and a search for identity and place. "Naipaul is like Biswas, who having no tradition to turn to, must create his own. And this tradition has its roots in the rootlessness of West-Indian society rather than in the well-established European and Indian societies."[16] Unlike Naipaul, Mr. Biswas's lifelong ambition is the ownership of a house to provide security and comfort. It is therefore appropriate that Naipaul should have made a 'house' the central and guiding symbol of the novel.

In the novel, the house becomes a kind of inverted fictional embodiment of Naipaul's own personal need for change and escape. While his father's experience becomes the story of any postcolonial man displaced from his origin by chance or choice, his Mr. Biswas's 'unhoused' condition and alienation are the problems of every contemporary diaspora which is presented in the autobiographical design of the novel. The novel succeeds in transcending the individual self by universalizing the issue of alienation with a Naipaulean cry for identity in the postcolonial world. An autobiographical study of the novel reveals how the life history of Seepersad and his son, V.S. Naipaul, is similar to that of Mr. Biswas and his son Anand who fails to absorb the Caribbean climate. Yet the novel is a tragic epic, densely populated, rich in variety and felt life, full of humour and beaming with vitality. It becomes visibly clear in *A House for Mr. Biswas* that the fictional embodiment of Naipaul's own personal life is assimilated and absorbed into art.

NOTES

1. M.S. Nagarajan, "Home and Exile," *The Hindu*, May 5, 2002, p. 4.
2. *The Sunday Times*, May 26, 1963.

3. Gamini Salgado, "V.S. Naipaul and the Politics of Fiction," *The New Pelican Guide to English Literature*, Vol. 8, ed. Boris Ford (London: Penguin, 1983), p. 316.
4. "Prologue to an Autobiography," *Finding the Centre: Two Narratives* (London: Andre Deutsch, 1984), p. 72.
5. Manjit Inder Singh, *V.S. Naipaul* (Jaipur: Rawat, 1998), p. 114.
6. V.S. Naipaul, *A House for Mr. Biswas* (Harmondsworth: Penguin, 1969), p. 22.
7. John Thieme, "A Hindu Castaway: Ralph Singh's Journey in *The Mimic Men*," *Modern Fiction Studies*, 30: 3 (Autumn 1984), p. 507.
8. William Walsh, "V.S. Naipaul: Mr. Biswas," *Literary Criterion*, 10: 2 (Summer 1972), p. 29.
9. Lillian Feder, *Naipaul's Truth* (New Delhi: Indialog, 2001), p. 40.
10. William Walsh, pp. 33-34.
11. William Walsh, *V.S. Naipaul* (London: Oliver and Boyd, 1973), p. 30.
12. Shashi Kamra, *The Novels of V.S. Naipaul* (New Delhi: Prestige, 1990), p. 85.
13. Albert Camus, *The Rebel: An Essay on Man in Revolt*, trans. Anthony Bower (New York: Vintage, 1956), p. 52.
14. B.K. Das, "From Slavery to Freedom: A Study of V.S. Naipaul's *A House for Mr. Biswas*," *Aspects of Commonwealth Literature* (New Delhi: Creative, 1995), p. 102.
15. Bruce King, "Protest, Alienation and Modernism in the New Literatures," *The Literary Half-Yearly*, 28: 1 (January 1987), pp. 6-7.
16. Anthony Boxill, *V.S. Naipaul's Fiction: In Quest of the Enemy* (Fredericton, New Brunswick: York Press, 1983), p. 24.

Identity Crisis in *A House for Mr. Biswas*

AMAR NATH PRASAD
Jadgam College, Chapra

V.S. Naipaul's *A House for Mr. Biswas* is a beautiful work which deals with the theme of isolation, frustration and negation in a colonized society—a society that turns cruel and callous to the aspiration of the protagonist, Mr. Mohun Biswas. The book also deals with a number of physical or spiritual maladies, e.g., the clash of cultures between the old and the new in a multi-racial society; a quest for identity in a conservative framework and, above all, the protagonist's dry and monotonous journey full of many jerks and jolts. In technique and style, the novel seems to conform to the metaphoric structure, though a bit wanting in proper structural unification as we see in James Joyce's masterpiece, *The Portrait of an Artist as a Young Man*. Like any other great novelist, he tries his best to weave his material through the colorful threads of art and beauty, symbols and images, irony and pathos. To him, ideas are more important than plot. He admits: "I preferred the natural way of describing how, at different stages as one's life capacities, one looked at one's place in the world. And one does this through the series of narratives and the linking of themes and emotions."[1]

The primary business of V.S. Naipaul as a novelist is to project carefully the complex fate of individuals, societies and cultures. To him, fiction is an instrument of analysis. Perhaps this is why most of his novels revolved round the recurring themes of colonial psychosis, individual's search for identity and clash of culture. Naipaul's fiction, as R.A. Singh thinks, acquires "three dimensional structure—historical, social and psychological."[2]

Almost all the works of V.S. Naipaul have a clear-cut influence on Indian life and culture. His union background gives him the multiple experience of a marginalised culture. He uses such words and phrases and creates such a situation that easily take the reader back to Indian myths and tradition, culture and civilization. Naipaul takes a very keen interest in a colonial ethos. Sometimes, he becomes autobiographical in his approach. The writer himself had to face many ups and downs in order to assert his identity in a disinherited tradition. He admits: "Living in a borrowed culture, the west Indian, more than most, needs writers to tell him who he is and where he stands."[3] It is this cultural disinheritance that made Naipaul a great writer of commonwealth literature. His anger, frustration and futility sprung from his sense of disinheritance. As a matter of fact, the secret of Naipaul's art lies not in his personal attachment to the establishment—individual, tradition, culture, but in his creative detachment beyond geography, history and ethnicity. In this respect he is a bit different from his contemporary West Indian writers like Mill Moltzer, George Lamming and Wilson Harris. Naipaul has tried his best to project in his novels a sustaining course for all those who are rootless or homeless. Keith Garebian rightly holds the view: "Naipaul explores landscapes in order to provide characters with a real home, a true place of belonging so that they will not continue to be homeless wanderers, unsure of themselves and their fates. But the mythology of the land is tinged with embarrassment, nervousness, hysteria and pessimism, all products in some way of Naipaul's own history as a colonial with an ambiguous identity."[4]

It is to be noted that the theme of identity crisis rings the note of almost all the major works of Naipaul. The characters portrayed in his world are mostly rural and poor. They have to undergo a lot of trials and tribulations, ups and downs. They long for a free and fair existence but unfortunately they are not able to cross the boundary of the colonial society. *A House for Mr. Biswas* gives such characters wings to fly freely in the open sky and assert their own existence. *The Middle Passage* records the author's impressions of colonial society in the West Indies and

South Africa. *An Area of Darkness* reflects semi-autobiographical account of a year in India. *India: A Wounded Civilization* is an extended study of the author about the miseries and sufferings of the general mass of India. This account shows the author's sympathetic attitude towards the downtrodden. *The Mimic Men* is the story of Ralph Singh, a disgraced colonial minister exiled from the Caribbean island of his birth. When he comes to politics, he finds himself cut up in the upheaval of empire. In other words, he was badly enmeshed in the turmoil of two large events.

A House for Mr. Biswas is a well-known work by V.S. Naipaul. It deals with the story of Mr. Mohun Biswas, who is born in the village of Trinidad at the hour of midnight, an inauspicious hour in that country. He is predicted by the pundit to be a lecher, a spendthrift and a liar. But this does not happen. Just after the birth of the protagonist, the family is split. His two brothers are sent to some remote places for earning bread. Mr. Biswas, along with his mother, goes to his sister Dehuti. He is admitted to the mission school where he studies mathematics and other subjects. Alec is his intimate friend. He also devotes his time to painting.

The second phase of Mr. Biswas's life can be seen as an apprentice. He is kept with Pundit Jayaram, a Hindu priest. He learns a lot of things from Jayaram but unfortunately this relation does not last long. Mr. Biswas was accused of theft of gifts. He was badly pulled up by the Pundit. He leaves his Guru in disappointment and goes to his aunt Tara to find out employment and monetary help. Tara is highly sympathetic to Biswas. She gets him employed in a rum shop run by her husband's brother, Bhandat, a man who was addicted to wine-drinking and forgery. He cheats his customers by giving them unmeasured drinks. One day Mr. Biswas is charged by Bhandat of stealing one dollar from his pocket and is turned out of his shop.

One day when Mr. Biswas was walking along the main road, he came across Ramchand with whom his sister Dehuti had run away. Ramchand escorts Biswas to his sister. There he gets the job of a painter. It is only during Christmas days that he gets plenty of work. Though his mother told him to get married but he refused to do so as he was not employed permanently. He goes to Hanuman House at Arwacas where he happens to meet Shama, the sixteen-year-old daughter of Mrs. Tulsi of Tulsi Store. He falls in love with Shama and they get married. Biswas begins to live with his wife in the Hanuman House with other sons-in-law of Mrs. Tulsi. Very soon he finds that the place does not suit his taste and temperament. His married life doesn't prove to be successful. He develops a mental complex due to the uncongenial family atmosphere. Shama is always ironical towards Biswas and treats him like a prisoner. By this time, Shama is pregnant. Mr. Biswas has to sell his goods on credit to his customers. As a result, the shop is paralyzed. Shama delivers a female child, Savi, and three years later a male child, Anand. Tulsi House appoints Mr. Biswas as an overseer at Green Vale at twenty-five dollars a month. But here too Mr. Biswas is not satisfied with his work. During Christmas, he presents a doll's house to his female child Savi. This presentation shows his inner desire to have a house of his own. The house also suggests his urge for freedom and security. So he starts making a house there. After completing the house (though half-house), he goes to live there. Here he feels at ease and fully relieved of his depression. But this does not go on for long. He suffers from strange fears. On a dark rainy night, he receives a mental shock in his incomplete house and is carried to the Hanuman House. After treatment, he gets the job of a Newspaper reporter in Port of Spain and brings his family in one of the houses of Tulsi family. Once again his life is revitalized when he gets another government job as a Community Welfare Officer. He takes some money from Ajodha to build a house. Thus, his long cherished dream for a house is fulfilled. But very soon misfortune knocks at his door. Ajodha's loan begins to multiply. The community welfare department is also abolished. He begins to suffer from depression. He dies at the age of forty-six.

One of the dominant themes which emerge from the reading of *A House for Mr. Biswas* is the theme of the cultural clash—the difficulty of adjustment of the protagonist in Tulsidom, his constant yearning for a life of liberty from the Hanuman House. The ideals of Hanuman House are, to some extent, very close to Ayemenem House in Arundhati Roy's *The God of Small Things* where the male characters prevail over the female ones; where conservatism and patriarchal domination rule the roost; where outsiders are rarely adjusted in patriarchal framework. This house can also be compared to Wuthering Heights of Emily Bronte where Heathcliff, like Mr. Biswas, has to undergo many undeserved miseries and sufferings. The opening of the novel very well expresses the inner conflict going on in the mind of the main character. Naipaul observes: "Mr. Biswas was forty-six, and had four children. He had no money. His wife Shama had no money. On the house in Sikkim Street Mr. Biswas owed, and had been owing for four years three thousand dollars. The interest on this, at eight percent, came to twenty dollars a month, the ground rent was ten dollars."[5]

Mr. Biswas was trapped in the clutches of Tulsidom. He had a dream of his own house. The house of his dream is highly symbolic. It is an archetypal symbol, which connotes stability and permanence, something solid in life. It represents also Mr. Biswas's partially successful attempt to escape from the ancient matriarchal order and medieval norms into a more western, private and candid state of life. Moureen Warner Lewis is of the opinion that in spite of the clash of cultures in Tulsidom, Mr. Biswas struggled for asserting his identity: "Into this apparent monolith of conversions, prejudices and conservatism, then, Mr. Biswas barges. He openly disapproved of many of the Tulsi practices and policies. He even challenges their religious belief and associates with Hindus of another sect with whom the Tulsis disagree. . . . The religious ambiguity and syncretism and, in some cases, even neglect of traditional religion, is one of the earliest aspects of cultural confrontation with which Naipaul deals in his novel. And he progressively shows the sometimes subtle, sometimes obvious, in which the western-oriented Creole culture of Trinidad corrodes Hindu traditional customs and beliefs, and the shifting of attitudes and psychological bewilderment this produces."[6]

In brief, the spirit of selfishness and rivalry was deeply rooted in the Hanuman House. But due to a highly disciplined system it was suppressed. This is why the members of the family are always seen flinging sarcasm and irony on any matter related to the protagonist. Mr. Biswas felt silent pangs of restlessness in the company of the house. The house was nothing but a slave house. Gordon Rohlehr rightly remarks: "Hanuman House reveals itself not as a coherent reconstruction of the clan, but as a slave society, erected by Mrs. Tulsi and Seth who need workers to help rebuild their tottering empire. They therefore exploit the homelessness and poverty of their fellow Hindus and reconstruct a mockery of the clan which functions only because they have so completely grasped the psychology of a slave system."[7] In other words, the Tulsi family was just like the West Indies 'constructed of a vast' number of disparate families, gratuitously brought together by the economic need of a 'high caste' minority."[8] In this house men are needed for two reasons—husbands for Tulsi's daughters as well as labourers for Tulsi's estates.

The status of women in the Hanuman House was very miserable. They have little real say in the affairs of the house. The Tulsi daughters of two generations ago had to abide by the rhythms and rituals of life. It is only on occasional funerals or on seasonal wedding parties that they get relief from the tedium of daily lives. In *The God of Small Things*, we get the same attitude in the big Ayemenem House where Ammu, the main female character performs the role of a tragic figure humiliated and insulted by her father, ill-treated and misbehaved by her husband. Naipaul is undoubtedly a writer of great worth who very well knows the art of blending both truth and beauty. Naipaul's world is the world of loneliness and homelessness set against a dry, sterile landscape. It is a world of "homeless nomadic migrants, making middle passages from Africa or India to the West Indies thence to England and back again, for, after three hundred years, there is no society and no system of values in which they can take root."[9] Against this crucial and critical background, the characters of Naipaul are seen struggling for permanence and stability—Mr. Biswas's desire for a house, Mr. Stone's scheme for the aged and Ganesh Ramsumair's desire for education and religion.

It is interesting to note that Naipaul has developed his own concept about fiction. His approach to novel is a bit different from that of Conrad who seeks only to explain, to theorize and moralize about an event rather than to allow a situation to describe the happenings. Conrad is so much pre-occupied with facts that there is little room for the readers to enter into action. Naipaul observes: "Conrad's value to me is that he is someone who sixty to seventy years ago meditated on my world, a world I recognize today. His achievement derives from the honesty which is part of his difficulty."[10] Naipaul says that novel as a form no longer carries conviction: "And so the world we inhabit . . . goes by unexamined, made ordinary by the camera, unmediated on; and there is no one to awaken the sense of true wonder. This is perhaps a fair definition of the novelist's purpose, in all ages."[11] Naipaul has a very poor opinion about ostensibly objective kind of literature, a documentary approach to reality. He accepts a balanced human expression, which is the heart of a true artist. He is of the opinion that in art there must be a form, a metaphoric structure and the thought must be expressed through the medium of art and beauty. He believes in the theory of a camera, which exactly mirrors the reality. But he is dead against obscene photograph. He opines: "The violence some of us are resisting is not the violence which is a counter of story-telling. It is the violence, which is clinical and documentary in intention and makes no statement beyond that of bodily pain and degradation. It is like the obscene photograph. It deals anonymously with anonymous flesh, quickened only by pleasure or pain; and this anonymity is a denial of art."[12]

Judged on the above conceptions, *A House for Mr. Biswas* fully conforms to the ideals of the novelist. It has fine symbolism and images which weave the theme into the garland of art and beauty. The language comes as naturally as a rivulet comes from the mountain. The miseries and sufferings faced by Mr. Biswas have natural conformity with the general human being placed in an alien land dominated by a colonized society; it is not the untold sufferings and thwarted desires imposed by powerful Fate or Providence which is a dominant note of Hardy's novels. Rather it is just a natural process of a man's life, which is a fusion of both happiness and sorrow, rough and sublime.

To sum up, Naipaul's *A House for Mr. Biswas* culminates the early phase of Naipaul's artistic development. The story of Mr. Biswas is the general story of man. Tortured by communal pressures and threatened by an unstructured society, the protagonist is in constant suspension, ever ready to assert his identity but failing to do so in the long run.

NOTES

1. Qtd. R.A. Singh, *V.S. Naipaul: A House for Mr. Biswas* (Bareilly: Prakash, 1999), p. 22.
2. *Ibid.*, p. 2.
3. V.S. Naipaul, *The Middle Passage*, p. 73.
4. Keith Garebian, "V.S. Naipaul's Negative Sense of Place," *The Journal of Commonwealth Literature*, Vol. X, No. 1, Aug. 1975, pp. 23-24.
5. V.S. Naipaul, *A House for Mr. Biswas* (Penguin, 1969), p. 7.
6. Maureen Warner Lewis, "Cultural Confrontation, Disintegration and Syncretism in *A House for Mr. Biswas*," *Critical Perspectives on V.S. Naipaul*, ed. Robert Hamner (London: Heinemann, 1977), p. 97.
7. Gordon Rohlehr, "Character and Rebellion in *A House for Mr. Biswas*," Hamner, p. 87.
8. *Ibid.*, p. 87.
9. David Ormerod, "In a Derelict Land: The Novels of V.S. Naipaul," Hamner, p. 162.
10. V.S. Naipaul, "Conrad's Darkness," *New York Review of Books* (Oct. 17, 1974), p. 17.
11. *Ibid.*, p. 21.
12. V.S. Naipaul, "The Documentary Hereby," *Twentieth Century*, 173 (Winter 1964), qtd. Robert Hamner.

The Immigrant Experience of Displacement, Exile and Homelessness in *A House for Mr. Biswas*

M.L. PANDIT
IGNOU, New Delhi

The commonwealth literature of today is a by-product of the nineteenth century British Empire. Whichever part of the world the English eventually withdrew from, they left behind the legacy of their language and literature. The English works of the creative writers of the erstwhile colonies of the Empire are now vying for honours with the very best that England is producing. The most talked about writer in the English-speaking world today is Salman Rushdie, who thrives on the controversial content of his fictional works. But the true successor to the legacy of Charles Dickens, perhaps the greatest English novelist of all times, is V.S. Naipaul, an expatriate from Trinidad, who chose to make England his home. For nearly forty years, he has been entertaining his readers all over the world with a mixed bag of writing that combines fiction with travelogue, journalese and autobiography. Apart from his mastery of the English language, the judicious mix that Naipaul provides is spiced with the flavour of humour, irony and satire that links him with his illustrious predecessor of the Victorian age.

There is, however, one thing that distinguishes Naipaul from Dickens, and that is the background of his colonial antecedents. While it is difficult to dissociate Dickens and his works from London, there is no single city in Trinidad, England, or even India with which you could associate Naipaul. In absolute terms, he belongs to none of these three nations, though all the three contributed to the forming of his sensibility as a writer. The complexity of his multi-faceted yet exclusive personality is a significant contributory factor to the diversity of appeal that one finds in his literary works. The West Indians regard him as an English man because of his British education; the English look upon him as an Indian for his ancestry and the colour of his skin; and the Indians refer to him as a West Indian writer. This is, sometimes, confusing to the research scholars, who would like to approach him as a writer pure and simple. That is how it is in the last decade of the twentieth century, when sociology, history, politics, reality and literature are talked about in the same breath. Much of this controversial debate, today, is due to the question of identity, which crops up again and again in the context of works of literature. It should be a useful exercise to focus attention on the basic problem of the origins of a writer, something that ultimately determines both the complexity and individuality of his work.

The roots of Naipaul's early writings like *The Mystic Masseur* (1957), *The Suffrage of Elvira* (1958) and *Miguel Street* (1959) lie in his Indian background originating in the mixed society of Trinidad. It was a society of the South Asian immigrants, who went to the West Indies in the nineteenth century as indentured labourers to replace the Africans, who became free after the abolition of slavery. Some of these poor labourers, taken away from the remote villages of U.P. and Bihar in India, were put to work in the sugarcane farms of Trinidad. Attracted by the incentives of better wages and avenues in another part of the British Empire, they willingly forsook their homes and hearts, kith and kin, to explore the possibilities of success in an alien land. But the journey across the seas meant a traumatic break from their moorings, traditions and beliefs. On reaching the new country, and after going through the experience of settling in, they invariably tried to revive their links with the land of their origin. Hence, they retained their Hindi speech at home though forced to speak English in the streets, and also continued to follow the Indian social and religious practices in Trinidad or other parts of the West Indies, wherever they were settled. This is evident in the Trinidad works of both V.S. Naipaul and his brother, Shiv Naipaul. The obvious conclusion arrived at even by a casual reader is that these two writers are projecting their sense of displacement, exile and homelessness in their works.

In V.S. Naipaul's *A House for Mr. Biswas* (1961), we encounter three generations of the Indian immigrants in Trinidad, i.e., Bipti and Raghu, Sharma and Mr. Biswas, Anand and his siblings. They correspond to Naipaul's own grandfather, who initially emigrated from India; father, who was born and bred in Trinidad, and worked in the education department there; and Vidiadhar Surajprasad himself, who went to England on a scholarship for university-education in 1950, and settled there to become a writer of international reputation. This tells the corresponding story of the other West Indians of Indian origin who live in Trinidad and Guyana, and yet retain links with the motherland of their ancestors. Even now they "come home" when they return to India to visit their relations on places of worship they regard as holy. The trauma as well as joy of such a "return" was experienced by V.S. Naipaul and M.G. Vassanji at different times in their literary careers. It is hard for the expatriates to break their links with India, though most of them no longer speak Hindi or any other Indian language. The predicament of the original immigrants is sensitively expressed by Naipaul in *A House for Mr. Biswas:* "They could not speak English and were not interested in the land where they lived; it was a place where they had come for a short time and stayed longer than they expected. They continually talked of going back to India, but when the opportunity came, many refused, afraid of the unknown, afraid to leave the familiar temporariness. And every evening they came to the arcade of the solid, friendly house, smoked, told stories, and continued to talk of India."[1]

When one is not quite sure of where one belongs, it is of utmost importance to have a roof over one's head. This is a desire of universal nature—Naipaul highlights this basic human yearning by making it the central theme of *A House for Mr. Biswas.* In doing so, he is not only voicing the cherished desire of his protagonist, but of all the other Indian immigrants in Trinidad, who wished for a part of India in the foreign land where they lived.

Mr. Biswas's ambition is to possess an exclusive house, a home for himself and his family.

The achievement of this dream would give him a sense of security, warmth and independence, denied to him since his birth in a village in Trinidad. This yearning is symptomatic of his sense of displacement and rootlessness. In spite of the limitations and flaws of the house, he draws satisfaction from the fact that he has paid the cost of the house in full, and that nobody could evict him from his safe haven of peace. To Mr. Biswas, this freedom is a great contrast to living in the houses of the Tulsis, the upper middle class family of his wife: "And now at the end he found himself in his own house, on his own half-lot of land, his own portion of the earth." (8) At the age of forty-six, Mr. Mohun Biswas dies in his own house. During the many years of his active life in different parts of Trinidad, he acquires many things, which he could call truly his own, the fruits of his own labour. "But bigger than them all was the house, his house. How terrible it would have been, at this time, to be without it: to have died among the Tulsis, amid the squalor of that large, disintegrating and indifferent family—to have lived even without laying claim to one's own portion of the earth." (13-14)

The conclusion is obvious. Every individual in the world, however low his social and economic status, desires to possess some space that could be his very own, his house or home. This desire is more evident in people who, for some reason or other, are displaced from their origins and for whom homelessness is an everyday phenomenon. The realization of their rootlessness forces them to create a solid home-space even in an alien land, just as Mr. Biswas does at Port of Spain. Through him, Naipaul speaks for the displaced people all over the world.

NOTE

1. V.S. Naipaul, *A House for Mr. Biswas* (Harmondsworth: Penguin, 1969), p. 194.

In a Free State: Into the Fourth Dimension

SHASHI KAMRA
IGNOU, New Delhi

In his earlier novels, Naipaul has followed recognizable patterns of the tradition of the novel, staying close to the novel of sensibility. He has regulated the distance between the protagonist, narrator, author and reader to ensure that the dominant vision of each novel is that of the narrator, leaving the novels open-ended. Though there are dramatic and literary resolutions in the lives of the protagonist and the narrator, respectively, in each novel—the latter arriving at a centre of stillness, however temporary. Naipaul, by depicting the narrator as the controlling agent of the novel, suggests other stories with different narrators and different endings. However, even though it is the narrator's vision and pain which is prominent, it is the protagonist's existential reality that dominates the story, the narrator/author being present by implication or intrusively and the artist's vision being a critical assumption of the reader based on the dramatic/ psychological structure of the novel.

Juxtaposing conflicting political, social and personal realities as the differing existential situations in the lives of the narrator and the protagonist, the author conveys his overall vision of a fragmented world in which individuals and societies are trapped in their own unreal realities, meeting reality only tangentially. For the artist, it is a painful experience of alienation as well as a challenge to his vision and art to project a sense of possibility, a sense of 'home' and a harmonious world order from an awareness of fracture, isolation, lack of community and finally total disorder.

In a Free State makes a statement about the relationship between experience, vision and art as a third world reality. The distance between these aspects of life is regulated by the capacity and circumstances of the concerned individual. It is therefore as much a description and a vision of external expatriate reality as a pictorial projection of the working of the artist's mind and his use of materials and techniques: of the genesis of the novel. These are complementary processes: the novel grows out of the experiences of life as well as of the processes of art. The experience of expatriation is seen as a common feature of life today. Today, as never before, the third world has become aware of its anonymity and unimportance which is as much a consequence of its historical past as of undeniable contemporary political, social and economic pressures. In an increasingly shrinking, industrialized and automated world as more and more individuals and peoples begin to feel unnecessary and obsolete, the trust for survival acquires greater urgency and obstinacy. Through a work of art, the anonymous mass man achieves an identity, affirmation and individuality. The artist focuses his attention on the real world forcing people, who are becoming increasingly alienated from it, as they seek release from present tensions by living in the past or future, to pay attention to it. The novel no longer represents a slice of life but becomes an activating agent in the development and fulfillment of man's desire to achieve selfhood.

Therefore, in this novel, the relationship between the protagonist, the narrator and the author is of no consequence for the vision projected is a single one; the awareness of the protagonist growing into that of the narrator and the artist. The emphasis is as much on the quality of the vision as on its use as a means for describing a single developing awareness. One sees the emergence of the personality of the narrator as artist in his own right, not used by the author to project his own ironic vision. The narrator projects his own reality as the protagonist and the artist. He juxtaposes his experience with accounts of varied third world personalities who, though important to themselves, can be seen as typical, common and general, for these are people controlled by their circumstances. He parenthesizes these three accounts between extracts from his journal giving the unquestionable impression that these accounts have significance only in relation to the narrator's experience/vision. He is protagonist/narrator in the journal extracts and author narrator in the three stories.

Unlike the earlier narrators, he visualizes the consciousness of the protagonist as part of his own particular awareness. Santosh's loss of an ideal self, Dayo's brother's loss of a complete love and Bobby's sense of a loss of a supporting environment, all, as a consequence of a growth in knowledge through disillusioning interaction with reality, reflect analogously the lonely tramp at odds with his environment deeply conscious of his vulnerability. The tramp is the only character with whom the narrator empathizes. Every character in the book seeks by self-exposure through narration to fill in the void and thus repossess the self and the world. The protagonist calls a halt to his despair and the narrator achieves status as an artist. His journal, descriptive, reflective and meditative, focussing on a community of exposed, vulnerable people, leads to and becomes part of the novel.

It is the distinct function of the narrator to create the contingent world as objectively as possible. He is a *craftsman,* very much a part of the world he creates. The needs of narration—logic, precision, clarity and verisimilitude—of necessity restrict the narrative to the reality of the narrator and therefore bias cannot altogether be eliminated. The artist rises above him to present the ambiguity, variety and palpability of a flexible reality in a state of flux which alters the moment it is asserted. The artist uses the narrator to arrest one such moment in all its multiplicity to give an overall vision of contemporary man: his failures, successes and possibilities.

Naipaul's vision is not an eternal truth about life, death or love or other universal constants arrived at intuitively. It is a moment of individual existential despair which extends its jaundiced understanding to cover the world. This despair illuminates a moment of time before it becomes history. The narrator builds up an understanding of this despair. It is revealed as a consequence of subconscious rational processes at work long before the moment of its emergence to consciousness. The actions of

Santosh, Dayo's brother, Bobby and the tramp are ordered by a particular logic even though it leads to disorder, break-up and anguish. Illumination comes to each of them only through a re-tracing of their lives, juxtaposing time present and time past. Though this understanding leads to a reduction of life, it provides them with a hold on it by establishing a sense of continuity in an otherwise fragmented existence. Naipaul is not a pessimist though his vision is such. A vision attained through rational processes, conscious or subconscious implies a search for possibilities measured against and defined by actualities.

This fullness of vision is created through projecting, by implication, a wider world and placing the narrator's world in it creating ironic tensions. Naipaul achieves this through the metaphorical vibrations set up by the titles of his novels: *The Mystic Masseur, The Mimic Men, A House for Mr. Biswas, A Bend in the River, Guerrillas* and *In a Free State;* by the use of epilogues and prologues as in *A House for Mr. Biswas* and *In a Free State,* epigram in the *Guerrillas* and section headings as in *A Bend in the River.* The relationship between the narrator and the artist is comparable to the relationship between a world of order and that of mystery, between one of mason and that of intuitive awareness. Naipaul presents these not only as contrary but also as complementary awareness, the presence of the one implying that of the other.

In a Free State is a composite of first person reporting of events experienced by the narrator and made available to the reader as pages from his journal and three fictive accounts. The first two are in the stream-of-consciousness mode. The third is a dramatic, third person account with emphasis on chronological detailing of journey by car as Bobby's growth in awareness as he travels with Linda through 'no man's land.' One sees the modern intellectual sensibility unable to be totally involved as experience is accompanied by simultaneous analysis of it. This exterior structure of the book, so evidently composed of disparate items, is loosely held together thematically by the latent relationship between absurdity and freedom, and structurally through the deliberate use by the narrator of his journalistic non-fictional accounts as parentheses for the fiction.

The surface structure then consists of five episodes. Each episode is in itself a complete story with a narrator, a protagonist, an action, a resolution, a mood and a vision. Each story reflects a total situation in its own context but a partial one in that of the novel. As analogues for the narrator's experience, unhesitatingly depicted in the prologue and the epilogue, they build up a novel of sensibility with emphasis on mood and subjectivity. They reflect a latent single vision whose genesis is in the experience of existential futility of the narrator while defending the dignity of the Arab urchin against the Italian tourist who baits the hungry child with food as a form of amusement in the rest house at Luxor. His personal frustration illuminates a particular truth about his contingent world: neither the oppressor nor the oppressed have a concept of personal and human dignity. It is a remnant of the past in the narrator's own personality which makes his action a wasted gesture:

> Perhaps that had been the only pure time, at the beginning, when the ancient artist, knowing no other land, had learned to look at his own and had seen it as complete. But it was hard, travelling back to Cairo, looking with my stranger's eye at the fields and the people who worked in them, the dusty towns, the agitated peasant crowds at railway stations, it was hard to believe that there had been such innocence. Perhaps that vision of the land, in which the Nile was only water, a blue-green chevron, had always been a fabrication, a cause for yearning, something for the tomb.[1]

The surface structure directs the attention of the reader to the narrator's subjective world, his dilemmas and his vision as a man and artist. It also presents the narrator's wide and varied experience of the world. Geographically, it covers the important world: Bombay/Washington, Trinidad/London, African Reality (actual and imagined, black and white) and Cairo and its environs. Within this important world of business and power politics, the narrator views a cross-section of contemporary humanity in the grip of contemporary culture in which power and money are the criterion of importance. The panorama ranges from the most deprived and dispossessed, the third world's third world—people like Santosh, Dayo's brother, Arab urchins, Egyptian soldiers returning defeated from Sinai, Greek refugees, the tramp—at one end, to the materially sound and secure people like Bobby and Linda, the Lebanese businessman, the American and European tourists and sons of affluent Egyptians studying abroad. An ironic touch is added by the inclusion of the comfortably well-off Communist Cninese Circus at Luxor, distributing gifts, handshakes, money, medals and picture postcards of Chinese peonies—one empire replacing another. The rich and the poor can never meet though separated only by the distance of a deck on the steamer! Ironically, as the narration proceeds, the important aggressive world recedes and the subjective reality of the unimportant emerges as the significant fact of each story. Washington, London and the African State become less than meaningful when Santosh is faced with the powerful reality of his body and his mortality, Dayo's brother with the insubstantiality of his all-embracing love for Dayo, and Bobby, the colonial administrator, with the insecurity of the compound!

The narrator hence presents contemporary reality, the 'thing in itself' as a vast 'no man's land' in which those who grab, or scavenge or indulge themselves possess the original freedom of Alexander or Crusoe who to themselves are the only living realities in the world. This world is indifferent, if not hostile, to the subjective reality of the sensitive, reflective third world man who in his own orderly and imaginative fashion seeks to possess the world. Simultaneously, the narrator also presents an emphatic image of the protagonist of each episode, literally and literarily in a 'free state,' detached from contingency as a result of a destructive encounter with reality.

In placing the 'free' world and the 'free' protagonist side by side, the depth of the latter's disillusionment is presented. The freedom of the upper deck of the steamer and the tourist rest house at Luxor, viewed from a distance, is the one aspired to and is also partially achieved by Santosh, Dayo's brother and Bobby. However, for these 'island innocents,' the distance coalesces security with success. Only as they approach it do they realize the antithetical nature of these two realities. For with success life for these people has come to a standstill. In order to arrive, they moved away from a 'home' but having arrived they do not 'belong' and so are stranded. But paradoxically, like a gift from the gods, their loss becomes the condition for their growth in self-awareness bringing with it the freedom of vision and perspective. Their sense of individuality, of subjective apartness from the world, may be painful but at least it combines the conditions of 'home' with those of freedom.

In Naipaul's fiction, the greatest traps to self-expression are well-defined social systems; the greatest freedoms can be practised only in situations which represent no man's territory. The maximum aggression and the greatest growth in self-awareness occur when contingent reality, in losing its contours, loosens its grip on man.

The narrator develops the multiple metaphorical implications of a 'free state' only by releasing settings from geographical, historical or social definition; here people form groups through chance, proximity or immediate purpose, without any deep 'ties that bind.' We see people for whom the security of a 'room,' a 'home,' a 'flat' or a 'hideout' is beyond comprehension, for they are the secure of the earth, alongside people who have just lost that security. Their loss is so great that the centre of gravity shifts from the future to the past as something they can cling to. The present remains in danger of non-existence. It is the narrator who make the present existent by recording the faint thrusts individuals make to assert their presence, to leave a mark on the world. The wasted gesture acquires a meaning and a context. *In a Free State* plays on 'free states' in order to discover the only freedom that man can own with dignity, that of possessing his own awareness—and watching himself grow—as it alters, expands and contracts responding to experience.

In the extracts from the journal, the steamer and the tourist rest house near Luxor are 'no man's land,' for, temporarily social and political restrictions are suspended for their inhabitants. No decisions have to be made or action initiated. The passengers on the steamer, whether there for pleasure or in anxiety, cannot do much except wait. The steamer is either a temporary security or a convenience for people for whom nationality (home) is a confusing or at best an indifferent issue. There are the refugee Greeks who were Egyptian citizens deported to Greece and now reentering Egypt as tourists; the Lebanese businessmen, whose main business is 'frankly money' wherever they can make it, Spanish night club dancers on a similar business and Egyptian students returning from Germany; the tramp, who has been travelling for thirty-eight years, having a fair knowledge of distinctive national traits, yet says: "But what's nationality these days? I myself, I think of myself as a citizen of the world." (9)

For these people, the concept of home has lost some of its original force but they still seek to create centres of the security it implied. They converse in a mixture of languages and accents, their own and acquired. It is the incongruity of this gathering that strikes the narrator. Together, they do not form a community, nor do they stand out as individuals. They congregate in temporary groupings, distinguishable racially, as a crowd, seeking idle entertainment. Whatever the purpose of the journey, the people on the upper deck mean to enjoy themselves and the tramp becomes a focus of attention by his odd, self-conscious and solitary appearance:

> It was to be like a tiger-hunt, where bait is laid out and the hunter and spectators watch from the security of a platform. The bait here was the tramp's own rucksack. . . . But Hans smiled and explained the rules of the game as often as he was asked.
>
> The tramp, though, didn't immediately play, Hans remained at his post. . . .
>
> Then the news came that the tramp had reappeared and had been caught according to the rules of the game. (15)

For the refugees crowded on the lower deck, the steamer is also literally no man's land. Nationality means security and they mean to acquire one as soon as possible:

> They had the slack bodies and bad skins of people who ate too many carbohydrates. Their blotched faces were immobile, distant, but full of fierce, foolish cunning. They were watch-big. As soon as the officials came aboard, the refugees began to push and fight

> their way towards them. It was a factitious frenzy, the deference of the persecuted to authority. (19)

Similarly, the rest house at Luxor is a no man's land catering to all irrespective of nationality. Money is the only criterion of importance. People who congregate here are all tourists who have no stakes in the land and have left behind all notions of social responsibility and humanity in their own countries. Out for pleasure, they are in a 'free state.' The rich tourists, constituting the world of the poor Arab child, are indifferent to his horrifying condition. In mocking him, they mock themselves.

The enforced 'free state' of Santosh, Dayo's brother and Bobby, brings only an awareness of negative existence: survival at its bare minimum. Loss of an identity leaves them as no man's land. Santosh, having once been 'a part of the flow' discovers an initial identity through his reflection in the mirror, seeing himself as the hubshi woman sees him, as an attractive man. Besides this, he discovers other freedom/identities through other people's eyes (his employer, Priya) of money, status, achievement and citizenship of U.S.A. Pursuing other people's definitions of freedom and self, he discovers that he has gained what other men desire at the cost of a loss of an older ideational identity. Marriage to the hubshi woman is an extreme self-degradation from which he is unable to recover:

> I am a simple man who decided to act and see for himself and it is as though I have had several lives. . . . Soul Brother. I understand the words; but I feel, brother to what or to whom? I was once a part of the flow, never thinking of myself as a presence. Then I looked in the mirror and decided to be free. All that my freedom has brought me is the knowledge that I have a face and have a body, that I must feed this body and clothe this body for a certain number of years. Then it will be over. (57-58)

Despiritualized, for the only dimension to his past life as a servant has been a religious one, he feels non-existent, in a free state, dead before he has actually died. The spark of life that remains illuminates the trap of doubt, regret and humiliation into which he has fallen and it urges him to repossess his self and the world through reflection, trying to establish a continuity between an imagined and an actual situation. The maximum freedom available to the Santoshs of the third world is freedom from economic and social pressures: the knowledge and nourishment of the body.

For Dayo's brother, insanity is the freedom which is available from a too harsh, too complex reality. His journey to attend Dayo's marriage to an alien, fraught with the pain of separation and a final breach with a meaningful existence, a final unimportance, is made bearable by withdrawal into a world of his own creation in which he journeys unsystematically through a happier past life. Past and present, Dayo and Frank, West Indies and London, collapse, coalesce and become interchangeable in his confused consciousness. His resolution, courage and faith have given way under pressure of loss of hard-earned money and disillusionment at Dayo's abuse of his love. His moments of sanity (dignity and selfhood) coincide with the recurring image of Dayo's earlier attractiveness and the recurring reminder of the purpose of the present journey to attend Dayo's wedding. The one had given meaning to his life, the latter breaking off his last links with any desire to live: condemned forever to a free state, utterly destitute, unable to form new ties. For Frank does not understand; he himself has broken links with his family after his sickness and he has finally realized the temporal reality of Dayo's love:

> I know that he love me, that now it is time, but that it will not be true as soon as he go out of this room, that he will have to forget me. Because it was my idea after my trouble that nobody should know, that the message should go back home and I was dead. And for all this time I am the dead man. (102)

Paradoxically the affluent, stable colonial life of Bobby and his like is rudely disorganized by independence. Civil War has torn the country apart and no one knows for whom he is working. There is the king, the President and the haunting presence of the colonial master, the white man. Having freely discarded their European identity in sympathy with the 'natives,' the expatriates discover they have nowhere to go, rejected and regarded suspiciously by both societies. The 'civilization' they opted for was illusory, imagined and a mockery of Africa and Europe. For Bobby and Linda, the once familiar land becomes strange and hostile as they journey through it, as they note each aspect afresh with a growing sense of danger. At each stage of the journey, an illusion is discarded regarding the past and white superiority leaving them exposed and vulnerable. Finally, the absurdity of Bobby's humiliation at the hands of the President's soldiers at the police outpost to what had once been the king's territory, strips him of his last trace of an established superior identity out to help an under-developed country. He appears as ludicrous and as unbelievably a puppet-like figure as the naked Africans running by the roadside—hardly real. Deprived of the supports of culture and civilization, what matters is how fast one can run for shelter in order to survive. There in the shelter, the final shock awaits Bobby. The absolute security becomes temporary as the houseboy, responding to the political temper of his tribe, turns 'cheeky.' Bobby's unconscious return to the role of the colonial master in his determination to dismiss the African houseboy is a final submission to a despised past and the loss of a carefully nurtured self. The white bachelor master and black servant relationship of love and loyalty was a unique feature of the colonial civilization. Having lost this, Bobby has nothing further to lose. These white expatriates in the third world, expiating for the colonial authoritarianism of their fathers by seeking equality with the African, find themselves rejected by both, living on the frontiers of both societies. Motivated by some hidden sense of responsibility, they end up 'free.' Having travelled through no-man's territory, realizing that in this chaotic state each man was out for himself, their only security is in the moving car or in the compound. It is only when he stops and gets out of his car to walk down to the check-post office that Bobby realizes his mistake. Safety is in keeping moving. When a 'dead-end' is reached, journeys are recreated to give a sense of life and purpose. Bobby knows that he will have to leave. Till then, as a safety measure, he will have to do without Luke, his houseboy.

The narrator, journeying literally on the steamer and with the tourist group in Egypt and figuratively with the protagonists of the three stories, never identifies himself. In their account from the journal does the narrator state his nationality or purpose for the journey. His journal is not dated. Uninvolved and unnoticed, he observes, notes and ruminates. His style of writing is 'free,' without any commitment to form or philosophy. This 'free state' is unintentionally lost in a moment of involved action, to be replaced by despair, a vision and a novel.

In *In a Free State* we see people who, having travelled linearly, have arrived at the limits of their known world with "no other place to drive to." (234) Having shed their past and with no further pressure of the future, they are in the present in a 'free state.' No man can live consistently in the present as no man can face continuously the glare of the searchlight. Reality is lighted up intermittently as by the steamer's search light in *A Bend in the River.* Man exists not only by facing the present directly but by approaching it obliquely, negating its force by moving backwards and forwards in time. A fresh perspective on the present makes the past seem a freer state. Linking present indignity to a past dignity through reflection makes the present pain and humiliation bearable. Having attained an economically free state, they discover its ironical, paradoxical contexts—the iron hand in the velvet glove. Freed from their immediate problems, they are also freed from their immediate contexts as well. Trapped in contingency, searching for existence, they are temporarily stranded in non-existence. The whole movement of Santosh's reflections and Dayo's brother's ruminations follows this pattern. Bobby, not really knowing whether he is moving backwards or forwards, away from or towards safety, finding a friendly landscape turning hostile at every stage of the journey, finally insulted by the man closest to him, finds safety in non-existence, in reverting to a role from being an individual. The 'free state' of the narrator of the journal soon evolves into the stricter role of the narrator/artist of the novel. The requirements of his art and his purpose set limits on his subject matter and restrict logically the narrative horizon of the novel. The reader has the vision of a 'trapped' freedom, an anonymity sought and achieved.

The reader may read each of the episodes for its own value. He can view the lives of Santosh, Dayo's brother, Bobby and Linda empathetically as extraordinary, isolated case histories. But he is compelled to interpret the book in terms of the meaning given to these stories by the prologue and the epilogue and perspectivize his interpretation through the experience of the narrator/artist. Thus the reader's final vision of *In a Free State* is controlled by the artist's.

Naipaul establishes, by manipulating the structural devices available to the novelist, a new form for the novel which places it in the mainstream of a man's life making it a necessary experience. Every man is a narrator and the germ of an artistic vision is nascent in the art of narration. As stated earlier, he relates the external and internal realities of the protagonist and narrator through the prologue and the epilogue. The narrator submerges after the prologue to re-emerge in the epilogue as a man with a developing vision who mobilizes his materials and tools to shape a unique novel out of his despair. Thus the state of tramphood—the free state of anonymity/non-existence—is concretized in the episodes and universalized in the form of the novel. Interpretation becomes more important than the story, and the fictive world, no longer revolving around the consciousness of the protagonist only, no longer remains within the pages of a book. Naipaul establishes a complex relationship between the protagonist, narrator, artist and reader, each one viewing an experience from overlapping positions which, like varying wavelengths, illuminate its different facets.

Below the surface of contingent reality and technical variety, one sees the developing novel possessing the requisites of coherence, sequence and imaginative truth. As is evident, coherence, in Naipaul's fiction, does not reside in the consistent use of a single point of view either first or third person. Sequence is not chronological or subjective time and imaginative truth is not a flash of the eternal or transcendent. Coherence in Naipaul's fiction is a function of bias. The bias of his protagonists and narrators is presented as limitation of vision suggested by the limits of their experience, ambition and power of expression. Hence limitation becomes a condition of alienation, loneliness and despair. The protagonist's and narrator's powers to conceive and express are linked positively to their experiences which they try to overreach but cannot transcend. (His characters do not alter radically by the end of the novel.) Sequence is more of a syntagmatic rather than a paradigmatic progression in his fiction. Certain similar ways of thinking, feeling and acting occur in totally unrelated peoples, cultures and situations enabling him to weave together as wide a geographical tapestry as he has done in *In a Free State*. Imaginative truth is the artist's vision possessed by the reader through recreative analysis. It is a momentary isolated truth which becomes eternal only because it leaves a lasting impression on the mind and is embodied in a work of art. Apart from the work of art, this truth had no existence, remaining a gesture locked in the mind of the protagonist—in a free state, unpossessed. The children being whipped are only puzzled when the narrator snatches the whip from the Egyptian server:

> The two Italians, fingering cameras, looked quite calm behind their sunglasses. The women in the party leaned back in their chairs to consider me.
>
> I felt exposed, futile, and wanted only to be back at my table. When I got back I took up my sandwich. It had happened quickly; there had been no disturbance. . . .
>
> The children remained where they were. The man from whom I had taken the whip came to give me coffee. . . . The coffee was free;. . . But even while he was talking the children had begun to come closer. Soon they would be back, raking the sand for what they had seen the Italian throw out.
>
> I didn't want to see that. The driver was waiting, leaning against the car door, his bare arms crossed. . . . I was expecting some gesture, some sign of approval. . . . He crushed his cigarette in the sand and slowly breathed out smoke through his lips; he sighed. But that was his way of smoking. I couldn't tell what he thought. He was as correct as before, he looked as bored. (244)

Thematically the title story of *In a Free State* anticipates *Guerrillas* and *A Bend in the River.* All three deal with the personal and social implications of political instability and power politics. Political power is not sought for its own sake as an assertion of national freedom. Eventually the deprived of the third world are beginning to realize that political power is the only tool of successful aggressive activity in defence of the self. And guerrilla tactics in war and politics is the only means of exercising a threatening control over powers—black and white, colonial and expatriate—which would push them back into colonial servitude. The metaphor is: hunt or be hunted.

In a Free State presents a different argument to the rest of Naipaul's fiction. Dialectically this novel stands alone as an effective question mark to the rest of his fiction. So far his novels have developed in detail situations of entrapment: entrapped individuals seeking release from intense immediate pressure which forbids any idea of the future or of freedom. In each case, it is the narrator who raises the question: what does freedom mean in the context of the lives of Ganesh, Harbans Singh, Biswas, Mr. Stone, Ralph Singh, Jimmy and Salim? The narrator emphasizes the hardly measurable distance the protagonist has moved in this direction because of the narrowness of his vision—"between attic and basement," "pleasure and its penalty" as Ralph Singh says. Yet he highlights the dignity of the effort as a moment of insight against a lengthy and vividly evoked landscape which is dead or disruptive of creativity. The houses that Biswas moves through are metaphors of entrapment. Contrastingly, hardly much space has been allotted to the house in Sikkim street which meant release. A major metaphor of entrapment in *The Mimic Men* is the houses and boarding house rooms in which Ralph Singh spends a large part of his life. The hotel room in which he finds a sense of release at the end of the novel received cursory attention. Similarly, Mr. Stone's house, for the larger part of the novel, conveys the impression of a prison. The narrator gives only a paragraph at the end describing it as the setting for a Mr. Stone who enters his house with a feeling of release and love for the black cat.

It is easy enough to analyze traps through the wisdom of hindsight. But what does it mean to be free? Can one truly express oneself in any situation without restraint? (This is a contradiction in terms for 'en situation' defines its own restraints of time and place). So far as the narrator/artist can see, to be free in the existing situation is an unenviable condition. For, to be free like Santosh, Dayo's brother and Bobby, without a wider vision than that of the self, is to be trapped in the self as one was earlier by circumstance, for it leads back only to one's own past. In *In a Free State*, we see the protagonist arriving at successive stages of being free from anxiety. Each free situation carries its own disillusionments. Each creates its own insecurities and necessitates further movement to the very limits of the literal and the literary in each context. "In a Free State" describes in detail Bobby's sense of security and freedom of action. The incident in the bar at the New Shropshire with the Zulu elaborates the gestures of a man at ease in his environment. The setback he receives when the Zulu boy spits at him does not disturb him unduly:

> Africa was for Bobby the empty spaces, the safe adventures of long fatiguing drives on open roads, the other Africans, boys built like men. You want lift? You big boy, you no go school?. . . When I born again I want your colour. You no frighten. You want five shillings?' (109)
>
> That evening he had broken all rules; the evening had shown how right his rules were. He felt no bitterness, no hurt.
>
> He didn't blame the Zulu, he didn't blame Linda. Before Africa, the incident of the evening might have driven him out adventuring for hours more in dangerous places;. . . But now he knew that the mood would pass; the morning would come. Even with Linda as his passenger, the drive remained. (110)

Throughout the journey, till the very end, Bobby and Linda are travel companions, sensitive to sights and sounds, indulging freely in light conversation, aware of each feeling as it passes through their minds. Bobby ignores or suppresses all impressions of impending danger. As Bobby and Linda move into the future, the new unknown Africa, his sense of insecurity deepens till they are almost in a panic to reach the safety of the compound. Hardly two pages are ascribed to the description of this safety which is part of the trap into which Bobby falls and from which it will be hard for him to release himself; Bobby's unconscious assumption of the role of the colonial master is not very relevant in his context: he has shifted into a world as fragile and exposed as that outside the compound:

> Bobby thought: I will have to leave. But the compound was safe; the soldiers guarded the gate. Bobby thought: I will have to sack Luke. (238)

Similarly Santosh's and Dayo's brother's sense of release is enlarged upon in the contextual setting rather than their traps till a final 'free' state is the trap of the alienated subjective life.

Finality for the narrator is the ultimate trap. He depicts each protagonist in a final state from which the narrator releases him through story telling. The despair of literal limits (of the void, of death) is counteracted by literary movement. Self-awareness adds the dimension of dignity to their personalities. We appreciate these failed men who can live with the knowledge of failure like the Egyptian soldiers on their way home from Sinai, "lost, trying to walk back home, casting long shadows on the sand." (246) The narrator of the epilogue sees himself as one such. Release, then, for the narrator is in the art of narration and in having an Idea. The demands of precision, order and semantics situates the end of the narrative in the beginning. And the Idea, separating from existence, becoming an abstraction, ends up as an absurdity. Both these requirements place restraints on the freedom of the narrator. For the artist, seeing the world as paradox, the greatest trap is the temptation to inaction and the highest free state is to reexamine an Idea and to act; to write another book.

The question raised by an overview of Naipaul's fiction, in which the fictive parameters are guided by considerations of entrapment and release, is what is the relationship between being trapped, being in a free state and the idea of freedom. Philosophically and psychologically, this can be restated as having a fresh look at the relationship that exists between existence, absurdity and self-awareness on the one hand and abstraction, freedom and non-existence on the other. Abstractions, urging a man in unknown directions, have existed, if at all, in the past. For abstraction engages the concepts of oneness, wholeness, purity and innocence which, as permanent features of life today, are beyond definition. They are the artist's vision of the past (245) which suggest 'nothing' for the future. Absurdity, both as existential anguish in the face of the void and the rational awareness of irony (the outer limits of subjectivity and objectivity) is the great turning point or dividing line where the trapped protagonist unites in his self-awareness, however briefly and lightly, the frontiers of freedom/abstraction with existence. Absurdity is a virtue and man's saving grace in Naipaul's fiction, promising the only freedom available today for his third world characters: that of growing individuation, whose parameters are limitless, outwards towards the world and inwards by reflecting in it. Thus entrapped and free states become conditions of awareness, ranging from the literal to the literary, and are not unalterables known and examined independently of the protagonist's existence.

We see the absurdity that is despair most vividly in Salim's condition. We see the absurdity that is the free state of non-existence portrayed in Mr. Stone: a monument to habit. The naked tribal Africans running at the edge of the road, viewed by Bobby in his moving car, are not only mirage-like but, if yet existent, render modern Africa an absurdity. The tramp, wandering meaninglessly round the globe, lives on the margin between existence and non-existence, a character with whom the narrator can readily empathize—aware of the world, wanting but unable to be a part of it.

Naipaul's little man is seen as one who makes great efforts, in spite of his almost insurmountable handicaps, to realign himself to an ill-defined present, ending up as a failure either in his own estimation or in that of his narrator. Hence Naipaul is considered to be a pessimist and is said to have a poor view of man. But this is a sweeping judgment of his fiction. His vision is focussed on a particular third world reality—the homeless man in search of an identity which dignifies. That he fails is also a particular truth of his situation today. But the fact that Naipaul's most endurable and lovable characters are travellers and explorers, that he uses the tools of analysis to sift for man's possibilities is an impossible world, that none of his protagonists ever commits suicide, is sufficient evidence of Naipaul's faith in humanity. What everyone's private heaven or hell is, is not his concern for no one can know another's existential anguish. But the fact that they face it distinguishes the individual from a faceless society. His protagonists, like Bunyan's pilgrims, are to be admired on the journey.

And it is in his next novel *The Enigma of Arrival*, that Naipaul's protagonist, grown worldly wise, ponders on the personal implications of the journeys he has undertaken. He examines the paradox of ceremonial departures and unheralded arrivals. Consciously leaving behind a world in which he is someone, certain that great things lie ahead, he arrives, unknown and insecure and builds a second life for himself. He has arrived. But, for reasons of ill health, he has to move again. So, ironically, the arrival has only led to the preparation for another departure.

NOTE

V.S. Naipaul, *In a Free State* (Harmondsworth: Penguin, 1978), p. 246.

Guerrillas as a Political Novel

ASHOK KUMAR BACHCHAN
L.N. Mithila University, Darbhanga

It is indeed difficult to define a political novel because it stems from the novel of ideas which goes back to the Victorian era itself. However, in recent times political novel has taken strong roots and has indeed assumed various forms. Irving Howe seems to be quite apologetic in using the term 'political novel' and he comments in his book *Politics and the Novel:* "Perhaps it would be more useful to say that my subject is the relation between politics and literature and that the term political novel is used here as a convenient short hand to suggest the kind of novel in which this relation is interesting enough to warrant investigation."[1] However, he defines political novel in the same book in these words: "By a political novel I mean a novel in which political ideas play a dominant role or in which a political milieu is the dominant setting. . . perhaps it would be better to say a novel in which we take to the dominant political ideas or the political milieu, or a novel which permits this assumption without thereby suffering any radical distortion and it follows with the possibility of some analytical profit."[2]

Oxford Dictionary has defined a political novel as a fictitious political narration or a novel about imaginary politicians. Chaman Nahal, an Indian writer of the novel of ideas, has risked his own definition: "A political novel, to my mind, is a novel in which the novelist presents a political preference; it is a novel in which one type of political ideology is confronted with another or several others."[3]

According to Harish Trivedi, the editor of *Critical Essays* on American political novels, political novel can assume various forms. The political novelist sometimes appears in the role of a political historian, while at the other time, he may make use of political and social raw material on the basis of his first-hand acquaintance with them. Similarly sometimes political novel may be attempted as a case of demonstration of confrontation between the claim of a particular ideology and the right of an individual to live according to his own natural impulses. In some other cases, political novel provides an imaginative solution by creating a Utopia. Finally, in some form of political novel, the conflict may turn out to be between the claims of humanity over those of political systems. Racial politics and violence and the problem of cultural displacement and loss of identity may also be classed in the category of political novels.

It is clear that Naipaul cannot be placed in the category of a typical political novelist because in his novels there is no clear preference for one set of political values or systems as such. He does not seem to have a short-range goal nor he espouses a political doctrine or creed. He simply uses the political situation, facts of history and the new power structure to demonstrate that human beings are bound to suffer in the present transitional phase and yet they have no option but to carry on. His novels like *The Mimic Men, In a Free State, Guerrillas and A Bend in the River* suggest the same recurring dilemma of the expatriates. *Guerrillas* is one of the most powerful novels in which real life has been transposed into a brilliant novel of great power and precision. Karl Miller has rightly commented: "What we find in *Guerrillas* is a narrative of unfailing fascination which delivers to the senses of the reader a country very like the country he knows in the real world."[4]

In a way, *Guerrillas* continues the themes of *The Mimic Men* and *In a Free State* inasmuch as this novel is also a study of chaos and corruption leading to violence and destruction. However, for a while Naipaul once again returns to Caribbean island for his setting and explores the emptiness and despair of the modern world through his close examination of the political scene in a West Indian Island, independently governed but in reality owned by an American bauxite company. The novel revolves round the three main characters namely, Peter Roche,

Jimmy Ahmad and Jane. The plot of the novel is based on an incident of real life in which one Michael Defreites is once charged with the murder of a local youth and an English girl. The victims are found buried in the garden of Michael's house near Port of Spain. The English girl Gail Benson comes to Trinidad with her black American lover. It is found that Gail Benson has been stabbed and buried alive. Michael is tried for the killing and hanged for murder in 1975 in spite of protests by some leading politicians of Trinidad. Naipaul has made good use of the incidents which were given wide coverage in the Press. The character of Jimmy Ahmad is patterned after Michael Defreitus, a self-styled revolutionary of Chinese origin. The character of Jane, the English woman, is sketched after the murdered woman, Gail Benson. The third central character Peter Roche, a white liberal, who has suffered for his beliefs is, of course, Naipaul's persona and it is through his book that the main incidents are reported.

Guerrillas begins with a journey like *In a Free State* and the journey is undertaken by Jane and Roche from their house on the Ridge to Thrushcross Grange, the centre of Jimmy Ahmad's activity. The landscape describes the three main centres of activity. On the one hand, there is the Ridge, a California styled suburb in the hills enclosing the bay with company houses inhabited by those who can avail themselves of helicopters in times of emergency. On the other extreme, there is Jimmy Ahmad's absurdly named commune Thrushcross Grange. Jimmy Ahmed, through his awareness of Chinese origin, perhaps, likes to imagine that, like Heathcliff of *Wuthering Heights*, his father was also some kind of emperor or an aristocrat. In between the two extremes, there is the hot city, rotting in the core constituting the third zone of action. As usual, the setting is also used here as the principal metaphor for expressing the pathetic condition of people.

The first place of activity is the commune established by Jimmy Ahmad and the drive to the place by Jane and Roche makes it clear that the place does not have vitality or possibilities of growth. It is a curious blend of sweat, heat and dust and even the new housing estates provide a dreary landscape of unpainted boxes of concrete and corrugated iron visited by the naked children with dirty clothes. In fact, there is piling up of images of death and decay in the whole description of Thrushcross Grange. The drive to the landscape brings Peter and Jane to Thrushcross Grange where apparently an agricultural commune has been established by Jimmy Ahmad. But his main aim is to use the same for a cover for his guerrilla activities. V.S. Naipaul makes it clear that his agricultural experiment is a non-starter:

> The vegetable garden was knee-deep in weeds, with no sign of furrow or ridge. Neither Jimmy nor Roche appeared surprised. Jimmy, suddenly energetic, pulled back weeds, looking for what had been planted, and showing what had grown: deformed, pale aubergines, stunted Ochroes.[5]

Throughout the novel the parched dryness of earth is constantly emphasized through recurrent phrases like 'dry field,' 'baked earth' and 'seedlings yellowed in shallow boxes of dried earth.' The people of the Grange also embody the qualities of the vegetables they grow. They don't show any sign of the toils of a hopeful heart, but are pathetic witnesses to a sluggish decay. Jimmy Ahmad himself is unable to identify with the situation and he has to fight a personal war. This is because he is himself a half-cast-half-Negro and half-Chinese—and calls himself a self styled 'Haji,' a Muslim holy man to impress the people. Though he tries to organize a revolution through agricultural labour and unemployed youth, he fails in his attempt for obvious reasons. The novelist is quick to point out that there is a lack of sincerity in Jimmy's effort for the kind of life which he leads and there is a yawning gap between his precept and practice.

Sardonic observation on the deceit and hypocrisy practised by the native is significant: "But it is like being in England." (24) Moreover, Naipaul is also intelligent enough to suggest that a leader of the kind of Jimmy can be produced only against the background of wild disordered men tramping along old paths and living a sub-human life. Jimmy's artificial personality is created by his egotism and enthusiasm for the British press. Naipaul is, however, unprejudiced in portraying his central character and this accounts for the authenticity of the portrait of Jimmy. For example, a sophisticated political Meredith rightly views Jimmy as a threat to the American Government: "He's dangerous because he's famous, because he has a lot of that English glamour still, and because he's nothing at all." (142)

Naipaul has made use of Jimmy's diary to reveal his true character. As a matter of fact, Jimmy resorts to writing to escape the engulfing disorder and to alter in his mind the image of himself. To this extent Jimmy parallels Ralph Singh of *The Mimic Men* who also writes to impose order on his life filled with chaos. It is quite interesting that Jimmy does not use first person and the narrator of his life history is Jane, the English woman, whose approval he feels is quite important for achieving his individual identity. The real truth about Jimmy's attitude to the Negro people is revealed in the following lines from the diary:

> I wonder how a man of those attainments can waste his life in a place like that with all those good for nothing natives for whom to speak in all candour I can not have too high an opinion, seeing them shit everywhere, just like that just like animals, they don't even shit in the high grass but on the path, because wait for it they're afraid of snakes. (38)

The confession of Jane, however, refers to the complex character. At one level, they make one aware of certain special features of his personality such as his cold reserve, the perfection of his form and his sway over the black louts. Yet he suffers from a sense of shame which reads like a recurrent motive in the present novel. Jimmy wants to see himself as the leader of the black but he is always at pains to set himself apart physically from the blacks. He does not want to merge with them but he wants respect and obedience from the black louts. He has only some sort of relationship with Bryant, an ugly and distorted figure, but even that relationship becomes sour because of the arrival of Jane in his iife. The novel makes it clear enough that the attitude of the novelist to Jimmy is quite complex and this sets him apart from Jane. Jimmy is aware of the game played by the imperialists when they send things to the commune which they don't want. Perhaps the roots of Jimmy's ambition of becoming a leader lie in his childhood desire of becoming a waiter in a hotel meant exclusively for the white people. Jimmy's failure to become a leader of the people results in his sadism and he becomes violent and revenges himself on Jane, a white woman, by assaulting her and murdering her in the end. Ironically, Jimmy's failure is reported by the protagonist himself. The novel's title and its epigraph which echoes Jimmy's words is quite revealing:

> When everybody wants to fight there's nothing to fight for. Everybody wants to fight his own little war. Everybody is a guerrilla. (87)

Peter Roche is the next important character after Jimmy who is a white South African. He has suffered imprisonment for his views on the racial discrimination perpetrated by the white government. In the island he comes as a liberal humanitarian and he is engaged in supervising agricultural commune and in general improving the image of a firm which once traded in slaves. However, Roche, like Jimmy, is tentatively attracted to Jane and the latter after her frustration from him, turns towards Jimmy. Roche, in a way, resembles Bobby of *In a Free State* as both are liberals and want to do good to the people in a world where people are learning to forget their past. However, Roche is more mature and he has no illusion about himself or about political revolutions creating a new order. Certainly, of all the characters Jane receives the hardest knock and the writer's anger and satiric fury is in reserve for her. Jane is described in aggressively physical terms and it is constantly hinted that she is fatally confused and aggressively sexual. She is described as a woman who symbolizes distorted emblems of female sexuality. In a certain way, she parallels Linda of *In a Free State* who is described as a 'rotting cunt' by Bobby. By contrast, Jane is regarded as a 'rotten meat' and 'dirty cunt.' Nondita Mason points out: 'In both novels there is also a Swiftian emphasis on the sun-tanned coarse skin between woman's breast and abraded skin.'[6] Naipaul makes it also clear that Jane is fatally confused in her view about the native inhabitants because she judges things from a point of view convenient to her:

> She was privileged: it was the big idea, the one that overrode all the scattered, unrelated ideas deposited in her soul as she had adventured in life, the debris of a dozen systems she had picked up from a dozen men . . . she would return to London; that society which she had given up, and whose destruction she thought she had awaited, continued. . . . But she was privileged: she told herself that once a day . . . out of this contradiction between what she did and said and what she felt, out of this knowledge of her own security and her vision of decay, of a world running down, she moved from one crisis to another. (55-56)

Ultimately, Jane is made the sacrificial victim. The novelist has made very good use of Jane's shallow, sacrificial patronage to revolutionaries. At first, she feels ashamed of her own easy life and a sense of shame motivates her to support Roche and later on the similar feeling is at work in her infatuation for Jimmy. But Naipaul exposes her frivolity and lack of experience:

> Everything about Jane was simple, exaggerated and, oddly for a woman of twenty-nine, schoolgirlish. Of the simplicity of her views and her girlishness she seemed unaware; this absence of doubt, which was like an absence of self-knowledge, made her forceful and gave a certain solidity to her presence. (95)
>
> She hinted at a procession of lovers, a continuing violation; she spoke, with brutal detail, of the affront of her abortions. She spoke as though she had never exercised choice. Events, society, the nature of men, her own needs as a woman, had sent her out into the sexual jungle, to play perilously with the unknown. (97)

Hence it is no wonder that for all her daring cosmopolitan attitude, she is soon disillusioned with the island and its people. Sex becomes her only weapon which she uses ruthlessly in her rejection of Peter and her wooing of Jimmy. In fact, Jimmy has his revenge on her and he is full of hate for her and in one of the hardest scenes her murder is narrated in the most cruel and inhuman manner. Jimmy assaults her and hands her over to Bryant who backs her to death with a cutlass:

> Sharp steel met flesh. Skin parted, flesh showed below the skin, for an instant mottled white, and then all was blinding, disfiguring blood, and Bryant could only cut at what had already been cut. (243)

The minor characters like Adela, Stephen and Bryant are by-standers and they play their limited roles with competence. Adela, who lives on the Ridge as the maid-servant of Jane and Peter, symbolizes stability and faith among people without any conviction. Bryant and Stephen point out the futility and hope-less end of guerrilla struggle even though they follow Jimmy for quite sometime. Meredith stands out among the other characters and seems to be author's mouthpiece in a limited sense of the term. Once he tells Harry de Tunja that tourists cannot bring about any change in the situation: 'The setting may change, but no one will make a fresh start or do anything new.' (149)

In short, *Guerrillas* appears to be a very disturbing book about political corruption and political blunder culminating in enormous suffering to the people concerned. The novel is a bit pessimistic specially in the author's hint that any revolution is bound to fail in the third world countries when the 'mimic' re-bels are confused and are hardly capable of the management of the fall-out of revolution. Naipaul himself refers to a problem in writing this book. The problem is related to the use of sex and violence which Naipaul once dreaded and frankly expressed his incompetence in dealing with sex. But in his later novels, he seems to be writing with amazing detachment. Yet another fea-ture of the novel lies in the fact that nobody can be pinpointed in the novel as the real villain though everyone has weaknesses and flaws. Paul Theroux points out: "This is a novel without a villain and there is not a character for whom the reader does not at some point feel deep sympathy and keen understanding. No matter how villainous and futile he may seem."[7]

Karl Miller and Francis Wyndham have pointed similarities between Henry James's Princess Casamassima and Jane of *Guerrillas* and Conrad's *The Secret Agent* has also been quoted in this context. Similarly in their vision of fallibility and frailty of men, Conrad's *Nostromo* and Naipaul's *Guerrillas* share a common setting and problem. If *Nostromo* is about an incendiary South African town where foreign investment in Silver is the starting point of story, in Naipaul's novel we have similarly bauxite filling station governed by America. Even Naipaul was aware of the terrifying power of the book and after the publication of the book, he confided to an American journalist: "I can't face books like *Guerrillas*. I would like to write something more celebratory—a book of reconciliation and delight. I suppose in a very simple way, I mean something with happy ending."[8]

Guerrillas remains a very successful and integrated work of art. It is intellectually stimulating and presents, a bleak, but refreshingly honest view about the political situation in the developing countries.

NOTES

1. Irving Howe, *Politics and The Novel* (New York, 1957), p. 18.
2. *Ibid.*, p. 17.
3. Chaman Nahal, *The New Literatures in English* (New Delhi: Allied, 1985), p. 138.
4. Karl Miller, 'Scorn and Pity,' *New York Review of Books*, p. 5.
5. V.S. Naipaul, *Guerrillas* (Penguin), p. 21.
6. Nondita Mason, *The Fiction of V.S. Naipaul* (Calcutta: The World Press, 1986), p. 61.
7. Paul Theroux, 'An Intelligence from The Third World,' *New York Times* (16 November, 1975), p. 2.
8. Mel Gussow, 'The Writer without Roots,' *New York Times* (26 Dec. 1976), p. 22.

A Bend in the River: A Critical Study

ASHOK KUMAR BACHCHAN
L.N. Mithila University, Darbhanga

In *A Bend in the River*, V.S. Naipaul records his impressions of Africa and its inhabitants confronting an ethnic problem of displacement. It is a disturbing novel in which the smouldering fire of violence caused by acute frustration and anger finds a memorable expression. Naipaul gathered material for this novel during his visit to Zaire in 1965. He published an article in the *New York Review of Books* which provides much insight into *A Bend in the River*: "To Joseph Conrad Stanley Ville—in 1890 the Stanley Falls station—was the heart of darkness. . . . Seventy years later at this bend in the river something like Conrad's fantasy came to pass."[1]

Naipaul has discussed in the article how the original inhabitants of Africa lost their identity not because of encounter with forces of nature but ironically because of their contact with the forces of civilization. The setting in *A Bend in the River* resembles Congo or Zaire of the Sixties to a certain extent. In part, the political set-up reminds one of the African country described by Naipaul in an earlier novel, *In a Free State*. The revolution is over and the country is now ruled by a mysterious adventurer called the Big Man who is invested, in popular imagination, with both omniscience and omnipotence. The President holds the country in his grip by his rhetoric, guile, sorcery and of course, brute force. The landscape is barren, blighted and desolate symbolizing the chaotic state of affairs and indicating violence: "Too many of the places on the way have closed down or are full of blood."[2]

In *A Bend in the River*, the landscape is veiled in mysterious darkness. Naipaul, like Conrad, exhibits his skill of adding tension to the story through an evocative description of the dark and inaccessible terrain. The landscape extends into the heart of Africa. Like other novels, *A Bend in the River* has a reporter as a character. Salim is a young and sensitive man of Indian origin, lonely and displaced in his surroundings. He is compelled to leave his family and settle in an up-country town. He confesses that he did not belong to the place and his family came from the coast, which is not truly African. He remarks:

> Many miles of scrub or desert separated us from the up-country people: he looked east to the lands with which we traded—Arabia, India, Persia—These were also the lands of our ancestors. But we could no longer say that we were Arabians or Indians or Persians, when we compared ourselves with these people, we felt like people of Africa. (17)

Salim remarks with nostalgia, an uneasy feeling about his alienation from native Africans, in these words: "It was an Arab Indian-Persian-Portuguese place, and we who lived there were really people of the Indian Ocean. True Africa was at our back." (17) Salim realizes that his life in Africa is quite unstable and insecure, even though he has achieved commercial success. He recalls: "We had the occasional comfort of reward, but in good times or bad we lived with the knowledge that we were expendable, that our labour might at any moment go to waste, that we ourselves might be smashed up; and that others would replace us." (94)

Salim, thus, shares the fate of every uprooted tribe and, to a certain extent, he shares the fate of other natives who also constantly live in fear of being uprooted because of the recurrent tribal clashes. Naipaul observes: "To an African, a child of the forest, who had marched down hundreds of miles from the interior and was far from his village and tribe, the protection of a foreign family was preferable to being alone among strange and unfriendly Africans." (19)

In spite of all these troubles, Salim looks for a fresh start when his family base on the coast is threatened. The series of events, which compelled him to start a new life in the heart of the continent, however, do not turn out to be propitious or rewarding as believed by him in the beginning. Naipaul suggests very imaginatively through the description of the setting itself that Salim's effort is bound to fail. This kind of foreboding, a sense of doom, was also expressed in Naipaul's *Guerrillas*, where Meredith had sounded the alarm: "The setting may change but no one will make a fresh start or do anything new."[3]

Naipaul describes the site chosen by Salim for his fresh venture. Salim, of course, becomes the chief spokesman of the novelist. There are also three other voices which provide their own impressions and sustain narrative interests of the novel. They even enrich Salim's observation by adding to it or sometimes detracting from it. Salim is the most acute observer and at times his comments become confessional. He continues to explore something new even realizing that this attractive place is actually a death-trap. The vivid description of the site with its water-hyacinth surrounding the water is a suggestive image. Hyacinth is repeated quite a number of times, thereby acquiring a symbolical significance:

> The tall lilac flower had appeared only a few years before, and in the local language there was no word for it. The people still called it 'the new thing' or 'the new thing in the river' and to them it was another enemy. Its rubbery vines and leaves formed thick tangles of vegetation that adhered to the riverbanks and clogged up waterways. It grew fast, faster than men could destroy it with the tools they had. The channels to the villages had to be constantly cleared. Night and day, the water hyacinth floated up from the south, seeding itself as it travelled. (51)

In spite of its beauty the lilac coloured flowers stand for death and destruction and the image also symbolizes rootlessness apart from its damaging function of choking waterways. The narrator of the novel, Salim, drifts and floats through the surge of social and political changes like the self-seeding water hyacinth. Nandita Mason regards Salim as 'the dominant consciousness of the novel.'[4]

Salim recapitulates and senses frustration but at the same time he also accepts the bitter truth of colonial history. However, this does not stop him from asking the painful question at a crucial moment: "But where was the good place? I could not say. I never thought constructively about it. I was waiting for some illumination to come to me, to guide me to the good place and the 'life'; I was still waiting for." (102-3)

Indar, the son of a wealthy coastal moneylender, shares the pain of exile like Salim but his fate is a bit different because he has his British University degree to fall back upon. Thus, Indar is a man of two worlds and that accounts paradoxically for his survival as a citizen of the world. He seems to be telling Salim the secret of his success in the midst of flux and drift. He fails to secure a job in England and even the Indian High Commission refuses to employ him because of his divided loyalty. Thus Indar has no choice but to serve in Africa and he tries to get the approval of the President with his new ideas of progress. Indar, once again, comes back to London, the place which he has rejected once out of a feeling of insecurity. A few critics have found fault with Indar's portrayal as to them Indar appears to be play-acting and does not appear to be a person fighting for survival. Indar is a deluded man Naipaul tries to be protective towards him for that very reason.

Nazaruddin is another exiled man who shares the same family background. His daughter is betrothed to Salim. He is quite different from Indar. He is a survivor and, in spite of his taste for good things of life, has a genuine resilience and in-built capacity to bounce back. He even anticipates the future troubles and manages everything in a shrewd manner. He tells Salim: "You must always know when to pull out. A businessman is a mathematician. Remember that, never become hypnotized by the beauty of numbers. A businessman is someone who buys at ten and is happy to get out at twelve." (29)

Nazaruddin is essentially a man of our times and is perhaps Naipaul's nearest success to create a contemporary man. Naipaul regretted to a reviewer that contemporary writers have not been able to write about the interest of a particular period: "One must capture the interest of this period. I don't believe the world has at all been written about. The world is no new."[5]

Nazaruddin's perception about the Arabs, Asians, Europeans and Americans is acutely relevant and unflattering in the novel. Naipaul's world is not an imaginary one, it is frighteningly real. John Leonard has rightly emphasized Naipaul's strength as a novelist: "Unlike Saul Bellow or John Updike or Graham Greene or Joseph Conrad, Naipaul has not invented an Africa. He doesn't need an imaginative construction to dazzle himself or the reader into sentience. He reports and thinks and feels, and the field, the domain is suddenly full of vectors. The future is a ruin not yet achieved, 'no family no flag, no fetish' and no place to hide."[6]

Mahesh, an Indian trader in Africa, is another exile in the novel. Mahesh spends his blessed days along with his beautiful wife, Shoba. His whole effort is directed in asking his family life a bulwark against the assault of history. Naipaul observes succinctly: "Like many isolated people, they were wrapped up in themselves and not too interested in the world outside." (34)

Salim, the novelist's mouthpiece, is however, unimpressed and he feels that Mahesh lacks Nazaruddin's worldview. Mahesh is certainly a small merchant with his grim determination to carry on. Mahesh may be regarded as a survivor from a limited point of view because he pulls off a coup and even gets the Bigburger franchise. Still his survival was related to his casual outlook. In spite of his casual manner, Mahesh can't conceal his bitterness and at least once he remarks without any reservation: 'It is not that there's no right and wrong here. There is no right.' (99) These different viewpoints on the state of affairs in Africa combine to present a somewhat cohesive, though mainly negative, view of the expatriates in Africa. In his political novels, Naipaul appears to be nearer to Balzac and Conrad in his avoidance of sentimentalism and absolute fidelity to experience. His clear-sightedness is obvious in his portrayal of small characters like Zabeth, Raymond, Yvette, Ferdinand, Metty and Father Huisman. Though Naipaul sometimes appears to be suffering from certain in-built prejudices, yet he is certainly free from the more serious failing, that is the bane of sentimentality. Zebeth, in her physical description, appears at least from an outsider's view, a large exotic African woman from the dark interiors. However, Naipaul resists the temptation to treat her as a noble savage. He does not idealize her character, but all the same, she is presented as a woman of tremendous vitality and, what is more, essential sanity. This becomes clear when she warns Salim against the machination of the President: "He is killing those men, Salim. They are screaming inside and he knows they're screaming. And you know Salim that is not a fetish, he's got there." (232)

Metty whose name is a derivative of the French word which means a mixed race, has enough sanity and like Zabeth, he can see through the game of deception handled by the ruler. He has escaped from the coast after a bloody riot in which the Africans and Muslims are badly involved. Naipaul brings out the brutality of people involved in this senseless killing: "They were behaving, as though knives did not cut as though people weren't made of flesh." (37)

Naipaul denounces the motiveless malignity of people once again in his description of the murder of father Huisman, a missionary and true lover of Africa. Metty and Ferdinand, the latter being Zabeth's son, are meant for satiric exposures as both of them ape the manners of the colonial masters and try to imitate their skill and life-style, conveniently ignoring their own native resources and moorings. Naipaul's comment is pertinent: "This better life lay outside the timeless ways of village and river. It lay in education and the acquiring of new skills; and for Zebeth, as for many Africans of her generation, education was something only foreigners could give." (41)

Both Ferdinand and Metty spend their days in the town by indulging in wine and women. Naipaul presents the degradation of the colonial victims who suffer from crisis of values and even their western education does not ensure their future but leaves them more insecure in the end. Naipaul's comment is expressed through Salim in this manner: "Now I felt his affectations were more than affectations, that his personality had become fluid. I began to feel that there was nothing there, and the thought of a lycee full of Ferdinands made me nervous."

Ferdinand's trip to America also results into a failure. Ultimately Ferdinand comes back to Africa and joins the polytechnic at the Domain, a place which attracts many foreigners and European teachers. He ends up his career by becoming a Commissioner. It is the Domain which invites people like Indar, Raymond and, of course, Yvette at the bend of the river. All these three persons finally share the same fate but Naipaul's treatment varies. His portraiture of Raymond is fairly severe and he shows him to be a deadwood scholar who has "made Africa his subject because he had come to Africa and because he was a scholar used to working with papers, and had found this place full of new papers." (187)

Raymond in his fifties and his young wife, Yvette, share a marital discord and join the ranks of Bobby and Linda and they become the third European couple in exile to be treated by Naipaul. Yvette's background before her arrival in Africa recalls Jane's. Like her, she was also poor and ambitious and Raymond almost dazzled and seduced her by spending more money on dinner one evening than her father earned in a week. Thus Africa seems to be the land of her dreams for leading a glamorous life with balls and dinners at the President's mansion. She enjoys these privileges until Raymond falls out of grace with the President. At this juncture, like Jane again, she begins to fret and fume and realizes her mistake. Like the women-protagonists of the preceding political novels, Yvette resorts to mindless sex to escape the boredom and frustration of reality. As usual, Salim's sexual involvement with Yvette has been presented in a very cold-blooded, almost clinical manner. Salim has no illusion either when he is involved with Yvette and confesses:

> My wish for an adventure with Yvette was a wish to be taken upto the skies, to be removed from the life I had—the dullness, the pointless tension, 'the situation of the country.' It wasn't a wish to be involved with people as trapped as myself. (191)

Yvette parallels Jane in her sexual greed. The culminating scene between Salim and Yvette is almost similar as the one presented in *Guerrillas* between Jimmy and Jane. Salim is less violent than Jimmy and he does not kill her, but his behaviour is no less shocking. His contempt is clearly pronounced in his typical reactions: "At this moment I held her legs apart. She raised them slightly—smooth concavities of flesh on either side of the inner ridge—and then I spat on her between the legs until I had no more spit." (227)

The breakdown of Yvette and Salim's relationship is not at all unnatural because theirs was a temporary liaison born out of a need to fill their vacant and almost meaningless lives. Like previous novels, there are shades of homosexual relationship between Salim and Metty and this has been imaginatively suggested.

The marital life of Mahesh and Shoba, the beautiful Indian couple, does not seem to flower into an ideal relationship. Mahesh remains ignoble and half a man. Naipaul tries to account for the failure of the power of love in terms of the broader disintegration of social forces. His characters appear to be passive, numb and self-absorbed. Sometimes they look like puppets being acted upon by some other forces, while at other times they seem to be overacting. Even the President, Big Man, perhaps modelled upon Henry J. Taylor's protagonist, remains in the background and we are made aware of the fact through the casual remarks of the novelist and characters that he is also handled by certain big power.

Naipaul's acute detachment from his characters is quite remarkable in *A Bend in the River*. He does not side with the white or with the black. The officers are little better than their European counterparts and Naipaul comments about them: "With their guns and jeeps, these men were poachers of ivory and thieves of gold. Ivory gold—and slaves, and it would have been like being back in oldest Africa. And these men would have dealt in slaves, if there was still a market." (99)

Naipaul's treatment of the whole scene in the modern Africa has something to do with his travel book, *Loss of El Dorado*, where he speaks of the extinction of Chaguana's Indians by the Spanish conquerors and in *A Bend in the River* he presents a parallel situation and convincingly demonstrates that neither colonizers nor liberated savages alone have a monopoly on cruelty.

The structure of *A Bend in the River* reminds us of *Guerrillas*. There are three zones of action—the town at the bend in the river where Salim runs his dry goods' shop, the domain, an artificial enclave built for the big Man's White men, and lastly, the capital, the pretentious home of the Big Man. Naipaul starts by presenting a beautiful description of the place where Salim arrives with new hopes: "In the daylight—though the colours could be very pale and ghostly, with the heat mist at times suggesting a colder climate—you could imagine the town being rebuilt and spreading. You could imagine the forests being uprooted, the roads being laid across cracks and swamps." (14)

Naipaul, then, moves to the Domain, an artificial region, with the people who are equally artificial. The place is full of cracks and flaws. He has pictured the scene both realistically and symbolically:

> The building of the Domain had run up fast, and the flaws that lamplight had hidden were noticeable in the midday brightness. The plaster on the walls had cracked in many places, and in one place the cracks followed the stepped pattern of the hollow clay bricks below. . . . The windows were open; with no protecting roof, no trees outside, just the levelled land, the room was full of light and glare, and there was no feeling of shelter. (176)

The description brings out the artificiality of the place as well as the unnatural presence of the dwellers like Raymond and Yvette who have reached there to heal their souls and finally realized that it is no blessing for them. Salim rightly notes that in spite of Raymond's boasting of high connections, the latter is a defeated man and his home is a house of death.

The capital, the third zone of action, the place is deliberately shrouded in mystery just as the Big Man, the modern version of Kurtz. The novelist does not present the Big Man visually and only once the glimpse of his habitat is presented. Salim describes the city: "The city, while decaying in the centre, with dirt roads and rubbish mounds just at the back of the great colonial boulevards, was yet full of new public works. Large areas near the river had been turned into Presidential reserves—palaces with great walls, gardens, state-houses of various sorts." (259) In other words, the capital is a strange place with unusual combination of dirty roads, rubbish mound and colonial boulevards. The place also presents the image of the big man as Salim rightly feels at a certain moment that the President is bypassing the real Africa in his frenzy to radicalize the country. His failure is suggested beautifully through the imagery of water hyacinths which end their journey in the capital itself.

The climax of the novel shows that neither of the characters is destined to last and each one is bound to face a debacle. Even Salim finally meets with humiliation. In order to remove his boredom, Salim makes a trip to London to see Nazaruddin, his prospective father-in-law. But even London provides just a temporary relief. Naipaul has presented brilliantly the theme of rootlessness as the common destiny of the contemporary man. Salim comments:

> In the streets of London I saw these people, who were like myself, as from a distance. I saw the young girls selling packets of cigarettes at midnight, seemingly imprisoned in their kiosks, like puppets in a puppet theatre. They were cut off from the life of the great city where they had come to live and I wondered about the pointlessness of their own hard life, the pointlessness of their difficult journey. (238)

Salim is engaged to Kareisha, Nazaruddin's daughter, who settles herself as a Pharmacist in London. Nazaruddin himself comes to London after experiencing bitter tastes of life in Canada and Uganda. He is also cheated in London by the Algerians as he was previously betrayed in Canada. Hence Nazaruddin generalizes like every embittered man, his experiences of the world: "We've come here [London] at the wrong time. But never mind. It's the wrong time everywhere else too." (247) But Europe is not the last of Salim's disappointments as his homecoming also results into a disaster. His store has been snatched and given to a citizen Theotime. Salim is accused of smuggling and thrown into jail, but he is rescued by the new commissioner, Ferdinand, the son of Zabeth.

Salim leaves Africa for the last time on the river-boat and he notices some positive symptoms of violence in the air around:

> After the morning heat it had turned stormy, and in the silver-storm light the overgrown, bushy bank was brilliant green against the black sky. Below this brilliant green the earth was bright red. The wind blew, and ruffled away reflections from the river surface near the bank. But the rain that followed didn't last long, we sailed out of it. (286)

The bright colours mentioned in these lines refer to the possibility of explosion and a search light on the river shows a boat full of Africans and other natives who look like flying insects trying to escape both the bush and water hyacinths. Naipaul, in an interview with Hardwick remarked that the encroaching bush embodies "the breakdown of institutions of the contract between man and man. It is theft, corruption, racist incitement."[7]

It is obvious that in *A Bend in the River*, Naipaul presents a documentary account of the turbulent Africa undergoing drastic changes through war and killings. In such a situation, the sensitive individuals who stand for dignity and sanity can have nothing but complete isolation. But even this isolation promises security and order which is the dream of all aspiring individuals. Hence, Naipaul's characters finally hide in dark rooms while they have the whole world to move into and they turn inwards in self-defence.

Naipaul's political novels including *A Bend in the River* appear to be too cruel and tragic, the fact remains that they have not darkened or soured the author's compassion or his belief in the future of man. Naipaul simply demonstrates that such things have happened before and will happen again. Even if the future holds no promise of security, there is no room for nostalgia. Like Nazaruddin, Naipaul hints at the need of carrying on even in the midst of all confusion, chaos and violence.

NOTES

1. V.S. Naipaul, 'A New King for the Congo,' *New York Review of Books*, 26 June 1975, p. 24.
2. V.S. Naipaul, *A Bend in the River* (Penguin), p. 9.
3. V.S. Naipaul, *Guerrillas* (Penguin), p. 149.
4. Nondita Mason, *The Fiction of V.S. Naipaul* (Calcutta: The World Press, 1986), p. 106.
5. Mel Gussow, 'The Writer without Roots,' *New York Times*, 26 December, 1978, p. 22.
6. John Leonard, "A Review of the Novel," *New York Times*, 14 May, 1979, p. 21.
7. Hardwick, 'Meeting V.S. Naipaul,' *New York Times*, p. 36.

Finding the Centre: A Critical Study

G. SRILATHA
P.B. Siddharth College, Vijaywada

This, paper focuses on the first section 'Prologue to an Autobiography' in *Finding the Centre*, where V.S. Naipaul gives an account of how he began to write. He recollects his memorable childhood days and his admiration for his father's stories through which he learnt to write. His father's ambition was to become a writer. He was a journalist and a storywriter. But he failed to be a writer. He wished Naipaul would become a writer and this was decided when he was three years old. Later, when he started writing he took his father as a Guru, which is the focus of this paper. "For a Hindu who wants to be a pundit has first to find a Guru."

Naipaul's father found Macgowan as his Guru, who was a Managing Editor of Trinidad Government. It was he who taught him how to write. To begin with, the writer starts to write in which he has first hand experience to overcome the starting trouble. Naipaul's father does this by writing about Chaguanas, the place and people, which he was very familiar with. He was interested in the Indians of the countryside who were cut off by the language, religion and culture from the rest of the colonial population. He learned from Macgowan how to give a voice to his knowledge of Trinidad Indian life, which was his own. It was also the place where Naipaul's father's stories of village life were placed. In all his stories there was little 'story.' Much importance was given to the observation made by the writers. His stories celebrated Indian village life and the Hindu rituals that gave grace and completeness to that life. He wrote eloquently about setting and customs of his childhood and about members of his extended family. Each and every element was beautifully adduced in his story. It was this celebration that Naipaul enjoys in these stories, as the order of the working day, the labour of the rice-fields, the preparation of food and eating habits all have occupied a major role in his stories. Seepersad Naipaul's stories are a vital portion of his heritage to his son who considers them a unique record of the life of the Indian or Hindu community in Trinidad.

Naipaul, in *Finding the Centre,* says that he enjoyed the beauty of Indian village life, which he experienced through his father's stories, which played a prominent role in his writings. They remain green and fresh in his mind. When he met his father's relatives, he realized that they were the characters in his stories. It is like a fairy tale coming true. So reality with factual images made his stories very interesting. Naipaul's complete involvement in these stories is represented as "I set my fantasy of home, my fantasy of things, like the ritualized day, field, and huts, the mango tree, the simple flower, the lighting of fires in the evening."

Naipaul while reading his father's stories learnt that while visiting places and talking to men, the writer gains a lot of experience. Each story is a lessc and reading those stories itself is a process of learning for Naipaul. Slowly Naipaul resolved that he would become a writer. When he was eleven, he had no sign of talent but his father prophesied that he would be a writer. Hence Naipaul's mind was set to become a writer. His father's stories, he says, gave him "a way of looking, an example of labour, a knowledge of the literary process, a sense of the order and special reality that written words could be seen to create."

When it comes to the process of writing, Naipaul observes his father writing. He says that his father had written with great patience. He was calm before and during his writing mood. His first long story was read out to Naipaul. It was a greatest imaginative experience of his childhood. "I knew the story by heart, yet always loved to read it and hear it, feeling a thrill at every familiar turn, ready for all the varied emotions." This shows his complete involvement in the story and his keen observation power on the process of writing and the impact of a work. As a boy, Naipaul participated in the act of writing that remain his father's refuge, his means of restoring his fragile sense of self-hood. Inevitably, the self-confidence such trust could bestow on a child was tempered by his assimilation of his father's anxieties, the conflict produced in suppressing his own truth, his writer's identity and his simultaneous need to articulate it. It is not surprising that the son incorporated his father's fear of psychic dissolution along with his vocation.

Naipaul studied at Oxford with the help of government scholarship. It was there that he started writing. Writing was the part he has chosen in which he had to travel. When he was at Oxford he insisted his father to write an Autobiography. This was to encourage him as a writer. But some deep hurt or shame something still raw and unresolved in his experience kept his father from attempting any autobiographical writing. Hence Naipaul makes an attempt and succeeds.

As a child, Naipaul was interested in the history and landscape but he was not satisfied with his school history and geography. His thirst for knowledge on history was quenched when he worked on a history of the region for two years, where, by reading in the British Museum, the public record office, he tried to understand how his corner of the New World was capable of developing in many ways. The ideas of 'Once upon a time' which was vague and unclear during his childhood days became clear and it penetrates his mind to think of the place and people. As it is important for a writer to study the place before he writes. Naipaul travelled to some of the places of which he would write in his stories. By moving to places, he gained confidence to write.

Naipaul started writing in London. He was afraid if he would fail to become a writer, failing twice in his attempt to write novels he sat at the typewriter to try once more to be a writer. Naipaul narrates his first experience as a writer. He took long time to write the first sentence. Though he got an idea of what to write, he had a trouble in framing the first line. He overcame this problem by recollecting his father, who wrote about Chaguanas, the place and people which he was very familiar with. Similarly

Naipaul when he had the trouble of how to begin he was reminded about Bogart whom he knew from his childhood. Bogart's father and Naipaul's grandfather developed a bond of brotherhood which was honoured by their descendants. As a child Naipaul had divined Bogart's impulses. He had Bogart's story in mind, in his struggle to make the first sentence he was reminded of Bogart's being called by Hat. There was much in that call of 'Bogart,' which impressed Naipaul to think. After a long time he wrote the first sentence "what happening there Bogart, Bogart would turn in his bed and mumble softly, so that no one heard."

The first sentence was true. The second was creative. It was like magic, he started writing the story of Bogart. Unlike his father, it is from here that he developed his individuality and uniqueness in writing. He typed the story at Freelances where people chat. He listened to three numbers who responded to his story.

John Stockbride who worked for BBC Programme read the story and "John made a serious face and spoke as a prodigious prophecy about my future as a writer. It was his way of giving me a little blessing." Andrew Salkey, another writer, after reading the story suggested changing the early sentences. Gordon Woolford whole-heartedly accepted the story. Something in the story touched Gordon. He read the story line by line, assessing the words of the tone.

The responses that he received helped him in writing further. On the second day he was conscious of the suggestion he received for his first story. Especially Gordon's who suggested never letting the words get loose. He had already created an atmosphere of the life of the street. As his imagination grew, the stories become longer. Beginnings, and rhythms, do not come naturally, they had to be worked for. He puts lots of pains to exercise and practice writing to attain perfection.

Finally, with lots of efforts he had written a book and that had been the ambition for years. Later he learnt that having written a book is not to be a writer. He thought he should wait until he writes 3. When he had written 3, he thought he should wait until he writes 6. So step by step, book by book each time the urge to write another book grew stronger.

To become a writer, a noble profession, it was necessary to go back to begin with self-knowledge. Hence Naipaul traced his own childhood days and learnt as he grew. As half work of a writer is to find his subject on which he writes, the knowledge about the writer's own roots and his self helps him focus on his subject. The rest half of the work is sweated out with his creative mind. Finally, confidence blooms in the writer when the work is done. Thus by building confidence the writer advances to progress and attains perfection in his art. This phenomenon of writer's experience is beautifully brought out in Prologue to an autobiography. In the text Naipaul says: 'I travel to discover other states of mind' which reveals how the mind functions in the process of writing. The states of mind he investigates include his own as well as those of the people he is drawn to and comes to know.

Finding the centre has many meanings. Finding the centre of the narrative, the centre of the truth of every experience, the philosophical centre of one's belief. It is the link between the author's inner and literary narratives. The angle of perception of a writer should be both subjective and objective. In his growth he learns the art of writing. The struggle that he undergoes while writing is like churning within his self for words and rhythms. Each and every next book is an exercise of writing.

As an apprentice, Naipaul learnt from his father. From his childhood, his mind was occupied with stories written by his father. Slowly, when he grew up, he took his father as a Guru. Hence we observe that in his works, he incorporates his childhood experiences along with his creation.

The vocation of writing was gifted to Naipaul by his father. Naipaul's father passed away with the fear of not becoming a writer. That fear was also seen in Naipaul. The fear could be combated only by the exercise of the vocation. This is symbolically justified by the title *Finding the Centre* where Naipaul has taken writing as his profession. Even at the time of his family's distress by his father's death, his determination to write was strong. "My father had died the previous year. Our family was in distress. I should have done something for them, gone back to them. But without having become a writer, I could not go back. In my eleventh month in London I wrote about Bogart. I wrote my book. I wrote another I began to go back."

The last line I began to go back is significant to the title *Finding the Centre* where Naipaul represents his strong determination to write. He learnt from his father the art of writing, with rigorous practice and exercise of writing, he grows to attain perfection. His ambition of writing is fulfilled and his perfection is rewarded by his achievement of Nobel Prize for Literature.

NOTES

1. Lillian Feder, *Naipaul's Truth* (U.S.A.: Rowman & Littlefield, 2001).
2. V.S. Naipaul, *Finding the Centre* (London: 1984).
3. C.D. Narasimhaiah, "Somewhere, something has snapped," *The Literary Criterion*, September 1962.
4. William Walsh, *Naipaul* (Edinburgh; Oliver and Boyd: 1973).

Arrival and Departure in *Enigma of Arrival*

T. SARADA
P.B. Siddharth College, Vijaywada

Arrival and departure are the inevitable facets of all life. We arrive only to depart and many a departure (according to certain beliefs) is meant only to arrive. Echoing Henry Vaughan's poem "Retreat," Wordsworth mentions in his "Immortality Ode":

> The soul that rises with us, our life's star,
> Hath had elsewhere its setting,

Life is thus perceived as a cycle of births and death by certain philosophers, when all births lead to deaths and vice versa.

The ideas of "arrival" and "departure" if not perceived in these strictly philosophical terms, assume different connotations to the third world expatiate writers. Migration of the people for various reasons has far-reaching consequences on their lives. In the postcolonial situation, the withdrawal of colonial powers alone did not usher in signs of prosperity. The disillusionment following independence was hard to cope with: "As the rosy mists cleared, the tryst with destiny revealed the witches on the heath. Panic and disillusionment began to replace patriotism and hope. Feeling weak and cynical, the native decided to flee to Britain/France, the home country, the ideal county." (Kirpal, 26)

The escapist tendency is a consequence of the "psychological paralysis" (Kirpal, 26) that the expatriate writer faces on account of oppressive circumstances. Forced to live in another land for multiple reasons, the writer not only tries to get acquainted with the new land, but also attempts to retain his roots with the native land, described in psychoanalytical terms as an "oedipal-tug." (Kirpal, 71) Apart from the country of his ancestry, and that in which he settles, the writer may also adopt another land which is closer to his sensibilities. V.S. Naipaul is one such writer who has his family roots in India, was born and raised in Trinidad and calls England as his "adopted home." Therefore, to writers like him, "the multi cultural situation is not only a subject matter, but a mode of perception as well." (qtd. Kirpal, 37)

So, an expatriate writer lives in a complex situation wherein his multi-cultural predicament offers both "place" and "place-lessness" Bill Ashcroft mentions how both these factors are intrinsic to postcolonial discourse. "By 'place' we do not simply mean 'landscape.' Rather . . . [it] is a complex interaction of language, history and environment. It is characterized firstly by a sense of displacement in those who have moved to the colonized, or the more widespread sense of displacement from the imported language of a gap between the 'experienced' environment and descriptions the language provides, and secondly by a sense of the immense investment of culture in the construction of place." (Ashcroft, 301) Restlessness, search for a steady centre, movement and travel are the salient features of expatriate fiction. Naipaul's thinly veiled autobiographical novel *Enigma of Arrival* (1987) explores the riddle behind arrival and departure at multiple levels.

The novel is about Naipaul's trip to England, especially Salisbury. His love for English literature through English education had made him perceive England as his "adopted home." Hence, he had always longed to move there. The first section of the novel is entitled "Jack's Garden," 'Jack' being a familiar name in England with its nursery-rhyme-like quality. The novel begins with a description of the river Avon. The topography and the landscape together form an integral part of Naipaul's consciousness: "the land had more meaning, when it had absorbed more of my life than the tropical street where I had gown up." (12)

Strangely, this arrival to a long-yearned land does not give him the extreme joy and a ready acceptance of the place as he had imagined. The novel is thus transformed into a physical and psychic expiation of the land in which he had dwelled for the past twenty years. Like the winter snow, he avidly describes as settling down in the landscape, he makes whole-hearted attempts to settle in England. But unlike the snow which successfully settles there, Naipaul continues to grope for a place in England. For the first time, he realizes how the process of assimilation is not an easy thing. The gap between imagination and reality dawns on him.

> But knowledge came slowly to me. It was not like the almost instinctive knowledge that had come to me as a child of the plants and flowers of Trinidad, it was like learning a second language. (32)

He understands the wide chasm that exists between spontaneous learning and deliberate effort. In order to enhance his effort to assimilate, he tries to sharpen his power of vision:

> I saw what I saw very clearly. But I didn't know what I was looking at. I had nothing to fit into. I was still in a kind of limbo. (12)

The "limbo" that Naipaul mentions is closer to what Wilson Harris mentions in his essay 'The Limbo Gateway': "Limbo . . . reflects a certain kind of gateway or threshold to a new world and the dislocation of a chain of miles. It is in some ways the archetypal sea-change stemming from the old world and it is legitimate." (qtd. Ashcroft)

Naipaul is stranded in a mental limbo since he is caught not merely in a single world but in the consciousness of three: India, Trinidad and England. Salisbury is no new land for Naipaul. He was acquainted with it through a painting by Constable in his third standard reader in Trinidad. His English education also strengthened his ties with England. But despite this exposure to England, he finds total assimilation impossible:

> After all my life in England, I still had that nervousness . . . that newness of response, still felt myself to be in the other man's country, felt my strangeness, my solitude. (12)

The incapacity to assimilate reveals to him the hitherto unknown deeper part of his unconscious self. An accompanied feeling of self-alienation further questions his rival there. Therefore, the walk through Jack's garden is filled with deep inquiry, probing not merely on the external landscape, but also into his inscape. He understands his "own strangeness and absurdity of the inquiry" and faces displacement at various levels. The very fascination for the English landscape could be perceived as a product of colonial enslavement which in its deepest sense could mean the whitewashing of the native's psyche. Critics brand this as 'Neo-colonialism' which means: "The existence of considerable foreign direction over a nominally independent nation. In its narrowest sense, this means a high degree of influence over a country's economic affairs. . . . Political and military policy as well. In addition . . . [it suggests] the predominance of the cultural values of the former colonial powers." (Magdoff, 890)

In Soyinka's play *The Lion and the Jewel* (1975), Lakunle, the village school teacher, is ridiculed for miming western ways. Although Naipaul's love for Britain cannot be perceived as a slavish craving for the white man's land, it is the love for a country which he feels is closer to his sensibility. He perceives the landscape as do Wordsworth and Keats. Avid descriptions like the "mud,' "cottage," "long Wet grass,' "hay," "warm smell," "sycamore," "beach," "oaks" etc. entice him. Like Keats, he assimilates the landscape with his five senses. But still, a total oneness with the country always seems elusive. Naipaul mentions that the title of the novel has been borrowed from a surrealist painting of George de Chirocco. Among the various paintings, he sees in a booklet entitled "The Little Library of Art," Naipaul is particularly fascinated by the one entitled "Enigma of Arrival." Explicating on the reason behind the choice, he mentions: "I felt that in an indirect poetical way, the title referred to something in my own experience." (91)

The title for the painting had been given by the poet Apollinaire. To Naipaul, the painting also suggests a sort of unsettledness which forms the core of his life. The painting connotes to him an ancient—Roman or Mediterranean—scene. The background consists of a wharf which lies beyond the walls and gateways. The mast of an antique vessel on the top suggests the ever-present journey motif. The two muffled figures (one native, other tourist) could then be interpreted as emanations of the same consciousness since both of them are "muffled," suggesting the deeper cloudiness in their lives. The journey therefore is a never-ending one. The three-dimensional painting consists of the earth and the vastness of space suggesting a greater travel in space and time. It is like his own journey. For years, he had dreamed of being in England, and once there, he wishes to move away from that place. "And just as once at home I had dreamed of being in England, so for years in England I had dreamed of leaving England." (95)

Originally, he planned to write a story under this title as "a sunlit sea journey ending in a dangerous classical city," with pointers from the Acts of Apostles, Appulius, Horace sad Petronius. But later a creative turbulence explodes in his head: "It is powerful . . . that threw me flat on my back in the presence of people, in a street; a crowded room. . . . Threw me into the posture of sleep in which I found myself when I awakened." (93)

The painting thus continues to haunt his creative mind. Moreover, the novel had come as a release from the creative fatigue of having written *A Bend in the River* (1979). The nightmarish internal dramatization makes him write a story concerned with the problems of assimilation in the adopted county. The identification still continues to remain elusive: "A stranger here, with the nerves of the stranger, and yet with a knowledge of the language and the history of the language and the writing." (22)

Various attempts are made by Naipaul to identify himself with the land. For instance, he indulges in historical fantasies. He also tries to deceive himself through the perspective that "all *was* well with the world." He tries to appreciate the past and the haunting sense of antiquity.

The past, then, is of immense significance to the third world expatriate writer. Shorn of his native roots and unable to completely settle down in the adopted land, he attempts to appreciate its past as an effective means of total identification (however unsuccessful it may be) The past is no ephemera. It is significant, since even unsuccessful attempts are both "diminishing" and "ennobling." Another way in which he attempts at identification is through the employment of sexual metaphors to prove his attraction to the land. Like Sandra in *Mimic Men* and Anne in *Half a Life* (2001), there is a temporary tryst with Angela in *The Enigma of Arrival.* But all these attempts yield little results, for till the end, he remains a traveller in search of a steady centre. But he does not give up travel. The author's foreword to *Finding the Centre* (1984) mentions:

> To travel was glamorous. But travel also made unsuspected demands on a man and writer, and . . . it soon become a necessary stimulus for me. It broadened my world-view; it showed a changing world and took me out of my own colonial shell; it become the substitute for the mature social experience the deepening knowledge of a society—which my background and the nature of my life denied me. (26)

Travel therefore widens his mental horizons and creates a deeper knowledge of the world in which he is living and also delivers him from his colonial existence. He may not be able to finally arrive at what he wants, but he continues to travel. The confusion, the persistent search and a continued willingness to travel is reflected in the language of the writer. The insubstantiality results in an unknown abstractness and even strangeness begins to modify the language of the expatriate writer which is in consonance with his experience. The novel, if probed deeper, is also a questioning of his arrival into the world of letters. Writing is basically a linguistic process. An introspection reveals that Naipaul's act of writing proves the Lacanian perspective of the distance between the word and its attempt at signification. Bill Ashcroft et al succinctly sum up this predicament of postcolonial writing: "The language always negotiates a kind of gap between the word and its signification. In this sense, the dynamic of 'naming' becomes a primary colonizing process because it appropriates, defines, captures the place in languages." (391) In this sense, Naipaul does define and render the place along with its language to authenticate his experience to himself and to his writing. But as Ashcroft et al further continue: "And yet the process of naming opens wider the very epistemological gap which it is designed to fill, for the dynamic mystery of language, as Wilson Harris puts it, becomes a groping step into the reality of place, not simply reflecting or representing it, but in some mysterious sense involved in the process of its creation, of its coming into being." (392) Despite the inadequacies of language, it does exist since language forms the primary mode of communication between individuals and also becomes one of the best ways of translating one's outer/inner experiences and a means of finding order to an otherwise chaotic experience.

Ever since he started writing, he apprehends the fact that there exists a gap between the man and the writer. Although the two physically refer to the same person, the gap arises in the course of the sensibility. For quite a long time, the 'man' and 'writer' remain different entities. In the second section, "The Journey," Naipaul mentions how he could already feel his two sides separating. But many experiences put together strengthen his act of writing. Despite the internal chaos, the writer in him is able to create. One can easily sense traces of a bildungsroman wherein one perceives the growth of a writer. The title "Journey" metaphorically indicates his sojourn into the world of writing as well:

> In my early days as a writer, when my talent was declaring itself, I had developed . . . this ability to concentrate and to compose in the midst of harassment . . . writing strengthened me; it quelled anxiety. And now writing restored me again. (156)

Writing continues to be his life force despite the prevailing creative confusions. At the time of writing *The Enigma of Arrival*, his mind remained fatiguely engrossed with *A Bead in the River* which was in the final stages of completion. He had been to Africa which he projects on Wiltshire. "I projected Africa on to Wiltshire. . . . The Wiltshire, I walked in—began to radiate or return Africa to me. So man and writer became one; the circle became complete." (156) The fusion between the man and the writer is essential to attain heights of mastery in the field. It is the "noblest impulse' in the colonial setting. It is the fountainhead of his existence, for, without it, he may perish.

The theme of "death" and "departure" is implied in the novel to a large extent. All life is born only to die. The pattern of the novel is circular. All the characters introduced in the first chapter, Bray, Pitton, Allen and the Phillipses die in the fourth section of the novel entitled "Rooks." The theme of mutability runs through the novel. The "idea of an unchanging life was wrong. Change was constant. People died; people grew old, everyone was aging; everything was being reversed or discarded." (34)

Death levels not only human life but also the landscape, flora, fauna, buildings and all perceptible forms of life on earth. Echoing Wordsworth, Naipaul also believes that every artificial intrusion of man into the natural world also is tantamount to death. Therefore, to this keen observer, death becomes an ingrained aspect of his psyche: To see the possibility, the certainty of ruin even at the moment of creation: it was my temperament." (52)

A number of synonyms are used to describe the all-pervasive aura of death. Words like "abandonment" "broken," "old,' "dying," "decay" "debris," "dereliction"; "ruin," "out-of-placedness," "neglect," "oddity," "unanchored," "strange," "junk," "mounds," "hidden," "unknown" and many such words prove that the arrival is meant only for a departure. It creates a sense of fear in him. Earlier, in his prologue to *Finding the Centre*, he mentions how as a child he had searched the book case of his father to find Marcus Aurelius, Epictetus and also many mystical and quasi-religious books. His father was sick. Earlier, he had taught him a line from Ella Wheeler Wilcox: "Even this shall pass away." (86) Naipaul calls it "classic consolation" since it could combat with the pains of all sorts, "of a moment, a day, life itself." Although his father never spoke to him about the nature of his illness, Naipaul could sense "his fear of extinction" which he had himself inherited. "That fear become mine as well. It was linked with the idea of the vocation, the fear could be combated only by the exercise of the vocation." (91)

Therefore, writing is an act which could purge in him the fear of death. This fear is a western one, a product of his existential angst. Born in Trinidad, inheriting Indian genes and having adopted England as his home, Naipaul finds himself nowhere. Thus, every arrival is questionable. Ralph Kripal Singh in

Mimic Men lives in a hotel in London. Having severed family connections, he lives a confined existence in a hotel. "I no longer yearn for ideal landscapes and no longer wish to know the god of the city. This does not strike me as loss. I feel instead, I have lived through attachment and freed myself from one cycle of event." (123)

Salim in *A Bend in the River* (1979) also moves from the east coast of Africa to Zaire in central Africa. He longs to disconnect himself from orthodoxy and rituals. Ultimately he is transformed into an existential individual. Like Ralph Singh in a hotel, he lives in a camp. Unable to stay in his old home and unfit to find a new one, his search remains endless. The angst is also a product of multiple levels of alienation. A displaced expatriate writer is basically alienated from his native land, from the land from which he has been uprooted, from the adopted land and also ultimately from himself. There prevails an "emptiness" in the midst of "spaciousness." The solitude he experience is also haunting: "I was more concerned with the strangeness of the walk, my own strangeness and the absurdity of my inquiry." (15)

To such a state of mind, death is a "felicity." Therefore, the last section of the novel entitled "The Farewell" is concerned with the death of his sister Sati. He confesses that the late thirties in his life is characterized by a fear of death. He experiences frequent violent explosions in his head. Initially, it is not any "specific fear of death" but a "great melancholy" with which he has to cope:

> This melancholy penetrated my mind while I slept, and then I awakened in response to its prompting, I was so prompted by it . . . that it took the best part of the day to shake it off. And that . . . added to the gloom preparing for the night. (309)

Thus, the idea of death always continues to haunt him day and night, whether asleep or awake. Slowly he realizes that they are one and inevitable. It continues to pervade his writings as a "motif all along." That was the motif of the story of Jack. The dental extraction he describes serves as an objective correlative to the emotion of death as it does in Eliot's *Wasteland*. Sati's death is rather revelatory to him. She had occupied a special place in his heart. In many ways she serves as a foil to him. Unlike him, she had "lived her life" at Trinidad and therefore feels more rooted. She had boldly lived the rich perils of her life, her father's illness, death, the racial and political changes in Trinidad, the anarchy of nineteen seventy and the oil boom. Therefore, here is a life of "success." Her death purges in Naipaul the Christian fear of death. Having understood his place in the larger scheme of existence he no longer fears anything.

> There was no ship of antique shape now to take us back. We had come out of the nightmare, and there was nowhere else to go. (317)

He understands that she had arrived only to depart. It reminds him of his father's death in 1953 when after the obsequies were performed, it left deep wounds in his brother's psyche. Both Naipaul and Sati place little value on rituals. But Sati's rites are performed in accordance with Hindu shastras. Her son performs them in a pair of jeans. Naipaul looks at the "Swahas," "shruddas," the pressing together of rice balls and other offerings with an ironic sense of detachment. One of the reasons is that the pundit, who performs these, offers little explanation to their queries. Naipaul understands that his nephew needed "support greater than the support of ritual." But still the rituals are followed since it would help them maintain their links with the past and ancestral roots.

> We were immemorially people of the countryside. . . . Living according to rituals we didn't always understand and yet were unwilling to dishonor because that would cut us off from the past. (386)

The sense of the past and antiquity is of great importance to an expatriate writer. It is one of the most effective means through which the individual tries to immerse himself with the land. In their connection, the times past and present are often fused to enable a feeling of continuity. Every incident and object in England reminds him of something or the other at Trinidad. His historical sense also throws light on some aspect of him: "Men need history, it helps them to have an idea of who they are." Despite his sincere appreciation of the history of the land, a total identification with it still seems a mirage. As he mentions in *Finding the Centre*: "Every place visited was different, every place opened in a new way. Always, at the beginning, there was the possibility of failure—of not finding anything, not getting started on the chain of accidents and encounters." (12)

Arrival and departure in the continued journey of life forms the core of the novel. Naipaul tries to arrive at various places—Salisbury, Trinidad and America. Yet he remains an unsettled wanderer. His moorings on the landscape are a metaphor for his moorings in his inscape. Lorangaka Losambe, an African writer, while expiating on the theme of expatriation, mentions how instead of seeing the characters as "assimilated, alienated or acculturated, it would be better to see the contradictions or trauma in these characters' personalities as expatriation problems." (qtd. Kirpal, 23) While Naipaul is not sure if the ultimate departure from the earth would lead to arrival once again, he is sure of the fact that all earthly arrivals would lead to departure and therein lies the enigma of his life rhetorically remaining unanswered.

NOTES

V.S. Naipaul, *Enigma of Arrival* (Penguin, 1987).
V.S. Naipaul, *Finding the Centre* (Penguin, 1984).
V.S. Naipaul, *A Bend in the River* (Penguin, 1979).
V.S. Naipaul, *Half a Life* (Picador, 2001).
V.S. Naipaul, *Mimic Men* (Penguin, 2001).
Viney Kirpal, *The Third World Expatriate Novel* (Sterling, 1989).
Bill Ashcroft et al., *The Post-Colonial Studies Reader* (Routledge, 1995).

A Way in the World: The "Unwritten" Narrative

RAMA DEVI
S.K. University, Anantapur

Naipaul's *A Way in the World,* though classified as a "fictional work" remains a rather strange hybrid, neither fish nor fowl, defying all classification written at an hour of dusk, a time for reflection, it is marked by a kind of mellowness which has actually made its mark in the previous work by Naipaul, *India: A Million Mutinies Now.* Naipaul himself classifies *A Way in the World* as "A Sequence."

The book is about fallen heroes in the afternoon of their lives awash with memories of youth, of fame and fortune. All the portraits sketched here are of failed revolutionaries and visionaries. There is Walter Raleigh, the man intent on ruling the Indians in America in the fabled El Dorado. And there is Francisco Miranda, the nineteenth century Venezuelan revolutionary, who spends most of his time in the courts of Europe while professing revolutionary ideas and who ends his life as a prisoner of the Spaniards. There is Lebanese, the Trinidadian Panamanian Community of the 1930s vintage, who is a permanent exile in London and romanticized in the social circles of London and New York. Lastly, there is an account on Blair, who rises from the clerkship in the Government House in Port of Spain to the post of economic adviser to a revolutionary socialist state in East Africa, where he is killed. It is a mocking account of the political ambitions of these semi-tragic heroes that the book turns out to be.

The stories within the book are chiefly accounts of people, some selected with great care from historical manuscripts and some drawn from memories that go back to Naipaul's adolescent years in Trinidad, his years in England while he was struggling to establish himself as a writer and the later years when he returned to the continent of his birth to look at in much the same critical way as he did India in *An Area of Darkness.*

Naipaul interweaves historical facts with works of fiction that go back to Marquez and Grass. Here are reflections of the great explorers—Walter Raleigh's doomed expedition to the Orinoco and Miranda's disastrous invasion of South America—that take back centuries to the colonial Africa of conquest and intrigue—of cultures subsumed, of people ravaged, of places laid waste by change. The book is not only about the conquered—such as the African slaves, the Amerindians, Indian immigrants—but also the conquerors, displaced colonialists, conquerors run around by their own failings: greed, and overweening ambition.

The book begins quite interestingly with Naipaul going back to Trinidad, that he left forty years ago and contemplating on his teenage years in Trinidad and finding "everything was strange and not strange: the suddenness of night, the very big leaves of some trees, the shrunken streets, the corrugated-iron roofs."[1] To go back home was, to him, to play with impressions, looking at a world "now sharp and small and not quite real, now standard size and real but blurred." (1) He culls one memory from the past and weaves a story out of it. Perhaps the most magical and poignant one in the entire book is the story of Leonard Side, a mortician and decorator of cakes and arranger of flowers. Though it is not more than mere retelling of a past incident, Naipaul tells it so well that everything that Leonard Side does leaves as firm an impression on the reader as it has on the narrator's mind:

> He was in a shiny, brass four-poster bed with a flowered canopy, and he was in green silk pyjamas. His little hairy fingers were resting on the satin or silk spread he was using as a coverlet. . . . There were crepe-paper flowers in a brass vase . . . and there were satiny cushions and big bows on two simple cane-bottomed bent wood chairs. I knew at once that a lot of that satin and silk had come, from the funeral parlour, and was material for the coffins and the laying out of the bodies. (6)

Leonard Side's idea of beauty-mixing roses and flowers and nice things to eat with the idea of making the dead human body beautiful—that has upset the narrator—upsets the reader also in the same way. This narrative entitled "Prelude—An Inheritance" sets the tone for the whole book in which a sense of going back in time prevails.

It is the early chapters that are most arresting as we see the young Naipaul in the Port of Spain. He was then an acting second-class clerk in the Registrar General's Department located in the Red House at the age of seventeen. The Red House was located between St. Vincent Street and Woodford Square. Most interesting to the young Naipaul was St. Vincent Street, the street of the newspapers—*The Trinidad Guardian,* wherein his father worked as a correspondent, and *The Port of Spain Gazette.* It was also the street in which Nazaralli Baksh, a tailor had his shop. In the same street was lodged the Police Headquarters, a British colonial building in the Victorian Gothic style. The Red House was the principal building of the administration built in the Italian style.

> It was one of the buildings that made Port of Spain Port of Spain. . . . On either side of the empty fountain big, free-standing, wooden notice-boards . . . served as screens, shielding clerks and typists and other civil servants from the gaze of the people passing to and fro. . . . The notice boards didn't carry government instructions. The pinned-up posters were about health care and the importance of vaccinations, things like that. (17)

Woodford Square, the most beautiful square in Port of Spain, a glorious thing of the town, was also one of the places where homeless people lived. Most of them were Indians who came as indentured immigrants in the sugar estates and now utterly destitute without any place to go to. They were without money, job, family and without the English language or any kind of representation. They were people who had been "lifted up from the peasantry of India and set down thousands of miles away—weeks and weeks of sailing—in Trinidad." (19) They were now tormented by the people of the town. The people saw it but never thought about it. Eventually they were all dead by the late 1940s, when Naipaul went to work in the Red House. His job was to make copies of birth, marriage, and death certificates for the purpose of maintaining records which were all stored in the Registrar General's Department. The volumes smelt of fish-glue, and hence the title of the chapter: "History: A Smell of Fish Glue." It was here, amidst these inhospitable surroundings, that Naipaul began his writing career.

His first essay on a black beauty contest was not received favourably by his colleague, a black woman typist, who told him: "If it was an Indian man you wouldn't have written like that." (27) The reference was to Naipaul's rather satirical treatment of the black master of ceremonies: his formal clothes, his ungrammatical speech and his vanity.

Some of the chapters and short pieces in the book, which are in fact very dense, are entitled "Unwritten" stories because, as the author himself says, "they are at once historical and invented. There's crust of fact but within that the writer's fantasy is working."[2] The first "unwritten story" in the book is titled "New Clothes," which is about the narrator's first visit to South America, to the wilderness of the Guiana Highlands, an Amerindian no man's land on the frontiers of Venezuela, Brazil, now known as Guyana. The narrator, in this section, writes about Lucas and Mateo, two young Indian boys who tell him about the 'Kanaima,' the spirit of death of the forests which inhabits the body of a living man and "Djukas" the descendants of the African runaways who had settled in some parts of the forest. The chapter ends with their showing of the clothes to the narrator, sent by an English man to their grandfather—"new clothes off three hundred and fifty years before, relic of an old betrayal." (67)

Drawing a distinction between himself and Joyce, Woolf and Lawrence, Naipaul points out in his interview with Aamer Hussein that he considers it appropriate for a postcolonial writer to "rethink" all forms including history and fiction. In that sense, he says his densely written stories are "Unwritten" because they are at once historical and invented and an account of civilization at a "hinge moment." As Naipaul points out, the diarist Pepys was a great new discovery. Thus the unwritten art of Naipaul in *A Way in the World* shows history as an interplay of various peoples, various traditions which intermingle but which retain their particularity. His accounts of the postcolonial societies, their cultural loss, replacement and borrowing and the particularity retained in an obliterating generality of incursion are cast in a form of narrative which, as Naipaul says, exposes the falsities of the literary novel that apply the George Eliot county society to Burma or India.

The following chapter, "Passenger: *A Figure from the Thirties*" is about Foster Morris, the writer of *The Shadowed Livery,* a book about Tubal Uriah Butler, a radical leader of Grenadines before the oil strike of 1937.

Foster Morris, a character from the British literary establishment, said of Naipaul's first novel *The Mystic Masseur,* "I have read your book and my advice to you is to abandon it immediately." (86) Naipaul was further advised by the same Foster Morris to read Chekhov, Hemingway, and Graham Greene. Curiously enough, the discouraging response was to act like a tonic on Naipaul that inspired him to make a fresh start as a writer:

> I thought I would turn away from what I had done, and go back to the beginning: try to see whether I couldn't make writing out of concrete statements, adding meaning to meaning in simple stages. . . . and I learned as a new truth what I really had always known, and what so far in my writing. . . . I had suppressed that comedy the preserver we in Trinidad had always known, was close to me, a double inheritance, from my story-telling Hindu family, and from the Creole street life of Port of Spain. (87)

The result was the somewhat Hemingwayesque *Miguel Street*—a vibrant anthology of street stories about life in Port of Spain. And still Foster Morris continued to patronize Naipaul's next novel—*A House for Mr. Biswas*—till Naipaul "could set this disciple-guru relationship aside" (97) and get on with the job of writing. After a gap of some years, Naipaul happened to meet Graham Greene in 1967 at Antibes, which meeting helped him gain a better perspective both on Foster Morris and on writing in general.

> He was precocious, as Greene had said. A precocious writer doesn't have much experience to work on: his talent isn't challenged. The quickness of such a writer lies in assuming the manner and sensibility of his elders. Foster Morris's runaway adolescent experience and his "rebellious" style as an undergraduate had disguised his essential mimicry, and later made it hard for him to find himself. (101)

Quite in line with Foster Morris's judgements about Naipaul's writings are those of Lebrun—a Trinidadian Panamanian communist of the 1930s, which of course are expressed in a metaphorical way in one of the Russian 'thick magazines.' It proved a revelation to Naipaul to be told about the essential "helplessness of his characters":

> He said I was writing about people impoverished in every way, people on whom history had played a cruel trick. My characters thought they were free men, in charge of their own destinies; they weren't; the colonial settings mocked the delusions of the characters, their ambitions, their belief in perfectibility, their jealousies. The books, light as they were, were subversive, the article said, and remarkable for that reason. (109)

Lebrun seemed to advise Naipaul rather indirectly to train himself, to look through the surface reflections at what lay below which Naipaul seemed to have set aside, like a 'comment misplaced' and of no value to him because it was "denying me—who relished it so much—the gift of comedy (the discovery of which was still linked in my mind with getting started as a writer)." (109)

Chapter V is devoted to the romanticized notions regarding Lebrun, a permanent exile, continuously "On the Run" in the social circles of London and New York. To begin with, he was a revolutionary. But he was not one of those men to whom power came. He disappeared after the elections as he had disappeared after the Butler oil field strike. When he was declared to be an undesirable immigrant by the Chief Minister of one of the West Indian islands, he fell into the role of an impresario of revolution which became his livelihood. Having no base of his own, he lacked popular following and had to attach himself to other leaders, simpler people in direct touch with the simple people who had given them power. And then after the excitement of the strike and the Charlie King affair he was bored. He was interned during the war. After that he became a member of the Legislative Council but preferred to stay in London. He had a great capacity for talk which opened doors for him all his life. But there was a hysteria there,

> the hysteria of the islands, expressed most usually in self-satire, jokeyness, fantasy, religious excess, sudden spasms of cruelty . . . the burning of Charlie King at the time of the strike in Trinidad and the almost religious, sacrificial regard for the victim ever afterwards. (129)

In extreme old age, Lebrun was fetched up in England, he was discovered as one of the prophets of black revolution. This role of the black spokesmen of the century pilgrimaging from one African country to another brought him a kind of fulfillment.

The chapter also throws light on Richard Blair who rises from the clerkship in the Government House in Port of Spain to the post of economic adviser to a revolutionary socialist state in East Africa, where he is killed. Naipaul seems to be mocking at the political ambitions of these semi-tragic heroes all along. And from them Naipaul goes seamlessly to the conventional heroes of history whose fame came from their claim to comprehend or conquer unknown worlds, as has been the case with the Western writers who made the West Indians see a vacuum in place of their own history. In London, their value came from their claim to be able to show the West another world that becomes more and more of a myth that quietly fails to interest, making these writers experience "disregard."

Regarding the conventional heroes of history, Naipaul chooses to recreate Walter Raleigh's second, failed expedition to his "El Dorado" in South America. This account of Walter Raleigh is followed by a fictionalized account of Francisco Miranda's attempted revolution in the nineteenth century Venezuela. Both men, at the end of their lives, are seen to be paying the price of having believed themselves to be larger than the worlds they claimed to see. These two adventurers, who in fact are the "Villains" in his early book, *The Loss of El Dorado* (1970), now become "tragic" heroes in the new, altered perspective.

Raleigh's journal, "The Discovery of the Large, Rich and Beautiful Empire of Guiana," and Miranda's private papers found a hundred years later by an American researcher in 1922 in the Bathurst Library in Cirencester in Gloucestershire are the principal sources of Naipaul's imaginative reconstruction of their horrendous lives. They "provide an oblique analogue to Naipaul's own explorations into the world's and his own numerous areas of darkness."[3]

In writing about Walter Raleigh in the chapter entitled "A Parcel of Papers, A Roll of Tobacco, a Tortoise," Naipaul adopts a remarkably novel technique. The contents of Raleigh's journal come as a conversation between Raleigh and his surgeon, at the time of his second adventure to El Dorado. This method happens to have the advantage of filling up those gaps that Walter Raleigh seemed to have skipped deliberately in his journal with the surgeon often referring to the contents of the Spanish records concerned. The surgeon is often found accusing Walter Raleigh of his atrocious behaviour towards the Spanish people and Indians. And, he, in turn provides the readers with first-hand information that he gets from Sir Walter Raleigh in the form of answers to his questions.

Accusing Walter Raleigh of his utter lack of concern for people like Francis Sparrow, Keymis who went to look for El Dorafio, the surgeon says,

> And look where it's brought you back. Look where it's got us all, waiting in this muddy Gulf for news, of your son and news of your lieutenant Keymis. From time to time during the day the Spaniards in Trinidad will fire off a shot to let us know they are watching. . . . Yet the day after you arrived you wrote to your wife that you could still be king of the Indies. (170-71)

And Raleigh replies thus:

> I rescued all the Trinidad Indian little kings or chiefs from the Spaniards. I was the first man here ever to punish the Spaniards for what they had done. I killed the Spaniards in Port of Spain and broke open the jail in their town in land and set the kings free, and their people burned the Spanish town. (172)

While the wait for the news about Captain Keymis and Raleigh's son (sent to San Tome, a Spanish territory in search of gold) continues, the surgeon refers to the journey of 1595,

> That journey of 1595 had begun with murder, it had ended with a massacre of your people and the stench of death in the ships. And all you had to show for it was sand. . . . You had to prove that you were not a fool, that you had found something more important than gold or booty. You had found a new empire for England, an empire of willing Indian subjects. So you wrote a difficult book, mixing up fantasy and history with your own real explorations. Everything on this side of the Gulf was real, everything on that side was fantasy. . . . The story was in the title; that was as far as most people would get. *The Discovery of the Large, Rich, and Beautiful Empire of Guiana, with a Relation of the Great and Golden City of Manoa (which the Spaniards call El Dorado) and Other Countries with their Rivers adjoining. Performed in the year 1595 by Sir Walter Raleigh Knight.* (177)

The next part of the story comes from the viewpoint of Don Jose, an aboriginal Indian, son of the former governor of San Tome who was sent by Captain Keymis to Raleigh to deliver a letter that carries the news of the death of Raleigh's son killed in an encounter with the Spanish people at San Tome. The anguish and suffering that Raleigh experiences becomes intensely pathetic as it comes from the point of view of his so-called enemy, Don Jose, who says: "When the surgeon left and we were alone in the cabin, the old man would go silent. In daylight and in darkness I could feel him grieving for his son and thinking of his own death." (194) Though he knew full well that there existed no gold in San Tome, he restrained himself from saying so for it was in this illusion or mad faith that the old man was hoping to find some meaning for his life that is yet to be lived out: "we had to bear with the general in his madness, that this madness was all that remained of his life now, that this rage had given the sick-man who had lost his son a kind of life." (197) Don Jose's concern and love for the old man, Walter Raleigh, till the very end of the latter's life is also suggestive of one of very significant themes of the story, that is, "the enemy becomes the man you love. The chain just goes on and on. You have to break the chain at some stage and say: I can't carry on living like this, it's too painful, let me get away."[4] As Don Jose admits: "It was strange I had hated Don Diego, the governor. Then I grieved for him. Now I began to grieve for the man who had killed Don Diego." (188)

The last lines of the chapter strike a particular chord though the music is not instantly recognizable. "I think, father, that the difference between us, who are Indians, or half Indians and people like the Spaniards and the English and the Dutch and the French, people who know how to go where they are going, I think that for them the world is a safer place." (205) It is true that the world is safer for those who know where they are going implying that the world is a safer place for the colonizer. The man who says these words is the aboriginal Indian who has turned out to be safer than all the people he has served. Though the world is safer, for those who come from Europe, it was not safer for Raleigh or the Spanish governor whom the speaker had served, and who died rather badly. Thus, though there is a truth about the lines quoted above, there seems to be an internal, a developing irony in it which is quite in line with the above-mentioned theme—that the enemy becomes the man one loves.

The chapter "A New Man," is about the author's references to the research that he made both before and after writing the book, *The Loss of El Dorado,* regarding the geographical and cultural histories of Venezuela and Trinidad, which "was an out crop of Venezuela; for three hundred years they had been part of the same province of the Spanish empire." (211) The narrator has many interesting things to tell, in this chapter, about the Cocoa Woods, oil fields of Venezuela and above all, about Manuel Sorzano, a Surinam-born carpenter settled in Venezuela who seemed to have found a gold hoard while working in one of the Old plantation barracks in Venezuela.

"In the Gulf of Desolation" unravels the story of Miranda. Behind this story is noticeable Naipaul's own strong desire to portray the slave society, the new calendars on this aboriginal land, and which was in fact the parent of the Trinidadian society in which he himself grew up. But the depiction is done in an indirect fashion.

Miranda, a Spanish American, who had left Venezuela after thirty-five years was called out from London by Bolivar and others soon after the start of the real revolution in Venezuela. When Miranda comes home, he does not see Negroes. On the very first day he arrives, he hears people outside talking a strange language and when he goes to the window he sees Africans working in the grounds. Miranda says: "This is a kind of homecoming for me, after thirty-five years. It is quite amazing. I know this rainy-season smell. . . . I feel I know this place very well. It is my own. It exists in my mind. But it is full of strangers I don't like the sensation. I feel a great gap." (253) Then he comes to the plantation house, and he smells the cocoa beans sweating, it is a smell from his childhood. Then he sees the girls in the distance moving strangely, dragging their feet through the drying beans. "They were 'dancing' the cocoa, moving slowly toes pressing down, through the beans." (303) That was work, to arrive at that solution in order to have the slaves always there, but not true presences.

To portray the slave society, Naipaul makes use of the story of Miranda and his attempted revolution in the nineteenth century as a gloss. It is an act of imaginative reconstruction and recovery of a lost history. Miranda's story is the story of a man who pays the price of having believed himself to be larger than the worlds he claimed to explore. At one point he is seen lamenting thus:

> It's strange, but I have never been in a situation like this before. In Caracas I was the son of a rich and prominent man. Even as a child I was known. I grew up feeling famous. Later in Spain I was an extravagant colonial, and then I was a captain in the Princess Regiment. I suppose I floundered for a while when I left the Spanish service and went to the United States. I had to pick my way,

> and I had to improvise all the time. But at the end of my time in the United States I had given myself a character that well-placed people could recognize. In England, France, Russia, I became known for my political cause. It is a very special cause I have always been somebody. Here now, so close to home; I see no kind of recognition in people's eyes, and I feel as though I am losing pieces of myself. (300-1)

Another dominant theme explored in these two sections—those on Walter Raleigh and Miranda—seems to be the theme of revolution and the idea of the revolutionary as a damaged man. The revolutionaries, about whom everyone, including the author, entertains some theatrical and heroic ideas turn out to be neither defiant, nor fierce, nor even full of faith: "They were more like people who had been dealt a bad hand, had taken a wrong turning, and who would somehow always be out of reach, always dealing with their private demons." (348)

Naipaul presents the reader with some material "sketched in strokes rather than painted in heavy colours."[5] He repeats things in different ways, thus making the reader remember what he reads. For instance, he repeats Miranda's story four times in the course of the book. He makes use of different points of view, and most of it comes in the form of an exchange of letters between Miranda and his wife, Sally. The method adopted to arrive at an illusion of knowledge makes it easier for the reader to approach unfamiliar material. To familiarize the reader with the unfamiliar material, the author repeats the contents again and again from different viewpoints.

The book which has rightly been called "A Sequence" opens in the Port of Spain with Leonard Side, a mortician, and after recreating the doomed adventures of such conventional heroes of history as Sir Walter Raleigh and Francisco Miranda (whose fame came ironically from their claim to comprehend or conquer unknown worlds), closes with the brutal murder of Blair in East Africa. What is unique about the book is the new kind of form that Naipaul has arrived at in order to deliver the truth, to deliver a form of reality especially when one is dealing with real people.

The book, *A Way in the World,* as the author himself says, turns out to be

> a way of dealing with all the strands of Caribbean or New World background, the place, and all the different stages of learning about it, as well. The learning is important, and the form I've arrived at seems to me truer and more natural than any artificial narrative. . . My story does have connections; they are associations. They are inseparable from the background.[6]

The citation implies that an interplay of associations—the landscape as well as the mindscape—plays a dominant role in the method invented by Naipaul in writing the book, *A Way in the World.* The interplay of associations makes everyone read his own book, depending on his own nature and his need for making it important for each reader in its own way. Some might pick up certain half-buried associations and not see others that are more prominent. It is this rare quality, the inventive narrative that makes the book unique even when the subject matter is to do with history that is factual and not fictitious or inventive.

NOTES

1. V.S. Naipaul, A *Way in the World: A Sequence* (London: Minerva, 1995).
2. Aamer Hussein, "Delivering the truth," interview with Naipaul, *Times Literary Supplement, The Hindu* (Sunday Magazine), 2 Oct. 1994, p. 6.
3. T.G. Vaidyanathan, "Call it a Naipaul," Review of V.S. Naipaul's *A Way in the World, The Hindu* (Sunday Magazine), Aug. 21, 1994, p. 3.
4. "Delivering the truth," p. 6.
5. *Loc. cit.*
6. *Loc. cit.*

Half a Life: A Critical Appraisal

SANTWANA HALDAR
F.M. College, Balasore

Half a Life (2001), the latest novel by V.S. Naipaul, the Nobel Laureate for literature for the year 2001, is set in three locales—India, England and Africa. Though the novelist writes at the beginning that the book is "not exact about the countries, periods or situations it appears to describe,"[1] the readers do not fail to count which are exact. A princely state in British India, untouched by colonial agitation, is the setting of the first part of the novel; the second is set in post-war London with its dingy West End Clubs and lonely pavements; and the third is set in a province of Portuguese Africa living out the last days of colonialism. These settings are not bare sketches meant for the background of an internal drama. These are integral parts of the novel, directly taken from life and rendered ironically, and with a sting of sarcasm. Be it a fiction like *The Mimic Man* (1967) or a non-fictional writing like *An Area of Darkness*, Naipaul's chief concern has always been the network of corruption, moral laxity and intellectual complacency, secretly destroying all human values. When the locale is America or England, as in, say, *A Bend in the River* and *The Enigma of Arrival*, Naipaul raises his finger at the dark corners of Western civilization. *Half a Life* is not an exception. Whenever he finds any discrepancy between the ideal norm and the existing one, he uses words which are what Brice-Parrain calls "loaded pistols."[2] He fires at pretences, moral laxity and other sources of corruption.

The protagonist of the novel *Half a Life*, Willie Chandran, born of a brahmin father and a scheduled caste mother, leaves India and goes first to England, and then to Africa, and the narrative veers accordingly. The first part of the novel is entitled 'A

Visit from Somerset Maugham.' The chapter records confessional life history of the protagonist's father who was almost universally accepted as a Gandhian saint, and who had the rare opportunity to be included as a saintly figure in Somerset Maugham's *The Razor's Edge*. The confession by Willie's father reveals his opportunism and pretences, "the spiritual source of *The Razor's Edge*"[3] being dragged to the ground. The myth of Indian spirituality created enthusiastically by some foreign scholars is thus deconstructed by Naipaul.

Willie's great grandfather belonged to the respectable priestly community which was once very rich and prosperous. The community began to be poor after the Muslim invasion in India, and the situation worsened after the arrival of the British. Forced by the pangs of hunger, Willie's great grandfather came to a big town where the maharaja was living. He managed somehow to get the job of a letter writer and became able to make a fair living. Eventually he and his son got respectable jobs as clerks in the maharaja's palace, and a better prospect was chalked out for Willie's father. Willie's father visualized a possible collapse of the easy life around the maharaja and his palace, and began to think of some new way to protect himself against that breakdown. He thought he was ripe for political action. But independent movement being illegal in the maharaj's state, he could not join politics. He started hating the studies; and sometime in 1931 or 1932 he heard that the mahatma had called for students to boycott their universities and the call suited him. He made a little bonfire of *The Mayor of Casterbridge* and other books which he had already started hating, in the front yard of the college, failing yet to raise any storm thereby. Feeling more useless than ever, he now fell upon the mahatma's call for removing casteism.

> The decision was nothing less than to make a sacrifice of myself. Not an empty sacrifice, the act of a moment—any fool can jump off a bridge or throw himself in front of a train—but a more lasting kind of sacrifice, something the mahatma would have approved of. He had spoken much about the evils of casteism. No one had said

> he was wrong, but very few had done anything about it. . . . My decision was to marry the lowest person I could find. (10-11)

Here is a keen observation and an ironic rendering of the way Mahatma Gandhi's message was distorted and exploited by the opportunists in India. Similar observations from Naipaul's non-fictional writing may be cited for confirming the view that Naipaul's intolerance with the distortion of facts in the writings of popular authors and the pretences of the common people is visible both in his novels and in his non-fictional works.[4]

In *Half a Life*, Naipaul hardly uses any derogatory word. The use of first person in the first section helps him to stray from his usual way of direct attack. The task of finding out the discrepancy between an actual sacrifice suggested by Gandhi and the fake one devised by Willie's father, is left to the readers. Naipaul only gives us the story as uttered by the character himself. Quite unaware of his moral degradation, Willie's father repeatedly refers to his "Sacrifice" which was criticized later by his son. He tells his son naively, that the possible bride, a backward girl in the college, coarse featured and noticeably black, was already sought. After a series of attempts to come close to the girl and propose to her, he got the information from the girl that her maternal uncle, a firebrand union leader, had seen them together and was going to take out a procession against him protesting thereby the ill-treatment of the upper class inflicted on a backward girl. Frightened and confused, Willie's father had to find a secret place for her at the back of the image makers' store house. To meet her expenses, he had to earn money as a tax collector in the Land Tax department, though that kind of servile labour had formed no part of his vision of the life of sacrifice. There was again no sympathetic understanding between the two. Distorting the thoughts on financial exploitation, Willie's father took the side of the cheats who, according to him, were being exploited by the system of tax collection and explained to himself that all this was a form of civil disobedience. "I became a kind of Saboteur, and it gave me great pleasure to think that in this office, without making any big statement, I was conducting my own kind of civil disobedience." (22) Ironically, he had big promotions: "It did not matter how badly I did my job, how much I sabotaged, they continued to promote me. It was like civil disobedience in reverse." (23) The readers may recall Naipaul's direct attack on Indian bureaucracy in his non-fictional writings.[5]

When Willie's father got repeated promotions, the principal in the Maharaja's College tried to get his daughter married to him. Willie's father then told his father, much to the latter's disappointment and rage, all about the backward class girl. When his father accused him of throwing their inheritance away, Willie's father took up the pose of doing sacrifice in the way shown by the mahatma.

> I said, 'Now is the time for sacrifice.'
> 'Sacrifice, sacrifice, why?'
> 'I am following the mahatma's call.'
> That made my father stop, and I said, 'I am sacrificing the only thing I have to sacrifice.'
> It was a line that had come to me the evening before. (24)

There could hardly be a better use of sarcasm for exposing the fact that from the very beginning Gandhism has been used in India as a facade to hide one's vested interest.

Naipaul's satire becomes more pinching when Willie's father escapes severe punishment for the corruption in tax collection under the protection of the backward movement. If was the backward girl's uncle, the firebrand union leader, who took out a procession of the backward people outside the palace or the secretariat, defending the cause of Willie's father.

> I know that if it wasn't for the firebrand, no amount of sanctuary was going to save me from the courts. It occurred then to me to do as the mahatma had done at some stage: to take a vow of silence. It suited my temperament, and it also seemed the least complicated way out. (28)

The news of his taking vow of silence spread and he became at once a holy man. A blending of satire and humour, as evident in these descriptions, differentiates Naipaul's art as a novelist from that of a writer of non-fictional works. The description of how the name of Willie's father became associated with the mahatma and his vow of silence, and the campaigning by the backwards for the upper class culprit's right to marry a backward girl provoke laughter and at the same time lay bare the pretences.

It was during the time when Willie's father remained detached from everything, thanks to his vow of silence, that Somerset Maugham and his friend came to visit him. They were accompanied by the school principal and Willie's father had every reason to be afraid of being exposed before the foreign writer. But the principal who belonged to the elite, was aware of his role as a good servant of the maharaja's tourist department, and he told the foreign writer what he wanted to hear. Hence he boasted about the 'bright prospects' Willie's father had, and which he mysteriously gave away, preferring the life of an ascetic. The headmaster is used by Naipaul for establishing the fact that the Indian intellectuals also contributed to the formation of the myth of Indian ascetics who give up the prospects of the materialistic world and aspire for the spiritual bliss.

Willie's father is rendered as a lampoon when he confesses that he could not stick to his vow of sexual abstinence.

> Privately, in the recesses of my heart, I took a vow of sexual abstinence, a vow of brahmacharya. Like the mahatma. Unlike him I failed. I was full of shame. (33)

And the gentle humour turns to be ludicrous hilarity in the confession that follows:

> My utter wretchedness, my self disgust can be imagined when. . . in spite of my private vow of brahmacharya. . . Willie's mother became pregnant again (35)

The first section, 'A Visit from Somerset Maugham' ends with a brief conversation between Willie and his father, and Willie expresses his contempt for his father.

This section is named after Somerset Maugham in order to highlight the fact that Maugham missed the reality while portraying an Indian ascetic in *The Razor's Edge*. In *An Area of Darkness*, Naipaul had referred to the influence of a book like *The Razor's Edge* on the Indian mind and criticized the Indian temperament. Naipaul had it, "In India thoughtful men have preferred to turn their backs on the here and now and to satisfy what President Radhakrishnan calls 'The basic human hunger for the unseen.' It is not a good qualification for the writing and reading of novels. A basic hunger for the unseen makes many Indians vulnerable to novels like *The Razor's Edge* and *The Devil's Advocate*, whose value as devotional literature is plain. Beyond this there is uncertainty.

Naipaul wants to replace 'the unseen' by the seen and thus the portrait of Willie's father reveals what he has seen in India. He came to India for the first time in the early Sixties, to search for his roots. His search for an alternative civilization sanctified by the Orientalist lore received a setback, as he was rudely shocked by the abject poverty, corruption, pretensions and intellectual complacency. His immediate reaction of utter disappointment was let loose and took the form of derogatory portrayals in *An Area of Darkness* (1964) and *A Wounded Civilization* (1977). In *India: A Million Mutinies Now* (1990), Naipaul's attitude to India seems changed, as the immediate reaction of disappointment has been over. In *Half a Life*, he attempts to render his feelings in an objective way. The portrait of Willie's father, who is given no name in the novel, is meant for a substitute of Somerset Maugham's Indian saint. Without using any derogatory remark Naipaul serves his purpose through ironic presentation.

The second section entitled 'The First Chapter' starts with Willie Chandran's experiences in mission school. He is ashamed of his father and gets irritated when somebody asks him about his father's career. The description of his mother's experiences as a child in her school is a direct attack on Indian caste system. In her school, Willie's mother found that a ragged and half-starved school servant was giving out water from a barrel. When a student appeared before him for water, he poured water into a brass vessel or an aluminium one. Willie's mother wondered in a childhood way whether she should get brass or aluminum. When she came to the servant no choice was offered to her.

> The ragged half-starved man became very angry and frightening and made the kind of noise he would have made before he beat a stray dog. (38)

And then he found a dirty tin in which he poured for the girl. That was how Willie Chandran's mother learned that in the world outside, aluminium was for Muslims, Christians and people of that sort, brass was for people of the caste, and a rusty old tin was for her. She spat on the tin and ran away.7 Willie inherited his mother's hatred towards the people of the upper caste. Mixed with that hatred was his disgust with his father, and he grew restless. As a child, he loved his mother and was eager to do something for her. But gradually, he began to look at his mother from distance. Tortured by desolation and hatred, he felt an urge to hide himself from others and longed to go to Canada from where the teachers in his school came. He even thought of being a missionary. All his secret emotions got released in the compositions which he had to write in his class. In one such composition about his holidays, Willie pretended he was a Canadian, with parents who were called 'Mom' and 'Pop.' Mom and pop had one day decided to take kids to the beach and the children with their new holiday clothes had driven off in the family car to the beach. Willie took all these details about foreign life from American comic books which were circulated in the mission school. This composition was awarded full marks, ten out of ten. Willie showed it to his mother and left it on the table in the verandah where his father used to take his morning coffee. Willie's father read the composition and understood his ambition. None of them mentioned the composition in their conversation, and Willie began to despise his father more than ever. Again, he left one composition for his father who got agitated after reading it. Willie seemed to challenge him through his compositions, but his father chose to remain silent. Willie began to think that he was not only a fraud but a coward. One day Willie expressed his desire to go to Canada, and even liked to be a missionary for that, much to the disappointment of his parents. As the bitterness developed more and more, Willie wrote a story entitled 'A Life of Sacrifice' which was a direct attack on his father in particular and on the brahmin community in general. Willie's father read the story and felt that his son's mind was diseased and again he followed the way of the mahatma.

> I cannot deal rationally with this kind of hatred, I will deal with it in the way of the mahatma, I will ignore it. I will keep a vow of silence so far as he is concerned. (47)

Naipaul's evaluation of Gandhi as expressed here is shared by a number of historians. When things went against him and he could not manage them rationally, Gandhi depended on his vow of silence.

Willie was however disillusioned when he saw a missionary magazine showing on its cover a picture of a priest with glasses and a wristwatch standing with one foot on the statue of Buddha and chopping it down with an axe. That picture exorcised the desire of being a missionary from Willie's mind; disappointed from all sides he even stopped going to school. Willie's father now tried his best to make an arrangement for Willie in some foreign country through corresponding to the famous foreigners who had come to visit his ashram. At last a place and a scholarship was found for Willie in a college of Education for mature students in London where the rest of the second section 'The First Chapter' is set.

Naipaul's assessment of London, rendered through Willie's sensibilities, is typical of the novelist who himself came to London for making a romantic career for himself as a writer in a purely literary region, and was a bit disappointed.

> He knew that London was a great city. His idea of a great city was of a fairyland of splendour and dazzle, and when he got to London and began walking about its streets he felt let down. He was disappointed by Buckingham palace. He thought the maharaja's palace in his own state was far grander, more like a palace, and this made him feel, in a small part of his heart, that the kings and queens of England were impostors, and the country a little bit of sham. His disappointment turned to something like shame—at himself, for his gullibility—when he went to Speaker's Corner. (52)

Almost a similar disappointment was uttered by the narrator in *The Enigma of Arrival* (1987) after he had arrived in Bard country. The narrator found that the river was called the Avon, not the one connected with Shakespeare.

Willie's struggle in London helped him to come close to reality. When he found no help from his father's friends who had gone to his ashram and had praised him highly, he understood that the world had not been easy for his father, This experience helped him to see his father in the proper perspective. Naipaul has also exposed the pretensions in London life through Willie's eyes. Willie found that the college was "full of various pieces of tradition, that the teachers and students were proud of but could not explain . . . it was a piece of make-believe . . . the old rules were a kind of make believe." (59-60) To this world of make-believe, Willie gets himself adjusted by remaking himself and his past. And he tells lies to remake his past, avoiding those elements of his life for which he had been ashamed.

> he speaks of his mother as belonging to an ancient Christian community of the subcontinent, a community almost as old as Christianity itself. He kept his father as a brahmin. He made his father's father a courtier. So playing with words, he began to re-make himself. It excited him and began to give him a feeling of power. (61)

Thus the character of Willie Chandran emerges as one who experiments with one pose after another, almost following the footsteps of his father, to place himself in a comfortable position.

Since his childhood, Willie had showed his competence in imaginary writings moulded in lucid language. This talent mixed up with his poses helped him to be a news correspondent and even a writer of short stories. His sexual experiences in London, on the other hand, helped him get confidence in himself. It was his friend Persey who acquainted him to the world of sex. Willie came in contact with Persey's girl friend June and came to know about his weakness as a man. He also compared his father's life-style in India to the life-style he himself has been acquainted with in London, and feels pity for his father. To his Indian sensibility, the world of sex appears rather brutal.

In London, Willie came in contact with a lot of people belonging to different races, who had come to London to try their luck. He learnt that people in London wanted West Indian chaps to drive the buses, but nobody in London liked to rent rooms for the accommodation of the black people. So some black people like Persey were encouraged to buy properties and rent to West Indian drivers. Naipaul has thus detected the maladies almost clinically, sparing none. Willie's script about the old Christian community in India, which was broadcast by the B.B.C. for the Commonwealth programme, is another example of falsity exposed in the novel. Willie prepared a fake story that was accepted without any verification. Willie wrote about "the feeling of separateness from the rest of India; no true knowledge of the other religions in India; the family's work in the British time as social reformers; people of Christian conscience champions of workers' rights. The writer's discovery of the tension between the old Christian community and the new Christian backwards, recent converts, depressed people, full of grievances." (77-78) Willie knew what was expected of him and did his job well. His imaginary description was accepted as fact. His report on an exhibition of woodcarving by a young west African is another example of falsity. Willie was sent as a reporter by the B.B.C to cover the exhibition and he made his script without any prior knowledge of wood carving. And for all such jobs he found himself in demand, and was able to change his financial condition. Naipaul's first-hand knowledge of the process by which news scripts are produced for broadcast by the B.B.C. enables him to offer a real story behind the screen, though this time a direct way of satire is kept aside.

Willie's friendship with Roger gave him double benefit. First, it was Roger who criticized the technique of Willie's stories and asked him to write on the model of Hemingway. Willie followed him and was benefitted. Secondly, Roger introduced him to his editor and other literary personalities, and helped Willie to get his book published. When Willie showed Roger some of his stories he wrote in his school days, Roger told him that he had not written real things, that his stories indicated that the writer was hiding something, Willie was mortified and felt burned with shame. Yet he wrote his stories on the model of Hemingway and Roger appreciated the changed version of the stories and asked him to carry on.

Roger also introduced Willie to his editor who, like the social figure Swann in Proust's work, liked to bring together dissimilar people. This occasion helped Naipaul to expand his theme into a study of different races including a study on interracial sex relationship. Willie is introduced to some 'modest' persons whose career is to pursue rich women. Naipaul also utilizes the opportunity of criticizing fake Marxism. Richard is called a bedroom Marxist. Explaining what he means by bedroom Marxist, Roga says:

> Marxism takes him to the bedroom, and Marxism stops in the bedroom. All the women he seduces knew that. They feel safe with him. It was like that in Oxford and it's still like that. The difference is that at Oxford it thrilled his common soul just to sleep with rich women, and now he takes large sums of money off them. Of course he's made his mistakes. . . . Richard is in publishing, quite rich now, and rising fast. As a publisher his Marxism makes him more attractive than ever. The more he takes off the ladies the more other ladies rush to give him. (91-92)

Exploitation in the name of Marxism is thus openly attacked in the novel. The naked picture of racism and sexual oppression in England reveals the uncompromising attitude of Naipaul.

Peter is another character who scored "notable success" in making money through his relationships with foreign girls. He is also exposed mercilessly:

> Peter's style is entirely different. His background is more modest, country estate agent and at Oxford he began to develop his English gentleman style. Oxford is full of young foreign women studying English at various language schools. Some of them are rich. Peter by some instinct ignored the university women and chose to operate among these people. They would have thought him the genuine article, and he, quicker than they, learning soon to sort the wheat from the chaff, scored some notable successes (92).

Naipaul has also shown how this sort of sexual relationship with other races changed the demography in some places. There is the African Marcus with his plan of having white grandchildren. As he says, his plan is not extraordinary. It is just repeating something that happened on a large scale in England a hundred and fifty years ago.

In the eighteenth century, there were about half a million black people in England.

> They've all vanished. They disappeared in the local population. They were bred out. The Negro gene is recessive one. If this were more widely known there would be a good deal less racial feeling than there is. (94-95)

The same history was repeated in South America, says Marcus: "there were large Negro populations in Buenos Aires and Uruguay in 1800. They disappeared in the local population. They were bred out. The Negro is recessive. Not many people know that." (97)

In support of Marcus's view, Richard gives an example from Thackeray's *Vanity Fair*. Thackeray's great London merchant wanted his son to marry a Negro heiress from St. Kitts in the West Indies. The Lady's fortune would have come from slaves and sugar. It is almost unthinkable that at that time a Negro heiress in London was greatly in demand. As Richards says, though Thackeray does not tell us anything about it, the Negro heiress would have married well and in a couple of generations would have been perfectly English and upper class. Richard also speaks of the possibility of a new reading of *Wuthering Heights* rendering Heathcliff a half-Indian child who was found near the docks of Liverpool. Naipaul has thus studied the past and future of interracial sex and marriage which adds a new dimension to the common racial feelings.

A detailed description of the race-riots in London is also given: "the race riots began in Notting Hill. The silent streets—with exposed rubbish bins daubed with house and flat numbers and with windows heavily curtained and screened and black—became full of excited people. The houses that had seemed tenanted only by the very old and passive now let out any number of young men in mock-Edwardian clothes who roamed the streets looking for blacks." (109)

In this background of racial riot, Willie was again affected by his earlier feeling of remaining hidden. As he found people casually saying, "Those blacks are going to be a menace," he felt at once threatened and ashamed. "He felt people were looking at him. He felt the newspapers were about him. After this he stayed in the college and didn't go out." (109) Willie's exceptional sensitivity as exposed in his encounters with the outer world including the world of sex that seemed to him to be brutal, is the central theme of the novel. Naipaul takes extra care in delineating how Willie came out of his fear of being exposed to the world—a baseless fear prompted by his extraordinary sensibility and an imaginative capacity—through his sexual experiences and his hankering for love. His conversations with the editor and the latter's reflection on life and writing helped Willie to realize himself and his past. The editor said that "Journalism is by its nature ephemeral," and that love is "the divine illusion." Willie was so influenced by the editor that in his next story he fitted the editor to the holyman (his father image) he had already written about in some of his stories:

> Up to this point the holy man had been seen from the outside: idle and sinister, living off the unhappy, waiting like a spider in his hermitage. Now, unexpectedly, the holy man showed his own unhappiness imprisoned in his way of life, longing to get away from his hermitage, and telling his story to a seeker from far away. (101)

The story grew in Willie's hand and took him by surprise, enabling him to look at his family and his life in a new way. Over the next few days he found the matter of many stories of a new sort. The stories seemed to be just waiting for him, and he continued writing for three or four weeks. And then he stopped writing. It was something like what the editor said 'romance with English literature.' A collection of those stories was however published. At the end of the second section, Willie gets the news that his sister Sarojini is going to marry a German and the section ends with Willie's realization that everything goes on a bias, that the world should stop, but it goes on.

The third and the last section of the novel is entitled 'A Second Translation.' It depicts Willie's first experience of love which seemed to have elevated him to some higher realisation of fulfilment and which was rejected by him after eighteen years. The section starts with Willie's self-analysis which was provoked by his sister Sarojini who came to spend some days with him. He does not like to go home for at home he will have to marry a Sarojini-like girl and have to fight the battle his granduncle, the firebrand union leader, fought. He liked neither. Through Willie's views on sex, Naipaul expresses some of his own. One such view is that the ancient Indian philosophical-practical way of dealing with sex was destroyed by the Muslim invasion and the thing became worse during the British period. The third section describes Willie's love for Ana, who had African-Portuguese parentage, and his decision to go to Africa where Ana inherited a luxurious estate house built after 1914 war. Willie stayed there for eighteen long years and then he left Ana for good telling her that he can no more live her life. Leaving Ana, Willie goes to Columbia where Sarojini is living and all the details about his life in Africa are told by him to his sister. Naipaul gets thereby the opportunity to remain detached.

Willie confesses that he depended on Ana for being a man. Her strength and authority supplying him with necessary sustenance. They became emotionally attached as they found similarities between their backgrounds. Ana's grandfather, a Portuguese married an African and later when he grew rich, he chose Portuguese sons-in-law. Ana's mother left her Portuguese husband and remarried a man of mixed race. Ana's father forged his wife's money and left the home. In her stepfather's home, Ana was seduced by him. Because of all these experiences, Ana developed a vacuum in her mind and longed for love that would remove her loneliness. She married Willie with the devotion of a loyal wife. Willie acknowledges that he found a complete acceptance.

Side by side with the description of Willie's internal growth as a man, the third section also acquaints us with coexistence of the people belonging to different races. There were the Portuguese, the African-Portuguese, the Arabs of Muscat and Oman, commonly known as Mohammedan. As it is expected of Naipaul, the corruption in the government offices and the social organizations, and the basic moral degradation of man have not escaped his eyes. When Willie lost his passport and Ana advised him to write to his home for another passport, Willie remembers the Government offices in India and Naipaul gets a chance to criticize the way the Indian bureaucracy works. Willie remembers a typical Indian office.

> the pea-green walls shiny with grime at the levels of head and shoulders and bottom, . . . the floor black with dirt, the pan-chewing clerks in their trousers or lungis, each man correctly marked on the forehead with a fresh caste-mark (his principal duty of the day), on every desk the ragged stacks of old files in many faded colours, poor-quality paper crumbling away—and I knew that I would wait a long time in far-off Africa, and nothing would come. (1588)

About the African Government, Willie says that the Government was authoritarian but the people had no idea about it. They felt it to be far away, something in the capital. The village people had contact with the Government only during the Sisal cutting season when the estate holders made their requisitions from the prisons, and the convicts, properly guarded, were sent for the dangerous work of Sisal cutting. It was doubly dangerous; the long black point at the end of the Sisal blade is needle sharp and poisonous, and the area remains full of venomous snakes. Only the convicts could be compelled to do such a work. This description lays bare the inhuman ways supported by the Government and the callousness of the affluent. The authoritarian way of the government is further criticized:

> There had been no challenge to our authoritarian but easy going government for many years, and it had grown strangely lazy. In his great security the ruler had grown to feel that the details of governing were a burden, or so it appeared; and he had farmed out or

> leased out important governmental activities to eager energetic and loyal people. Those people became very rich; and the richer they became the more loyal they were, and the better they did the jobs they had been farmed out to them. So there was a kind of rough logic and effectiveness in this principle of government (169)

This is the typical ironic way of disclosing corruption, adopted by Naipaul. The novel also supplies the readers with examples taken from life. Willie describe how Mr. Correia grew more and more rich, and then was in deep trouble when he was used as a scapegoat by the big masters. Naipaul has thus chalked out another area of darkness.

The description of the children beggars and the children prostitutes complete the picture of corruption in Africa. Willie receives first-hand knowledge of all this and proceeds towards a 'full man.' His affair with the manager's wife Graca and Graca's strange relationship to her husband have been carefully dealt. The sudden change in Graca's mind after the illness of her husband makes an end of her relationship with Willie. This change in Willie's personal life goes side by side with the political change:

> The colonial government in the capital closed down just like that; The guerrillas took over. The Portuguese population began to leave. The army withdrew from the town. . . . The army hadn't really wished to fight the African war and the life in the town remained normal right up to the end. (224)

The establishment of the local government brought new problems for the non-Africans. The ante-Portuguese guerrillas had the support of the black government over the border. The new insurgents had the support of the white government to the west. Willie became more and more afraid. He did not have the stamina to go through another war. And one day he told Ana that he was going to leave her as he had been tired of living her life. He did not deny that Ana had done everything for him. The novel ends with Ana's reply that it was not really her life either. This comment by Ana throws a new light on her character, her loneliness and desperate attempt to make a relationship being exposed.

The abrupt end of the novel has been justified by Roger the journalist in the second section, 'The First Chapter.' Roger tells Willie,

> I know your great namesake and family friend (implying Somerset Maugham) says that a story should have a beginning, a middle and an end. But actually, if you think about it, life isn't like that. Life doesn't have a neat beginning and a tidy end. Life is always going on. You should begin in the middle and end in the middle, and it should all be there. (83)

Naipaul began his novel in the middle, and ended it in the middle, distorting the age-old form. But he has consciously followed the traditional narrative style the kind of which had been followed by, say, Tolstoy, Balzac and Flaubert. Naipaul, however, remains least concerned with the explosion in the world of novel caused by the stream of consciousness technique of James Joyce, and later by the projection of the multiple reality by the Latin American masters. Naipaul's is his own way, traditional and yet unique. He chose to be traditional as he felt that his colonial world, mixed second-hand and restricted, could be better expressed in that way.

NOTES

1. Naipaul wanted to make it clear that Willie's father was not the exact person whom Somerset Maugham met in India. But the way Maugham generalized Indian ascetic was not a fact either.
2. Qtd. Jean-Paul Sartre, *What is Literature*, trans. B. Frenchman (Methuen, 1983), p. 14.
3. *Half a Life* (Picador, 2001), p. 3.
4. In *An Area of Darkness*, Naipaul criticized Gandhi openly: "The *Gita's* selfless action is a call to self-fulfilment and at the same time a restatement of degree; it is the opposite of the service which Gandhi the Indian revolutionary, is putting forward as a practicable day to day ideal. . . . Gandhi's obsessions . . . seem ill-assorted and sometimes unpleasant." (Penguin, 1964), p. 74.
5. Naipaul attacked the Indian way of running government whenever he got an opportunity. (*Gita's* selfless action) . . . has created a

psychology which will frustrate all improving plans. It has led to the Indian passion for speech making, for gestures and for symbolic action. Symbolization, tree planting week (seventy percent of the trees planted die from lack of attention after the speeches), anti-fly week (declared in one week before the flies came, . . . malaria eradication week, "Help Eradication Malaria" daubed in English, on the walls of illiterate Hindi-speaking villages) . . . when the crisis occurs as during the Chinese invasion, the symbolic nature of the structure is made plain." *Ibid.*, pp. 78-79

6. *Ibid.*, p 217.
7. Naipaul's realistic attitude is once more expressed in his study of the tribal life which had been secluded from the mainstream. "They did not know about the religion of the people of caste or the Muslims or the Christians. They did not know what was happening in the country or the world. They had lived in ignorance, cut off from the world, for centuries." *Half a Life*, p. 3.

V.S. Naipaul's Such a Long Journey in Search of Soil and Roots: A Study of *Half a Life*

SAVITRI TRIPATHI
Govt. P.G. Arts & Comm. College, Bilaspur

In a literary Kumbh-Mela in New York in Feb. 2000, Leela Jacinto said, "V.S. Naipaul's 23 odd works of fiction and non-fiction have won him virtually every conceivable literary award barring of course, the Nobel."[1] But now let us stop worrying; Naipaul won the Nobel Prize for literature in the month of October 2001. Naipaul is the seventh Indian or person with Indian roots to be awarded Nobel Prize and second for literature after Rabindranath Tagore. The Nobel Prize came soon after the publication of *Half a Life*, his latest novel in which he has gone over his familiar domain—people of mixed descent in three countries—India, England and Mozambique—struggling to find their identities.

Born in a Hindu Brahmin family in Trinidad in 1932 and the son of an Indian Civil Servant, Naipaul has been based in England since the 1950s, yet has spent much of his life travelling around the world and seeking answers and inspiration. Like other unfortunate Indians who had to leave their motherland and move abroad as indentured labourer, his grandfather Naipaul Pandey migrated to Trinidad from Gorakhapur District of Uttar Pradesh under some economic compulsions but he could not forget the cultural ethos of his country. His son See Prasad also had with him the culture and tradition, but V.S. Naipaul, the grandson of this family was not satisfied at all with Indian ways of living, speaks the truth without malice because perhaps he had 'Utopian view' in his mind. All this can be seen in his earlier novels on

India. He writes: "It still horrifies me that the people should put food for animals on plates that they themselves use."[2]

In two books on India: *An Area of Darkness* and *India: A Wounded Civilization*, Naipaul's views are very aggressive and the books are the best examples of his negative nostalgia but in his third book on India, *India: A Million Mutinies Now*, his negative attitude towards India becomes soft and he realizes that he cannot liberate himself from Hindu past. Naipaul considers himself "a man without no country" and thinks himself an outsider. This is the reason that he can write cruelly and accurately about any country.

Half a Life depicts his attachment towards India. The novel is partly autobiographical and describes the story of a man whose origin always remains with him. It is a beautiful work of Naipaul about half-developed societies. It presents the lives of the people of three countries—India, England and Mozambique. It is a story of a man who goes to England from India on a scholarship and feels alienated there. The novel has three parts. The story of the first part is told to Willie Chandran by his father and reminds us of the background of V.S. Naipaul. The novelist writes.

> I must go back. We come from a line of priests. We were attached to a certain temple. I do not know when the temple was built or which ruler built it or for how long we have been attached to it; we are not people with that kind of knowledge. We of the temple priesthood and our families made a community. At one time I suppose we would have been a very rich and prosperous community, served in various ways by the people whom we served. But when the Muslims conquered the land we all became poor. The people we served could no longer support us. Things became worse when the British came. There was law, but the population increased. There were far too many of us in the temple community. This was what my grandfather told me. All the complicated rules of the community held, but there was actually very little to eat. People became thin and weak and fell ill easily. What a fate for our priestly community! I didn't like hearing the stories my grandfather told of that time, in the 1890s.[3]

Willie Chandran's father, an idler student of B.A. at the university, had no interest in literature, hears the call of Mahatma "for student to Boycott their university," ultimately decides to sacrifice his life and joins Mahatma's call. To get Mahatma's favour and to turn his back on his ancestry; he lives with a backward caste girl. When his father came to know about his ideas of sacrifices and he refusal to marry the daughter of the principal of 'Maharaja College,' he says "you have blackened all our faces and now we will have to face the anger of the school principal. You have dishonored his daughter." (24) Though he had not touched either of them and had not gone through any form of ceremony with either of them, there were two women whom he had dishonored.

As a result of not marrying with daughter of the principal, he is charged with corruption and forced to leave the job of Maharaja's Land Tax Department. He takes shelter in the courtyard of the temple. He takes a vow of silence, which was a great help to him in that situation. He lives there depending on the bounty of pilgrims to the temple and thus becomes a holy man. But he could not keep on living at the temple forever. He becomes a man of establishment of his own and "privately, in the recesses of my heart I took a vow of sexual abstinences, a vow of brahmacharya." (33) But very soon he becomes the father of Willie and again after sometime the father of a daughter who was given the name Sarojini, after the woman poet of the Independence movement, in the hope that a similar blessing might fall on her and for whom he wished an international marriage. "This was the story that Willie Chandran's father told. It took about ten years. Different things had to be said at different times. Willie Chandran grew up during the telling of this story." (35)

In the second part of the novel, we come to know that Willie and his sister Sarojini go to the mission school as their mother had had her education there. As Willie grew up, he, with the help of one of his father's friends and without any idea of what he knew, goes to London for higher studies. Uprooted from his own culture, Willie reaches London but is unable to get fulfillment anywhere. He comes in contact with many friends but cannot adapt to the culture of that place. Cut off from his roots and culture, he aimlessly floats like a survivor of a shipwreck, trying to find security but finds none anywhere. Naipaul deals with the crisis arising out of a change of environment, which is known as cultural shock. Cultural alienation today is a world phenomenon. A tree torn of its roots and transplanted somewhere else does not form healthy roots nor does it have normal growth. It needs soil and air of the place of its birth. It is only in one's own culture that one can find fulfillment. In spite of all his efforts to get used to the new environment, Willie is overtaken by the feeling of alienation. Willie in hope to get something that will place him both 'in and apart' from the world, he "was drawn to England to the immigrant community of post-war London, its dingy West End clubs, lonely pavements and sexual encounters, and even to the eccentric milieu of the English writer."[4]

Willie makes friendship with Percy Cato, a boy of Jamaican mixed parentage. They are both exotics and on scholarship. Percy Cato had an Indian grandmother. He lives bohemian immigrant life of London of the late 1950s and meets some frightening men. In one bohemian party, he meets a 'fattish' young man with a beard who worked for B.B.C. Willie on his advice writes a script and receives acceptance from the producer. They become friends. Willie again writes some stories about India and Indian themes. He sends these for publishing but after two or three weeks these come back. Thus Willie fails to establish himself as a writer: "let the book die. Let it fade away. Let me not be reminded of it. I will write no more." (123) He feels fulfilled when he meets Ana who is an admirer of his stories. She was young small and thin and quite pretty. Before meeting Ana, Willie was leading a half-life. He was in search of completeness: "And what was most intoxicating for Willie was that for the first time in his life he felt himself in the presence of someone who accepted him completely. At home his life had been ruled by his mixed inheritance. It spoilt everything. (125)

The period of his scholarship ends and Willie realizes that he believed the magic, becomes pathetic and thinks that college will throw him away: "My life is going to change completely. I will have to look for a place to stay. I will have to look for a job. It will be a different London then." (130) Ana comes in his life as a guide and protector. As he had nowhere else to go and did not want to lose Ana, so he goes to Africa with Ana. There he does not feel exotic and finds a complete acceptance. He feels 'first experience of love' that might bring him the fulfillment he so desperately seeks. His wife Ana leads him to her home, a province of Portuguese Africa, a country populated by desperate businessmen and their frustrated wives all uncertainly living out the last days of colonialism.[5] Ana came in his life like a flash of light guided him in his life. In her company he gets fulfillment. She was his anchor and Willie says to his sister Sarojini that it may be because of something in our culture that in spite of all appearance 'men are really looking for women to lean on.' Ana was timorous, so they matched each other and found comfort in each other company. He says: "Ana was important to me because I depended on her for my idea of being a man." (142) But very soon, Willie realizes that the world he had entered was only a half world and friendship is developed between Willie and estate manager Alvaro, the Corrieas who takes him to a big warehouse, where men and woman were dancing. He drinks beer and is invited by a girl. Fascinated by her extraordinary look, he follows her and feels 'a new idea of sex,' a new idea of his capacity and knows 'another kind of satisfaction.' He does not feel that he has betrayed Ana. During the visits to warehouse, he sees Julia's daughter, Ana's little maid who met Willie the first time on his arrival at Ana's estate house. Very soon Willie finds less and less pleasure in sex and thinks that the act of sex which used to excite him had 'grown mechanical.'

Willie meets Graca-Carla's convent school friend, the wife of the new manager. He feels strong desire in her eyes: "How terrible it would have happened, if I had died without knowing this depth of satisfaction, this other person that I had just discovered within myself." (205) But these sensuous affairs end. One day, Willie, amazed at himself, at the person he had become, says that he faces poor Ana every day without any shame. One day, he slips on the front steps of the estate house and become unconscious. When he woke up, he found himself in Military Hospital in town, among wounded black soldiers with shining faces and fire-red eyes. Post-Independence civil war starts and he feels: "The physical pain of my damaged body was like the other pain that had been with me for months and perhaps for years." (227) When Ana came to see him, he says, 'I am going to leave you. I have given you eighteen years. I can't give you any more. I can't live your life any more. I want to live my own.' Finally, he leaves Ana and goes to Berlin to his sister Sarojini.

Thus Willie, uprooted from his own culture, cannot get any permanent fulfillment anywhere. He fails to adjust anywhere and ultimately comes to live with his sister. Willie leads a half-life. His sister Sarojini is also living a half-life, wandering here and there with her German husband whose occupation is to make films. Willie's friend Percy Cato too is leading a half-life and has no proper place to stay. Willie and Percy Cato belong to the same background. Willie had not really known what to make of a man "who appeared to have no proper place in the world." (62) Greca and her husband also lead a half-life. They move from town to town, house to house and job to job. It was very difficult to establish himself as "The local rich people controlled everything and didn't allow the poor man to live." (209) Almost all the characters struggle for existence but fail to find perfection or completeness.

V.S. Naipaul speaks the truth without malice. There is honesty in his writings. He always writes about real things because he believes that the writer should not have any secret. A great poet, critic and Nobel Prize winner T.S. Eliot also believes in depicting the harsh reality of 'inner voice.' Naipaul feels agony in half-developed societies and pines for 'Utopia.' But it is impossible to have completeness. Naipaul calls himself a man without a country and an outsider who is in search or roots. He writes clearly about societies not because he is against any country or religion in particular but against 'Avidya' in general. He wants to see a complete and developed society. He has written cruelly and accurately about our defecating masses, our filth, and our pollution, our poverty and confusion in his earlier novels. We become angry but is it not true? Naipaul at first never called himself Indian but now he calls India 'a home of my ancestors.'

Thus the novel shows that a man may pick up ways and habits of better civilized societies but his own background forms a base of all his growth and achievement in later life. One can find fulfillment only in his own culture. "He is to a very high degree a cosmopolitan writer, a fact that he himself considers to stem from his lack of roots; he is unhappy about the cultural and spiritual poverty of Trinidad, he feels alienated from India, and in England he is incapable of relating to and identifying with the traditional values of what was once a colonial power."[6] The story tells us that uprooted from his own culture, man feels identity crises, because one cannot cut off from his own culture, neither can adopt fully the foreign culture. "*Half a Life* is a devastating work of exceptional sensitivity, grace and humour. In its depiction of love fulfilled and thwarted, in its vision of the half-lives quietly lived out at the center of our restless world. V.S. Naipaul's new novel brings its own unique illumination to another aspect of our shared humanity."[7] The language of the book has dignified simplicity. It has its own style. Unaffected by literary fashion and models, he has wrought existing genres into a style of his own in which customary distinctions between fiction and non-fiction are of subordinate importance.

NOTES

1. *The Sunday Times of India*, Review, Feb. 20, 2000.
2. V.S. Naipaul, *An Area of Darkness* (Penguin, 1964), p. 47.
3. V.S. Naipaul, *Half a Life* (London: Picador, 2001).
4. *Ibid.*, cover jacket.
5. *Ibid.*
6. *Times of India*, New Delhi, Oct. 12, 2001.
7. V.S. Naipaul, *Half a Life*, cover jacket.

Exile, Alienation and Cultural Tradition: A Study of *Half a Life*

PARMANAND JHA
C.M. College, Darbhanga

V.S. Naipaul, the widely acclaimed finest living writer of English prose, is the seventh Indian or person with Indian roots to be awarded the Nobel Prize and the second, after Rabindranath Tagore, for literature. Born in Trinidad, of Indian parentage, educated in Port of Spain and Oxford University, Naipaul has to his credit more than fourteen works of fiction and ten works of non-fiction. He is one of the finest winners of the prestigious Booker Prize (in 1971, for *In a Free State*) and was knighted by Queen Elizabeth in 1990. Living in England, he alternates between a country home in Wiltshire and a flat in the Knightsbridge locality of London. A relentless explorer of the traumas of postcolonial change with a moralist's outrage, Naipaul, in all of his writings, "focuses on individuals attempting to escape Fate, for Fate belongs to a world of magic, myth and ritual where the past exists but not history, a world which provides a sense of wholeness and belonging but proscribes ambition and curbs freedom. His heroes strive for the latter, for self-awareness and for change. This could also be a metaphor for peoples and nations."[1] The Swedish Academy citation rightly remarks, "He is to a very high degree a cosmopolitan writer, a fact that he himself considers to stem from his lack of roots; he is unhappy about the cultural and spiritual poverty of Trinidad, he feels alienated from India, and in England he is incapable of relating to and identifying with the traditional values of what was once a colonial power."[2]

Half a Life, Naipaul's latest novel, published just before the Nobel Prize came his way, portrays and evaluates the lives of the people of mixed descent in three countries—India, England and Portuguese Africa (modelled on Mozambique) and their struggle to discover their identities. Partly autobiographical, the novel delineates the traumas of a tainted and troubled past, of attempting to find some meaning and purpose of life. It beautifully analyses the pangs of the exiles, their living a half-life, their sense of alienation, and their cultural traditions. "*Half a Life*," writes Maggie Ball, "has been over eight years in the making and combines many of the traditional Naipaul themes such as cultural alienation, the concept of national literature, how we define ourselves, with an unusual narrative structure."[4]

The story of the novel, moving through three different settings and three different eras, is told by three narrators. The first part of the story is told to the hero, Willie Chandran, by his 'self-deluded' father. A Brahmin by birth, coming from a line of priests (5), Willie's father decides to join the Mahatma's campaign against casteism and marries a 'backward' girl, very low in caste, as a supreme gesture of sacrifice, 'not an empty sacrifice . . . but a more lasting kind of sacrifice, something the Mahatma would have approved of.' (10) Even as he takes the vow of sexual abstinence, a vow of 'brahmacharya' (33) he fathers a son and a daughter in quick succession. The son is Willie Somerset Chandran, the middle name taken from the visit by the famous English writer Somerset Maugham to his ashram; and the daughter is Sarojini, named after the 'woman poet of the independence movement.' The stigma of marrying below caste, the disappointment of the college Principal who wanted him to marry his daughter, the fear of the fire-brand uncle of his wife and his own shell-shocked parents forced him to leave his job in the Land Tax Department of the Maharaja and find shelter in the courtyard of the temple. Subsequently he set up his own ashram and began living the life of a 'holy man.' "This pantomime of high intention and pathos subsumes the story of Willie Chandran's father's life; his stints in the Maharaja's Land Tax Department, his refuge in melancholy and his eventual career as a bogus holy man. Curiously it stands Naipaul's own most poignant story on its head; the story of his first father's ambition and failure."[5] This was the story that Willie Chandran's father told. It took about ten years. Different things had to be said at different times. Willie Chandran grew up during the telling of the story (35).

It is at this point that the omniscient author intervenes to narrate the second part of the story. Having inherited the shaded, undistinguished ancestry in 'an undefined place in pre-independent India,' Willie Chandran sets out on a journey of life. Disillusioned with his stay at the Mission School and his parents, and uncertain of his future, Willie obtains, with help from one of his father's contacts, a scholarship to a college of 'education for mature students' in London. He arrives in England to find himself on the fringes of the 'special passing bohemian-immigrant life of London of the late 1950s. 'The immigrant community of post-war London, its dingy west-end clubs, lonely pavements and sexual encounters and even the eccentric milieu of the English writers captivate as much as frighten Willie. He is portrayed here as a young man 'with nothing to his name but his promise as a writer, drifting aimlessly, groping for a voice.' Egged on by his creative triggers and armed with the advice of his publishing friend Roger, Willie begins to recreate himself with little lies in his stories, modelled on the borrowings from 'old Hollywood movies' and the 'Maxim Gorky trilogy from Russia.' Reviewers, however, dismiss his book of short stories as a 'nondescript savoury' and he quickly abandons his plan to be a writer. 'Let the book die, let it fade away. . . . I will write no more." (123)

Willie's life in London is fraught with many a frightening experience. He suffers from alienation and emptiness in being in the metropolis, 'a sense of being without history or understanding, the difficulty a writer from the colonies faces in finding material and his shocking sexual encounters.' He sleeps with prostitutes and friends' girl friends only to discover his own sexual incompetence. "Willie realizes that his own failures mirror those of his father's and that these personal failures mirror the failure of colonialism; Britain losing India and Portugal losing Mozambique."[6] Willie, however, finds love in a chance encounter with Ana, a mixed race girl from Africa and admirer of his abandoned book. They meet in his hostel-room. Willie has been a little tense and nervous before her arrival. But 'as soon as he saw her, all his anxieties fell away, and he was conquered.' (125) The most intoxicating thing was 'that for the first time in his life he felt himself in the presence of someone who accepted him completely.' At home his life had been ruled by his mixed inheritance. It spoilt everything. Even the love he felt for his mother, which should have been pure, was full of the pain he felt for their circumstances.' (l25) His experience of love with Ana, he hopes, might bring him the fulfillment he so desperately seeks. With her, he travels to her home in a province of Portuguese Africa 'a country populated by desperate businessmen and their frustrated wives, all uncertainly living out the last days of colonialism.'

The eighteen years of Willie's life with Ana in Africa recounted by him to his sister Sarojini forms the third and final part of the story running into 87 pages. At Ana's estate house in Africa, Willie feels like a stranger but draws sustenance from Ana: 'It may be because of something in our culture,' Willie reflects, 'that in spite of appearances, men are really looking for women to lean on.' (141) And further, 'Ana was important for me because I depended on her for my idea of being a man.' (142)

Willie gets along passionately with Ana, who helps him to live with 'a new idea of sex,' a new idea of his capacity. He experiences with her 'some genuine excitement, some moments of sexual discovery.' 'We each found comfort in the other; and we had become very close, not looking beyond the other for satisfaction, not knowing, in fact, that another kind of satisfaction was possible.' (189) But he does look beyond Ana for satisfaction when in the company of Alvaro, the Correias' estate manager, he visits the converted warehouse on the edge of the town, the blue bulbs and the dance floor and little cubicles and sleeps with a small, young girl who 'with her extraordinary look of command and aggression, need filled eyes, body becoming all tension' revives him and thus helps him recover from all the shame and incompetence of his earlier sexual encounters in London. Returning home, he doesn't feel that he has betrayed Ana in any important or final way. He feels that split-second still locked away in his mind. These furtive visits to the warehouses continue for some time until one day when he spots among the 'rouged and dressed up girls,' Julio's daughter. Ana's little maid who had evinced some interest in him on the very first morning of his arrival in Ana's estate house. Recalling the day, Willie feels that 'that was the day when I betrayed Ana, sullied her, as it were, in her own house.' Willie's visits to the 'places of pleasures' cease to give him any real pleasure now. This was partly due to the 'worry about seeing Julio's daughter again.' 'But the main reason was that the act of sex there, which used to excite me with its directness and brutality, had grown mechanical.' (195) He tries to renew his lovemaking with Ana 'hoping to recover the closeness that had once seemed so natural' (195) but it doesn't work. Soon, at a weekend lunch party he meets Graca, Correias' new Manager's wife and Carla's Convent school friend who has 'disturbed eyes' and looks at him 'in a way that no woman had looked at me before.' (198) He makes love to Graca in the deserted cobra-infested German castle. "It would have been terrible," Willie thinks afterwards, "if he had died without knowing this depth of satisfaction, this other person that I had just discovered within myself. It was worth any price, any consequences." (205) This stormy affair is, however, short-lived. Willie's sensual life receives a setback when he realizes that he has not been living his own life all these years. Africa's brutalities intervene to dry up his sexual urge. He slips one day on the front steps of Ana's estate house and becomes unconscious. He wakes up later to find himself in the military hospital in the town 'among wounded black soldiers with shining faces and tired red eyes.' Post-Independent Civil War has broken out in Ana's land. When she comes to see him in the hospital, Willie tells her that he is going to leave her: 'I have given you eighteen years, I can't give you any more. I can't live your life any more, I want to live my own.' (136) He leaves Ana, leaves Africa and thus arrives in Berlin, at his sister's house.

Willie discovers, as he narrates his life in Africa to his sister in Berlin, that 'there was something in the African heart that was shut away from the rest of us, and beyond politics.' A large part of that something happens to be raw sexual abandon. "Willie's submission to sexual desire is wholly believable for the very reason that he has previously been stunted into half-life by the constrictions of caste in India and class in England. Africa releases him into sensuality."[7]

A major theme running through the novel and supported by its structure is that of 'exiles living a half-life.' The story of the first forty years of the life of Willie Chandran, living in exile, first in London, then in Portuguese Africa in the years leading up to independence and civil war seems to suggest that man's search for wholeness is only half-successful. "The displacement of the novel's characters, from Willie through to the other exiles he comes into contact with, and how they manage this disappointment forms the tension in the story."[8] Willie's circle of acquaintances in London consists of many an exile that lives in a 'half-and-half world' and suffers the pangs of alienation. There is that smartly dressed Percy Cato, a Jamaican of mixed parentage, 'who appeared to have no proper place in the world' (62) and who becomes Willie's guide to the city; Marcus, the West Indian, West African with his plans for a white grand child; and, of all people, Ana who looks like an extension of Willie's own existence, mirroring his own sense of being on the outside of life, 'homeless without a direction back.' Her autobiographical tales of 'Luisa' also mirror Willie's half-lies about his own background. All these exiles are living a half life or are looking for a life and perhaps having to borrow a life, never living life to the full. Even Sarojini, whose life remains largely untold, is homeless, wandering from one city to another with her German filmmaker husband. Her life is no more her own than Willie's. Sarojini's drift is more poignant than Willie's, because she has hardly anything to fall back on. Willie has his stories and a hope of finding some purpose in life: 'All that he had was a belief in magic—that one day something would happen, an illumination would come to him, and he would be taken by a set of events to the place he should go.' (122) Willie discovers some purpose in life, though temporarily, through his sensual associations and sexual encounters in Ana's Africa but he realizes their futility soon after as these happen to be experiences in external settings and cannot be permanent for him. Near the end of his African life when Ana proposes they should go to Portugal, Willie replies, 'Even if we go to Portugal, even if they let me in there, it would be still your life. I have been hiding for too long.' (227) And Ana's assertion, 'Perhaps it wasn't really my life either' suggests that even those who seem to be living their own lives don't really have more of a personal life than an exile.

Allied with that of exile and alienation is the theme of cultural tradition. In a recent interview with Farrukh Dhondy, Naipaul remarked, "My concern in the book [*Half a Life*] is also the historical side of things. Willie runs away from his background, and even when he gets to Africa, this Portuguese province, he is reminded of the background from which he came."[9] Our origins always remain with us. The bonds of tradition are too steely to break. Trying to explain his sexual incompetence, Willie speaks on phone to Perdita, Roger's girl friend: 'But I have a need of you. It was bad last time. But I'll tell you. It is a cultural matter. I want to make love to you, but then at the actual moment old ideas take over and I become ashamed and frightened, I don't know of what, and it all goes bad.' (118) Later in Africa, Willie does not feel the excitement he has been seeking desperately with the small, young girl in the warehouses: 'I couldn't feel any longer for her. Even if I did, all the ghosts were already with me, the ghosts of home . . . all the shame and incompetence.' (187) Further, in a post-coital exchange in a Land-Rover in the bush, Willie whispers to Graca, 'I am smelling you on my body as I drive.' (205) At the same time, he remains aware that the life into which he has been initiated is not really his own. The 'sexual simplicities of his earlier days are replaced by the opening up of new senses by a life of sensation in the company of Graca and he feels helpless. At the same time now same half-feeling of the inanity of my life grew within me and with it there came the beginning of respect for the religious outlawing of sexual extremes.' (211) Rooted, thus, in his own cultural tradition, Willie finally fails to establish any fulfilling relationship through his escape from caste and class.

Willie's real life, however, lies in waiting for something to happen, like the characters in *Waiting for Godot*. Whether something really happens or not is not the issue. "There is no full life except for the life we live. We make and remake ourselves to suit our circumstances. Naipaul's *Half a Life* raises interesting questions about what life really is all about."[10] In a prose style that has the controlled edginess of Joseph Conrad in its evocation of a decadent yet curiously alluring frontier experience, *Half a Life* brings its own unique illumination to a novel aspect of our shared humanity.

NOTES

1. *The Times of India*, New Delhi, October 13, 2001, p. 14.
2. *The Hindustan Times*, New Delhi, October 12, 2001.
3. V.S. Naipaul, *Half a Life* (London: Picador, 2001).
4. Maggie Ball, "Slippery Substances," A Review of V.S. Naipaul's *Half a Life* (books on line telegraph.co.uk).
5. Soma Choudhary, "Taking Leads from His Own Life," *The Hindustan Times*, September 23, 2001.
6. Maggie Ball, "Slipping Substances."
7. Jonathan Bate, *Escape from Caste and Class* (booksonlinetelegrap h.co.uk accessed on October 24, 2001).
8. Maggie Ball, "Slippery Substances."
9. V.S. Naipaul, "Indian writers don't know why their country is in such a mess," An interview with Farrukh Dhondy, Cupidonline. com. Accessed on October 24, 2001.
10. Maggie Ball, "Slippery Substances."

Disorientation of Identity in *Half a Life*

BHAGABAT NAYAK
Kandarpur College, Cuttack

Vidiadhar Surajprasad Naipaul is one of the few prominent expatriate writers of our time, particularly writers with Indian background. He has emerged as the most eminent writer in English of the world after his winning the Nobel Prize for literature in 2001. As a journalist, novelist, writer of travelogue, and a great master in the art of non-fiction novel-writing, he has significant contribution to commonwealth literature or postcolonial literature and has secured his place in the literary map of the English-speaking world. With the exalted idea of the western literary canon, it seems that "He is a tireless but reluctant traveller, like an unsponsored explorer without a compass in his work as in his life—for his characters share his homelessness."[1] His writing has often been seen in the Third World as caustic and personal, but takes his readers into the farthest reaches of the third world-Africa, the Caribbean, Asia and the Central Asia and all the way to South Africa, to test one or both his obsessions: what it means to become and finally to be a writer; what happens to postcolonial societies when the imperial power recedes, leaving cruelty and chaos to fill the breach. Both in his writing and daily life he is a perfectionist, what he expects and writes about he is a Brown man of Indian descent born into the Black and Brown society of Trinidad. Unlike, for example, Salman Rushdie, whose literary referents were Guntur Grass and Gabriel Garcia Marquez, Naipaul cuts his teeth on the great masters of the nineteenth and the early twentieth century European fiction: Tolstoy, Balzac, Stendhal, Flaubert and Proust. If there is a fundamental urge to blaspheme in Rushdie, there is a search for a unified self in Naipaul. All the Naipaul readers are happy that his modernist moment may have passed but he remains perhaps the last great representative of a classic movement in English letters.

Being the author of some twenty-four highly acclaimed works of fiction and non-fiction, he has been held to controversy for his views on the Third World, on Islam or the destruction of Babri Masjid (at the International Festival of Indian Literature organised by the Indian Council of Cultural Relations, 2002). As a top-ranking writer in the English-speaking world today, Naipaul constructs an entirely new metaphor for dislocation, fragmentation, rootlessness and the quest for a viable identity. His Indian-Caribbean ancestry, the enigma of a decentred and disoriented experience in the explosive and disconcerting realities of the postcolonial world anywhere and everywhere, and the knotted relationship with his own cultural identity from Indian and his Caribbean and western identities help him to remain as a kind of literary outsider in the postcolonial realities. His clarity of vision is almost Swiftean as he has enjoyed his life in the century which is marked by the political upheaval, mass migration, colonization, revolution and, at the same time, by his typical extended family of Hindu India, bound by tradition, rituals, customs, and in a community where the roots had been severed and environment was alien and all-encompassing Hindu culture and its recollections of India had become more attenuated with each passing generation. In an interview with Rahul Singh, he says, "I was born in Trinidad, I have lived most of my life in England and India is the land of my ancestors. That says it all. I am not English, not Indian, not Trinidadian. I am my own person."[2] His writings are realistic and include the knowledge about cricket, movies of the Forties, snuff, architecture, fine wine, Indian art and politics, exploration, military strategy and the pictures of some countries with high-pitched tone of anger, harshness and severity of his statement as well as brilliant world-view.

Acknowledging his "colonial Hindu self" as a "man and writer," Naipaul projects his "autobiographical material into poignant fiction and his neuroses onto his narrators and characters."[3] The relations with the people he meets in his travels affect the very nature of his memories and enlarge his perspective on his heritage; the religion and customs of immigrants from colonial Indian who settled in colonial Trinidad. The idea of "universal civilization" came into formulation by his understanding of the cultural traditions of India, the Arab world of colonialism. Further, his conception of "Universal Civilization" is based on his belief in individual potentiality and individual responsibility which he has observed by associating himself with the hardships and aspirations: "the Whiteman's burden" in colonialism, the present western cultural dominance on other societies and the need of those societies to ape western practices and institutions. His claims as a seeker of truth are always contingent on his individual role in history and the possibilities of discovery within a particular time and place. Yet his truth is "Observing the intricate connections between the self and the observed world and its peoples stirs ambiguous memories and subliminal feelings that alter his responses"[4] and refer to an individual mind contending with barriers to its authentic interpretation of experience. Throughout his career he has transformed self-creation into a cultural lens and a literary method that constitutes his approach to truth, however, contingent on the changing prospect of contemporary history and his own evolving skill as its interpreter. He has been acclaimed for his penetration into the lasting impairment of the postcolonial societies, specially the deprivations of individuals who inherited a history of exploitation, and he has been criticized as "a reactionary loyal to imperialist values." He has been praised for his creative use of autobiography in his travel narratives and for converting autobiographical material into poignant fiction, Naipaul's protagonists emerge from different social classes. They are linked to each other and to their progenitor by an impulse to pursue truth about themselves and their world; however circuitous the cause. In its Nobel citation to Naipaul, Swedish Academy rightly remarks, "He is to a very high degree a cosmopolitan writer, a fact that he himself considers to stem from his lack of roots; he is unhappy about the cultural and spiritual poverty of Trinidad, he feels alienated from

India, and in England he is incapable of relating to and identifying with the traditional values of what was once a colonial power."[5]

It is interesting to mark how Naipaul has "invented stories" on truth with the setting of plot and places as "a form of social enquiry" in which his characters are presented as confused identities through different disorientations. *Half a Life*, his latest work, apart from being a fictional counterpart of the earlier three interrogatory Naipaulean passages—dark, wounded, mutinous—to India, is also perhaps in need of this low form of heraldry to appear as the anti-thesis of the spiritual, sympathy laden passages to India of Forster and Maugham. "It certainly tells a story, in fact several stories, but they seem unrealistic, like events in a nightmare, and the characters are like those glimpsed in one, briefly and horribly. Also like a nightmare, the book leads nowhere, and when it was over it . . . disappointed . . . greatly."[6] *Half a Life* reflects his fundamental social and cultural values in his psychological reactions to his immediate and extended family. Naipaul is consistently hostile toward mobilization for political change is believed by the evidence in various political movements, observation of corruption, brutality, and tribal hostilities like the slaughters in Rwanda and Bosnia. In the novel, he presents his protagonist's encountering of "half-made societies that seemed doomed to remain half-made." The fictional material and experiences in the novel are restlessly nomadic which Naipaul discusses on the themes of exile, dislocation, alienation, displaced histories and most painful dilemmas in the postcolonial societies in both fictional and non-fictional modes.

Half a Life is really an invention about the countries, periods or situations if it does not exactly appear to describe them. The novel is without any real surprise in which Naipaul portrays and evaluates the lives of the people of mixed descent in three countries—Trinidad, England and Portuguese Africa (Mozambique) and their struggle to discover their identities.

The book is about the confused identities, a theme that Naipaul discusses in almost all the books he has written—people coming from small places, smaller historical contexts and struggling with the looseness of their selves and their lives. The novel has three parts with different settings cast in different eras. Each part is a narration of an individual narrator. In the first part, Willie Chandran's father tells his story which took about ten years. Unlike the author, he comes from the line of priests. On the setting of the human drama, he is "self-deluded" by Mahatma's call in 1930s, gives up his English education, plans very deliberately the seduction of an untouchable Dalit girl "from the backwards," gets into trouble with everyone concerned, gets a job, marries the girl, renounces the world and joins in the campaign against casteism. He marries this backward scholarship girl as a supreme gesture of sacrifice, "not an empty sacrifice . . . but a more lasting kind of sacrifice, something Mahatma would have approved of."[7] Though he had taken a vow of sexual abstinence, a vow of "brahmacharya," (33) he marries this backward girl as a great sacrifice to liberate the people who were dehumanized, without shedding his caste prejudice and abhorrence of the "unclean." He enjoys his life in the measure of social distancing, and renouncing the world like his grandfather before him, whose activities Naipaul is careful not to disclose to the reader.

Willie's father sacrifices his life for a cause greater than life and perhaps the greatest in humanity. His life is charged with the philosophy of the Mahatma and he gets confused about the fate of the country during the freedom movement. He feels the ground beneath his feet falling by marrying a girl below his rank and fighting the petty caste-war, "I was irredeemably tarnished, a fallen man of caste, and my path of mockery of sacred ways." (32) Yet his confusion saturates with his Dalit wife, disoriented son, Willie Somerset Chandran whom he thinks of as "tainted" and desirable daughter, Sarojini, whom he finds repulsive. He keeps the middle name of his son since the visit by the famous English writer Somerset Maugham to his ashram in search of a saintly person, for his novel *The Razor's Edge* and daughter's as Sarojini after the patriot woman poet of the Independence movement. He waits to see how much of the backward Willie could be read in his son's features, and wishes that the blessing might fall on Sarojini like that of the great woman poet. The disappointment of the college principal who wanted him to marry his daughter, the fear of his wife's "fine-brand" uncle and his own shell-shocked parents forced him to leave his job. All this "has been a life of sacrifice" (36) and he sublimely says: "I am sacrificing the only thing I have tò sacrifice." (24) Conscious of his duty to his wife, he says to her "I have no riches to offer you. All I have are my friendship. That is my treasure" (36) and for his daughter he says "all I can hope for Sarojini is an international marriage." (36) He tells his life story of ten years during which Willie grows and goes to school, and starts reworking some of the stories he hears his father telling him, such as "A Life of Sacrifice" in which an old brahmin bound to sacrifice a child every year in order to retain possession of a treasure, finally ends up by sacrificing his own children through the subterfuge and malice of a tribal chieftain, the children of whose tribe he had been using for the purpose. Willie's father never got tired of telling him of his own "life of sacrifice" of whose ridiculous dimensions Willie seems to have become aware very early in his life. "This pantomime of high intention and pathos subsumes the story of Willie Chandran's father's life; his stints in the Maharaja's Land Tax Department, his refuge in melancholy and his eventful career as a bogus holyman. Curiously it stands Naipaul's own most poignant story on its head; the story of his father's ambition and failure."[8] Thus it appears that the first part of the book is quite Naipaulean and "delineates the traumas of a tainted and troubled past, of attempting to find some meaning and purpose of life. It beautifully analyses the pangs of exile, their living a half-life, their sense of alienation, and their cultural traditions."[9]

Naipaul describes the ancestry of Willie Chandran in pre-independent India. The ridiculousness of the significance ordinary men attach to their own lives is another topic dear to Naipaul, and that forms the second part of the story. It delineates that a life without any special significance is no better either, and that is what his father understands of Willie. Both Willie and Sarojini face a hostile and confused Mission School environment and family atmosphere that make their future uncertain. In the school, their friends have a degraded callings at their father and his business. "The teacher kept on smiling, waiting for an answer, and at last Willie Chandran said with irritation, 'You all know what my father does?' The class laughed. They laughed at his irritation and not at what he had said." (37) Willie goes to a college in England on scholarship. He finds himself in London on the fringes of the 'special passing bohemian-immigrant life of London of the late 1950s. In the immigrant community of post-war London, Willie grows up to despise his father and hate his mother. In the London literary underground he wants to be a writer, meets a number of people who lead uniformly intellectual and silly lives. There he begins to recreate himself as a writer and publishes a book of stories modelled on the borrowings from *Old Hollywood Movies* and the *Maxim Gorky Trilogy from Russia.* When the readers feel the book unreadable and reviewers dismiss, his disorientation starts and he abandons his plan to be a writer "Let the book die, let it fade away. . . . I will write no more." (123)

Willie's creative activity increases with the reading of a cheap history book of the world published during the war about the nationalization of Suez Canal and Krishna Menon's representing India at the international forums. He begins to recreate himself with some historical, some personal, some traditionally novelistic and some materials—part fact, part fiction as Roger says "a story should have a beginning, a middle and an end . . . if you think it, life isn't like that. Life doesn't have a neat beginning and a tidy end. Life is always going on. You should begin in the middle and end in the middle, and it should all be there." (83) He comes in contact with Percy Cato from Jamaica in London and is initiated into the city's bohemian underground. He sleeps with Cato's girl friend, visits a prostitute, gets to know Roger, sleeps with his girl friend and reworks some of the stories from India, shows them to Roger who asks him to take them to Richard who publishes them. As a "sexual athlete" in his different encounters, he discovers his sexual incompetence and comes to know how "sex is a brutal business." (71) In London, Willie understands two things: that he is free, that is, free to be much more than he could be within reason and remake himself and his past and his ancestry; he finds that his love with Ana, a mixed race girl from Africa, is true and sincere and for the first time in his life he feels to be in the presence of someone who accepts him completely. He realizes that sexual knowledge is required to make one's way in the West. He considers his love for his mother as pure but his experience of Love with Ana could bring him the fulfilment which he searches for desperately. Willie realizes that personal failures mirror those of his father's and that these personal failures mirror the failure of colonialism; Britain losing India and Portugal losing Mozambique. "We are in the late Fifties at this stage of the novel and we can see Naipaul using some of his own experiences here, especially when Willie works briefly for the BBC."[10]

Ana is the daughter of a plantation owner from an unnamed Portuguese colony in Africa. Willie is passionately involved with her, and it is she who helps him to live with 'a new idea of sex,' a new idea that he experiences with her, 'some genuine excitement, some moments of sexual discovery.' Unlike him, Ana is also a confused soul, a Euro-African from a Portuguese colony. With her, he cannot stay in Britain because there are no cultural codes available that would help him to live with his unbelongingness. In London, he is the little man thrust into a grandiose dimension of history merely by being present at a certain time in a certain place. In his relationship with Ana, Willie develops different perspectives on life, society and man-woman relationship. During his eighteen years of married life with Ana, he realizes that "in spite of appearances, men are really looking for women to lean on," (141) and admits "Ana was important for me because I depended on her for my idea of being a man" (142) and also "we each found comfort in the other; and we had become very close, not looking beyond the other for satisfaction, not knowing, in fact, that another kind of satisfaction was possible." (189)

Naipaul describes Willie's life with Ana in the third and final part of the story during the post-Independence Civil War period. He describes Willie's disorientation in life in the ruined and dying colony of Africa. Willie lives these eighteen years a perfectly useless existence, hobnobbing with other planters who are all stereotypes or caricatures and sleeping around with women, for pleasure in the converted warehouse on the edge of the town. But this act of his commitment to unscrupulous sex he does not feel any betrayal towards Ana and rather continues his visits to the warehouse until one day he spots the dressed up Julio's daughter. At the weekends, he visits the 'places of pleasure' in the deserted cobra-infested German castle and makes love to Graca without knowing the danger involved in this and the depth of satisfaction as "it was worth any price, any consequence." (205) With the break out of the Civil War, the colony is about to explode into a bloody revolution and Ana tells him: "Africans may not be afraid of you and me, but they are afraid of one another. Everyman has access to the fetish-man, and this means that even the humblest man has power. In that way they are better off than the rest of us." (159) This helps him to realize that he has not been living his own life, but rather existing all these years. This makes Willie leave Ana and Africa and he goes to Germany, to Sarojini who has married a German photographer with radical ideas. Naipaul describes Willie's alienation, disorientation and emptiness in the ruined and dying colony of Africa. Willie narrates his African experience in a brooding before his sister believing that there was something in the African heart beyond everybody and everything. He realizes how all through the years "Africa releases him into sensuality" as prior to this he had led a half-life in his submission to sensual desire, to confusion of caste in India and to class in England. Willie's experience and realisation of halfness in life are reflected in his trans-continental migration and multi-dimensional socio-cultural environment.

One of the major themes of the book is the half-life the exiles live. The author raises this important existential question in an autobiographical way through disorientation of Willie's life. Wherever he goes, he realizes that a man searches for wholeness but becomes only half-successful. Willie abundantly inherits the collective unconsciousness of the Indian ethos and therefore the Third World heritage—and is by no means a flag-waving propagandist for the erstwhile colonies of British imperialism. Willie strives to find but not to yield in the nature of his inward journey into the half-and-half world and is confused through the suffering and alienation. On the other hand, Ana looks like an extension of Willie's own existence, mirroring his own sense of being on the outside of life. The exiles in the novel lead a half-life or look for a life or hope to borrow a life, and never to live a life to the full. Willie desires to discover some purpose in life, though temporarily, through his sensual associations and sexual encounters in London and Ana's Africa. But he realizes the futility of life through his experiences in the external settings. Both Willie and Ana realize that exile is a half-life and they do not have more of a personal life. Willie is pre-occupied with varieties of dislocations, migrations, exile, the idea of being unanchored and displaced; the enigma of a decentered and disorientating experience in the explosive and disconcerting realities of half-London, half-Portuguese and half-and-half world with their different linguistic cultural ecologies, sociological hues and nostalgia. Willie tries to run away from his background but he is reminded of his origins that always remain with him as he cannot be out of his roots in the cultural tradition and his relationship with caste and class.

The novel is an invention of Naipaul, and does not present the exact countries, periods or situations that it appears to describe. It is a devastating work of exceptional sensitivity, grace and humour in its depiction of love fulfilled and thwarted, in its vision of the half-lives quietly lived out at the centre of our restless world. During the anti-colonial agitation, Willie Chandran's father stood at all odds with the world aspiring to greatness in an attempt to defy his post, he lived with a low-caste woman only to find himself at the mercy of his own fury. It appears on the blurb of the book how "From this unhappy union, the utterly compelling character of Willie Chandran emerges, oddly like his father, naively eager to find something that will place him both in and apart from the world. And so he is drawn to England to the immigrant community of post-war London, its dingy West End clubs, lonely pavements and sexual encounters, and even to the eccentric milieu of the English writer." Being confused in the postcolonial social matrix of Trinidad, Portuguese province in Africa and London "perhaps he is trying to say that to live in postcolonial countries addles people's mind. This is possible, but it is not a great discovery. And if, as the title suggests, Naipaul is saying that most people, in the true sense, only lead half a life, it is a statement of the obvious."[11] Willie leads half-a-life through his pilgrim's progress into the nether world of love in order to achieve a fullness of life. Drawing the reader's attention into the depth of the story of the novel, Naipaul describes Willie's journey to find out a place for himself in the world and his dilemma is that of a man who had to leave his background and find something else.

Naipaul as the sole model of Joseph Conrad is the most polemical among the contemporary writers, lauded for his objectivity in presenting the case of the history of exploitation though his detractors have vilified him as a reactionary and an apologist for neo-colonialism. His theme in the novel is related to caste, religion, culture, nationality, love and marriage. The title, *Half a Life*, is justified not only because Willie is close to fifty when he leaves Ana and Africa, but also because, as he tells Ana, he spent all his mature years trying to grab a life he could call his own, in the knowledge that the life that was given to him had become unbelievable. This is a predicament that one can identify with Naipaul himself, the scholarship holder from Trinidad, who came to know the miracle of fiction and left all dilemmas related to individual identities behind him. Naipaul speaks of the less fortunate, and the nightmares he was able to avoid. This is not really the top of the line Naipaul reaches mainly because one cannot write with spontaneity about things one doesn't have a first-hand experience of. His depiction of the Indian and the African episodes in Willie Chandran's life come across as the products of passionless calculation. The alternative to spontaneity is the abandonment of historical realism altogether. But Naipaul does not believe in that either. Thus, Naipaul's purpose is never didactic; he merely takes the historical situation as a setting for all kinds of human drama and activities which perhaps he is not careful to disclose to the readers.

NOTES

1. Paul Theroux, "V.S. Naipaul," *Modern Fiction Studies*, 30.3 (Autumn 1984), p. 450.
2. V.S. Naipaul, An Interview with Rahul Singh, *The Times of India*, 19 Feb. 2002.
3. Lilian Feder, *Naipaul's Truth* (New Delhi: Indialog, 2001), p. 1.
4. Feder, pp. 6-7.
5. *The Hindustan Times*, New Delhi, 12 Oct. 2001.
6. Dom Moraes, "Half a Novel," *The Hindu*, 4 Nov. 2001, p. 3.
7. V.S. Naipaul, *Half a Life* (London: Picador, 2001), p. 10.
8. Soma Choudhary, "Taking Leads from His Own Life," *The Hindustan Times*, 23 Sept. 2001.
9. Parmanand Jha, "Exile, Alienation and Cultural Tradition: V.S. Naipaul's *Half a Life*," *The Indian Journal of English Studies*, vol. 39 (2001-2002), p. 47.
10. Soumitro Das, "Enigma of Non-arrival," *The Sunday Statesman*, 30 Sept. 2001, p. 1.
11. Moraes, p. 3.

Demystifying India in *Half a Life*: An Analysis of Naipaul's Attitude to India

SANTWANA HALDAR
F.M. College, Balasore

V.S Naipaul's position as an Indian diasporic writer is unique. With his Indian-Caribbean ancestry Naipaul settled in London and his love-hate relationship to India has been revealed continuously in his non-fiction writings. The India that he presents in *An Area of Darkness* (1964) is in the process of decay, with its degraded and stupefied people seeking consolation in past glories and with its outmoded religion that legitimizes the suffering of the mass. Naipaul also praises, at the same time, the passivity and detachment highlighted as great virtues in Indian philosophy. *India: A Wounded Civilization* (1977) reinforces his conviction that India, wounded by a thousand years of foreign rule, has not yet found an ideology of regeneration. Yet, he expresses his hope of the possibility of a true new beginning in India at the end of the book. *India: A Million Mutinies Now* (1990) reveals a mellower tone of its author. The book records those voices from all sides of India which tell him that India has changed. A good number of persons taken from almost all the walks of life are seen by the author as parts of the "beginning of a new way for many millions, part of India's growth part of the restoration." In *Half a Life* (2000), again, on the cover page of which is written 'a novel' to avoid confusions, the author takes up the task of satirizing Indian spirituality, a theme popular among a part of foreign authors. The present article will discuss how Naipaul demystifies India in his latest novel.

Half a Life is set in three locales, India, England and Africa. A princely state in British India, untouched by colonial agitation, is the setting of the first part of the novel entitled 'A Visit from Somerset Maugham.' Almost the entire second part entitled 'The First Chapter' is set in post-war London with its dingy West End clubs and lonely pavements. And the third part called 'A Second Translation' is set in a province of Portuguese Africa living out the last days of colonialism. The protagonist Willie Chandran, born in India of a brahmin father and a lower class mother, leaves India and goes first to England, and then to Africa, and the narrative veers accordingly. The first part of the novel contains a confessional life-history of the protagonist's father who was almost universally accepted as a Gandhian saint, and who, as he claimed, had the rare opportunity to be included as a saintly figure in Somerset Maugham's *The Razor's Edge*. Through his confession, Willie's father is rendered as a fraud and Somerset Maugham is said to have based his Indian saint on that fraud, mistaking him for a great saint. The present article intends to show first, how Somerset Maugham portrays the Indian saint and creates thereby a myth of spiritual India, and then how V.S. Naipaul deconstructs that myth through the portrait of Willie's father. It will also be shown that Naipaul continues criticizing the Gandhian philosophy and the non-co-operation movement of Gandhi almost in the same way he did in his previous non-fiction works. Finally, Naipaul's criticism of the Indian approach to sex as revealed through Willie's experiences in England and Africa, will also be discussed.

Intertextuality is considered valuable by most critics in the genesis of narrative texts. Peter Verdonk and Jacques Weber explain intertextuality as "the way any spoken or written text, literary or non-literary, is produced and interpreted through our conscious or unconscious experience and awareness of other texts. These texts, in turn, will have their own intertextual dimension, and so forth Obviously, the texts in such an intertextual network can relate to each other for all sorts of reasons."[1] The 'reason' for bringing the intertextual element in *Half a Life* is obviously satire. Willie's father, a fake saint, tells his son how the famous writer came to the temple where he had been living as a mendicant.

> You must believe that I had said nothing to him at all. But then, perhaps eighteen months later, in the travel book the writer brought out, there were two or three pages about me. . . . Everything the Maharaja's headmaster had told about me was there, and a few other things besides. Clearly the headmaster had tried to win the admiration of the writer by saying very good things about my various vows of denial. . . . That was how I became famous. Not in India, where there is a lot of jealousy, but abroad. And the jealousy turned to rage when the writer's famous novel came out during the war, and foreign critics began to see in me the spiritual source of *The Razor's Edge.*[2]

A direct reference to Somerset Maugham's novel demands a query into the novel and a revelation of what is said there about the Indian saint. In *The Razor's Edge*, Laurence Darrell of Marvin, Illinois, alias Larry, went to India as a tourist and was greatly impressed by Hinduism. First he got to Bombay, and then to Benares. It was in Madura that Larry heara about the saint Shri Ganesha who lived in Travancore. When Larry went to Shri Ganesha's ashram, he saw the saint sitting in meditation on a raised dais covered with a tiger skin. Larry was surprised to hear from Shri Ganesha that he had been expecting Larry. At first Larry thought that his friend in Madura might have informed the saint of his arrival. But any such possibility was denied by Shri Ganesha himself who appeared to be a thought reader. The saint looked at Larry without speaking, and Larry did not know how long the silence lasted. Thus Larry expresses his experience:

> I don't know how long the silence lasted. It might have been for half an hour. It is the serenity that he irradiated, the goodness, the peace, the selflessness. I was hot and tired after my journey but gradually began to feel wonderfully rested. Before he had said another I knew that he was the man I'd been seeking.[3]

In *Half a Life* Willie's father also remains silent when he is troubled and has taken shelter in a temple. As he said to his son, his silence had nothing to do with the silent meditation of ancient Indian saints. It was a pose to save himself from outward hazards: "It occurred then to me to do as the mahatma had done at some stage: to take a vow of silence. It suited my temperament, and it also seemed the least complicated way out. The news of this vow of silence spread. Simple people who had come from far to pay their respects to the temple deity would now also stop off to pay their respects to me. I became at once a holy man." (28)

Naipaul cleverly links the 'vow of silence' to Mahatma's and criticizes thereby both the Gandhian philosophy and the make-believe world of the ascetic. Moreover, he criticizes the Indian intellectuals (the Maharaja and the Principal in the novel) who knew the facts but did not disclose it, as they wanted to oblige the foreign author. Naipaul's lash of satire is directed against this colonial tendency to gain foreign favour. In the novel we see that the Maharaja of the state, of whom Somerset Maugham had written flatteringly in his travel notes, obliged him through pretensions. Willie's father confessed,

> They [Maharaja and his men] pretended to see me as the writer had seen me: the man of high caste high in the Maharaja's revenue service, from a line of people who had performed sacred rituals for the ruler turning his back on a glittering career and living as a mendicant on the alms of the poorest of the poor. (3)

In actuality, Willie's great grandfather, a brahmin by caste, came from the interior village in starving condition and somehow managed a minor job in the Maharaja's court . When Willie's father was admitted into the local college, there was a prospect of job for him in Maharaja's court, and the principal in the Maharaja's college thought of marrying his daughter to him. Willie's father, shrewd enough to understand that the days of the Maharajas have gone, thought of a different career for himself. He got no interest in studies. For some days, he tried in vain for a career in politics. Sometimes in 1931 or 1932, he heard that the Mahatma had called for students to boycott their universities. He decided to follow the call. In the front yard of the college, he made a little bonfire of *The Mayor of Casterbridge*, Shelley and Keats, and the professor's notes, but no reaction was felt. His next thought was to marry the lowest person he could find. And he selected one coarse-featured, noticeably black girl belonging to the 'backwards' in the college. He thought of declaring that in her company he would live out a life of sacrifice. He continued to meet her in public places though he had begun to hate her voice. One day she told him that her uncle, a 'firebrand' union leader, had learnt of their affair and was going to take out a procession against him on the ground of 'caste oppression.' He was really frightened and wanted her advice. She told him that he should keep her hidden somewhere for the time being. He found a shelter for her inside the compound of a small factory and himself lived at home. To meet the expenses, he took a job in the Land Tax department of the Maharaja. The girl was demanding. She believed that people of higher caste had secret funds . She even found fault with him for destroying her career. Though Willie's father did not like the job, he was offered promotion. One day he disclosed to his father all about the girl and his father felt heart broken. When his father accused him of throwing their inheritance away, Willie's father told that he had accepted a life of sacrifice following the Mahatma's call. Though his father could be subdued, the principal who thought of marrying his daughter to him remained a threat. At that crucial time, he was being investigated for corruption during the service period in Land and Tax department. Being caught between the girl and the school principal, the firebrand and the threat of imprisonment, he took sanctuary in the famous old temple in the town where his grandfather had taken shelter in his days of trouble. This was how Willie's father got attached to the temple. In the meantime, the girl's uncle, the firebrand, took out a procession in support of him and he became "part of the cause of the backwards." (27) At that time, unable to face the situation, he started the "vow of silence" popularized by Gandhi. The character of Willie's father is thus sketched in a ludicrous way, and his claim, that Somerset Maugham's Indian saint in *The Razor's Edge* was based on his life, brings a serious charge against the credibility of the famous writer's assessment of Indian spirituality. The myth of Indian spirituality projected by Maugham is thus deconstructed by Naipaul. Moreover, laying bare the way of how Gandhi's message was exploited by persons like Willie's father for their self-interest, Naipaul criticizes the application of the Gandhian philosophy in Indian politics. It is made clear that Willie's father had no spiritual make-up. Rather, he was a materialist taking the pose of a devotee and the Gandhian practice of silence suits him best.

To turn on *The Razor's Edge*, again, Larry informs that in his youth Shri Ganesha practised very rigorous austerities, but he had never enjoined them on his disciples. Further, Shri Ganesha lived in a cave up the hill for many years, but finally has been persuaded to move down to the plain where some charitable persons gave him a plot of land and built a little adobe for him. Disciples gathered around from all corners to visit Shri Ganesha who sought to wear them from the slavery of selfhood, passion and sense Shri Ganesha taught his disciples that man has immense possibility and that wisdom is the means to freedom. He also taught that with work done with no selfish interest purifies the mind and that duties are opportunities afforded to man to sink his separate self and become one with the universal self. Larry was impressed not as much by his teaching, as by the saint himself. His presence was a benediction and he felt that he received something of illumination. Thus Larry describes his "illumination":

> I was suddenly released from my body and as pure spirit partook of a loneliness I had never conceived. I had a sense that a knowledge more than human possessed me, so that everything that had been confused was clear and everything that perplexed me was explained. (275-76)

Through the claim of Willie's father that Shri Ganesha was modelled on him. Naipaul suggests that Maugham was not properly briefed, and that he did not judge things for himself. The role of the Maharaja and his men in obliging the foreign author is a direct attack on the Indian intellectuals who are ready to eat the crow for gaining a foreign support. In his essay collection *The Writer and the World*, Naipaul accuses the Indians of hankering after the stamp of foreign approval. Thanks to this hankering, Willie's father in *Half a Life* is saved from the grudges of the principal and others in the Maharaja's court, who did not object to the way a fraud like Willie's father was projected as a saint before Somerset Maugham. A comparison of Shri Ganesha in *The Razor's Edge* and Willie's father in *Half a Life* thus throws light on Naipaul's intolerance of the idealistic version of India, popular with some foreign authors. As ever in his non-fiction writings, here too, Naipaul washes the dirty Indian laundry before the Western eyes, much to the discomfort of the proponents of spiritual India. Larry's appreciation of the chastity of the Indian saints, a quality that is supposed to enhance the power of the spirit,[4] is criticized through the confession of Willie's father who bluntly reveals his sexual indulgence.

> My utter wretchedness, my self disgust, can be imagined when with everything I have spoken about, and in spite of my private vow of brahmacharya, which represented the profoundest part of my nature, Willie's mother became pregnant for the second time. (35)

Ludicrous hilarity is the obvious result of such comments, and Naipaul's lash of satire mixed up with that hilarity produces the desired effect. Naipaul feels that sexuality has always been a taboo for the Indians, who are often unable to assert their individuality due to this taboo. And chastity being accepted as a great virtue in India, it is quite likely that the Indian people are unable to go against the law of nature and leading the life of chastity becomes a pose. Through Willie's sexual experiences in London and Africa and his realisation of the differences between the Indian and the Western approach to sex, Naipaul seeks to make his stand clear. After his first encounter with June in London, June said to him,

> A friend of mine says it happens with Indians. It's because of the arranged marriages. They don't feel they have to try hard. My father said his father used to tell him, 'Satisfy the woman first. Then think of yourself.' 'I don't suppose you had anybody telling you anything like that.' Willie thought of his father with compassion for the first time (69)

After each new sexual experience, Willie thinks of his wretched father in India who did not have the opportunity to enjoy sexual life, and was gradually absorbed into melancholy. Willie begins to sympathize with his father more and more, and becomes critical of the suffocating conditions in India. Through Willie's reactions Naipaul sends this message to India: life is to be accepted fully and naturally, and any pose or make-believe leaves one crippled and unable to enjoy life.

Naipaul has also exposed the much abused caste oppression in colonial India. That the lower class people were prohibited to cross the temple road while the priests in the temple were doing a long and taxing set of religious ceremonies, is informed by Willie's father in a casual manner. The description of the harassment of Willie's mother at the primary school lays bare the extent of humiliation to which the lower caste children were thrown. A half-starved school servant gave out water to the children from a barrel using a longhandled bamboo dipper and when a student appeared before him he poured water into a brass vessel or an aluminium one. Willie's mother wondered in a childish way whether she would get brass or aluminium. But when she appeared before him no choice like that was offered to her . The servant became angry and "made the kind of noise he would have made before he beat a stray dog." (38) Some of the children objected and then the man found a rusty and dirty tin into which he poured water for the girl. That was how the girl learned that in the world outside, aluminium was for Muslims and Christians, brass was for people of caste and a rusty old tin was for her. She spat on the tin and to avoid the beating of the servant, ran out of the school. Naipaul's assessment was that the lower class people in India were excluded from the mainstream. They did not know about the religion of the people of the caste or the Muslims or the Christians. They didn't know what was happening in the country or the world. They had lived in ignorance, cut off from the world for centuries. (39) This rendering comes from the pen of one who is intolerant of all sorts of make-believe and of exploitation and corruption in any corner of the world.

Naipaul's intolerance of the corruption in different sectors in India is also manifest in *Half a Life*. Describing Willie's experience in the audit section where he had to look out for corruption among the tax collectors and surveyors, Naipaul reveals the trend of exploiting the poor among the affluent:

> Officers would take the land tax from poor people who couldn't read and not give receipts and the poor peasant with his three or four acres would have to pay the tax again. Or he would have to pay a bribe to get his receipt. It was endless, the petty scheating that went on among the poor (22).

From an Indian point of view this type of portrayal may appear derogatory. Critics even observe that this type of portrayal reflects Naipaul's disappointment at his failure to find out in India an alternative civilization sanctified by Orientalist lore, a civilization with which he could identify himself. But the complexity of Naipaul's mental make-up may not be interpreted in terms of the search for identity. As Edward Said observed, the days of "binary oppositions" dear to the nationalists and the imperialists being over, the new alignments across borders, types, nations and essences are rapidly coming into view and the fundamentally static notion of identity are becoming useless.[5] Further, during the time that sees globalizing process, it is hard for a diasporic writer to find out his real identity. Naipaul's attempt to demystify India and his direct attack on the corruption going on in India may be best appreciated if his literary work viewed is as the conscience of human kind. All through his literary career be made a search for reality, or rather a real history of mankind in different lands. The urgency with which he demystifies India is a proof of his concern for revealing the history of India devoid of all illusions.

NOTES

1. Peter Verdonk and Jean Jacques Weber, ed., *Twentieth Century Fiction: From Text to Context* (London: Routledge, 1995), p. 248.
2. V.S. Naipaul, *Half a life* (London: Picador, 2001), p. 3.

3. W. Somerset Maugham, *The Razor's Edge* (Pan Books in association with Heinemann, London, 1976), p. 272.
4. Ibid, p. 280. That the author also supports Larry's view is evident from the author's attitude to him in the novel.
5. Jean-Paul Sartre, *Being and Nothingness*, trans: Hazel E. Barnes (London: Methuen, 1972), p. 49.
6. Edward Said, *Culture and Imperialism* (London: Faber, 1993), p. XXVIII.

The Novels of V.S. Naipaul: Quest for Order and Identity

N. Rama Devi

The book analyzes Naipaul's quest for order and identity in his novels with the third world setting, namely *The Mystic Masseur, The Suffrage of Elvira, A House for Mr. Biswas, The Mimic Men, In a Free State, Guerrillas, A Bend in the River* and *A Way in the World.*

ISBN: 81-85218-006-4 **Rs. 300**

The Novels of V.S. Naipaul

Shashi Kamra

The study makes an inquiry into Naipaul's fiction as an experimental recreation of the third-world consciousness. It is one of the pioneering studies on the mind and art of Naipaul. It has detailed chapters on *The Mystic Masseur, The Suffrage of Elvira, The Mimic Men, A House for Mr. Biswas, Mr. Stone, The Knight's Companion, Guerrillas, A Bend in the Ganges* and *In a Free State.*

ISBN: 81-85218-12-9 **Rs. 300**

The West Indian Fiction

R.K. Dhawan, ed.

The West Indian fiction constitutes a major segment of the world literature written in English. The term 'West Indian' here seeks to represent Guyana, Jamaica, Trinidad and Barbados, the larger territories of the English-speaking Caribbean. The literatures of all these nations have certain common features which contribute to the sense of a unity. Whileas there is a considerable work in the areas of poetry and drama, the West Indian literature is best known for the fiction it has produced. George Lamming, Wilson Harris, Samuel Selvon and V.S. Naipaul are amongst the most significant novelists of the twentieth century. The volume highlights the contribution made by these writers. It also discusses the work of other writers including Jean Rhys, Roger Mais, Cyril Dabydeen and Jamaica Kincaid.

ISBN: 81-7551-044-7 **Rs. 400**

Modern Indian Fiction:

History, Politics and Individual in the Novels of Salman Rushdie, Amitav Ghosh & Upamanya Chatterjee

P.S. Ravi

Indian English novel has undergone a significant deveopment in keeping with recent trends in contemporary fiction worldwide. The book explores these developments in terms of themes and technigues through a selection of novels by three leading contemporary writers: Salman Rushdie, Amitav Ghosh and Upamanuy Chatterjee. It focuses on the emergence of a new cosmopolitan consciousness through the study of a close interaction between the historio-political contexts and the individual and the resultant search for identity in a complex world. The book examines the attempts of these versatile authors who, in order to express complexities of contemporary experience, adapts techniques of postmodernist fiction. Investigative in approach, it offers new insights into the fast-growing area of Indian fiction in English.

ISBN: 81-7551-117-6 **Rs. 400**

Discussing Indian Women Writers: Some Feminist Issues

Alessandro Monti and R.K. Dhawan, ed.

The central objective of the book is to discuss the theoretical investigations carried out by Indian women writers in their works and to arrive at a deeper understanding of feminist contentions. Fiction by women constitutes a major segment of the contemporary Indian writing in English. It provides insights, a wealth of understanding, a reservoir of meanings and a basis of discussion. The feminist literary critics strongly believe that women must create a literature of their own, in which feminine sensibility could consider and confront the peculiarly feminine issues and experiences. The book discusses major Indian women writers, including Anita Desai, Nayantara Sahgal, Shashi Deshpande, Rama Mehta, Arundhati Roy, Manju Kapur, Kamala Das, Mahasweta Devi, who have given a graphic picture of Indian woman in their works. The conflict between tradition and modernity finds a prominent place in the portrayal of women. The new woman depicted in these works refuses to conform to age-old traditions and truly represents the Indian culture that is at the cross-roads of transition.

ISBN: 81-7551-128-1 **Rs. 500**